The Legal, Professional, and Ethical Dimensions of Higher Education

The Legal, Professional, and Ethical Dimensions of Higher Education

Mable H. Smith, RN, JD, PhD
Associate Professor and Attorney at Law
Old Dominion University
Norfolk, Virginia

LIPPINCOTT WILLIAMS & WILKINS
A **Wolters Kluwer** Company

Philadelphia • Baltimore • New York • London
Buenos Aires • Hong Kong • Sydney • Tokyo

Acquisitions Editor: Quincy McDonald
Managing Editor: Helen Kogut
Editorial Assistant: Marie Rim
Project Management: TechBooks
Director of Nursing Production: Helen Ewan
Art Director: Carolyn O'Brien
Senior Manufacturing Manager: William Alberti
Compositor: TechBooks
Printer: R. R. Donnelly, Crawfordsville

9 8 7 6 5 4 3 2 1

ISBN: 0-7817-5204-3

Library of Congress Cataloging-in-Publication Data

Smith, Mable H.
  The legal, professional, and ethical dimensions of higher education / Mable H. Smith.
     p. cm.
  Includes bibliographical references and index.
  ISBN 0-7817-5204-3
1. Education, Higher—Law and legislation—United States. 2. Education, Higher—Moral and ethical aspects.
I. Title.
KF4225.S628 2005
344.73'074—dc22
                                                                                    2004018126

Care has been taken to confirm the accuracy of the information presented and to describe generally accepted practices. However, the authors, editors, and publisher are not responsible for errors or omissions or for any consequences from application of the information in this book and make no warranty, express or implied, with respect to the content of the publication.

The authors, editors, and publisher have exerted every effort to ensure that drug selection and dosage set forth in this text are in accordance with the current recommendations and practice at the time of publication. However, in view of ongoing research, changes in government regulations, and the constant flow of information relating to drug therapy and drug reactions, the reader is urged to check the package insert for each drug for any change in indications and dosage and for added warnings and precautions. This is particularly important when the recommended agent is a new or infrequently employed drug.

Some drugs and medical devices presented in this publication have Food and Drug Administration (FDA) clearance for limited use in restricted research settings. It is the responsibility of the health care provider to ascertain the FDA status of each drug or device planned for use in his or her clinical practice.

LWW.com

Richardean Benjamin
Chair, School of Nursing
Associate Professor
Old Dominion University
Norfolk, Virginia

Yvonne D. McKoy, PhD, APRN-BC, DABFN, FACFE
Associate Professor
Coordinator of Psychiatric-Mental Health Nursing
Former Coordinator Graduate Forensic Nursing
Xavier University Department of Nursing
Cincinnati, Ohio

Reviewers

JoEllen Dattilo, RN, PhD
Associate Dean for the Undergraduate Program
Georgia Baptist College of Nursing of Mercer University
Atlanta, Georgia

Catherine Dearman, RN, PhD
Professor and Chair, Maternal Child Health and Project Director
University of South Alabama
Mobile, Alabama

Sharon Denham, DSN
Professor
Ohio University, School of Nursing
Athens, Ohio

Marjorie Dobratz, RN, DNSC
Professor and Program Director, School of Nursing
University of Washington
Tacoma, Washington

Linda Foley, PhD, MSN, RN
Associate Chairperson
Nebraska Methodist College
Omaha, Nebraska

Lauren O'Hare, EdD, RN
Assistant Professor of Nursing
Wagner College
Staten Island, New York

Mary K. Proksch, EdD, MS, RN
Associate Professor
Winona State University—Rochester Center
Rochester, Minnesota

Evelyn Stiner, PhD, CFNP, RN
Chairperson, Department of Graduate Nursing
Alcorn State University, School of Nursing
Natchez, Mississippi

PURPOSE OF THE TEXT

Faculty in higher education environments face many legal, professional, and ethical issues from grade appeal to denial of tenure, to conflicts with faculty and administrators, to sexual harassment, to giving extra points to prevent a student from failing. Legal issues comprise a significant component of the daily operations of colleges and universities. Content in numerous chapters of this book provides a foundation for understanding the rights of students, professors, and the education institution. An understanding of the legal, professional, and ethical frameworks governing higher education institutions will help educators avoid and/or correctly address many of the issues that arise in these institutions.

This book is written to provide graduate students and faculty with an introduction to basic concepts and principles of the legal, professional, and ethical dimensions of education. It is designed as a primary textbook for graduate students seeking a certificate or degree in the educator track and can be used as a reference and resource for faculty in higher education who must constantly make defensible decisions in many areas of practice. There are no prerequisites to the use of this book.

The foundation of each chapter, with the exception of the chapter on ethics, is on legal cases from the U.S. Supreme Court, federal courts, and state courts. Landmark cases, usually from the U.S. Supreme Court, are discussed in detail, because they provide the foundation for analysis and decisions on subsequent issues. Although many of these cases are dated, they contain valid and applicable law that provides the foundation for present day cases.

ORGANIZATION OF THE TEXT

This book organizes and conceptualizes the range of legal, professional, and ethical considerations pertinent to educators in higher education institutions. It discusses trends in the evolution of law, analyzes legal cases, extrapolates legal principles from case law, and discusses the significance of these legal principles for educators. The professional and ethical dimensions of higher education are also addressed. This book contains nine chapters and is divided into three parts.

Part 1 The Legal Framework of Higher Education Environments

Part 1 consists of four chapters and addresses the legal framework governing faculty in higher education institutions.

Chapter 1 provides the faculty with information on the legal status of students, which provides the basis for lawsuits against faculty and the educational institution. In the course of teaching, evaluating, and disciplining students, faculty must understand the constitutional protections and contractual rights that students are afforded, so as to not infringe on those protected rights.

Chapter 2 addresses the legal protections afforded faculty in higher education institutions under the First Amendment. The First Amendment protects freedom of speech, freedom of the press, freedom of religion, and the right to assemble. Faculty must understand the dividing line between constitutionally afforded protections for speech, organizational affiliations, and so on and behaviors that can result in institutional-imposed discipline or punishment.

Chapter 3 addresses the immunity from lawsuits provided to the institution and its faculty under the Eleventh Amendment of the U.S. Constitution. In some instances, faculty may be afforded immunity from lawsuits. However, faculty must also understand the limits of their ability to sue the institution for its alleged violations.

Chapter 4 provides faculty with an understanding of their employment status within the institution as it relates to appointment, promotion, and tenure. Rights afforded faculty under the terms of their contract, handbook, policies, and the Fourteenth Amendment of the U.S. Constitution are discussed. The chapter also includes content on discrimination.

Part 2 The Professional Framework Governing the Educator's Role

Part 2 consists of four chapters and addresses the professional framework governing faculty in higher education institutions. It explores the primary dimensions of the faculty roles as it relates to teaching, scholarly productions, and service.

Chapter 5 establishes the legal foundation of the professional roles and addresses professional competence, faculty-faculty relations, and faculty-students relations. The foundational basis of the faculty-student relationship is addressed in detail.

Chapter 6 addresses the teaching dimension of the educator's role. The traditional role of educators is explored and used as the basis for understanding the nontraditional classroom of today and the expectations and challenges of teaching in today's colleges and universities. The various media for teaching and evaluating students are discussed in this chapter.

Chapter 7 discusses the roles and expectations of faculty as they relate to producing and generating knowledge. In the realm of scholarly activities, many legal issues arise related to copyright and patents. This chapter discusses the professional dimension of scholarship, within the auspices of a legal framework.

Chapter 8 addresses the service component of the educator's role. Service to the university, community, and profession is discussed.

Part 3 Ethical Framework of Higher Education

Part 3 consists of one chapter and addresses the ethical framework governing faculty in higher education institutions. Ethical theories and principles are presented and discussed. Application of these theories and principles as they relate to higher education is presented using numerous case scenarios.

SPECIAL FEATURES OF THE TEXT

Each chapter includes features that help the reader gain a fuller understanding of the content.

- **Chapter Outline**. A chapter outline has been provided to give the reader a clear understanding of the organization of the chapter content.
- **Case Scenarios.** Each chapter begins with a scenario based on legal, ethical, and professional issues to draw the reader into the chapter content.
- **Critical Thinking Questions with Responses.** Critical thinking questions follow each scenario and a full discussion of each question is found at the end of each chapter.
- **Implications for Educators.** This feature highlights pertinent professional concepts that are developed in the chapter. It also summarizes important key legal concepts that are discussed in the chapter.
- **Strategies to Avoid Legal Problems.** This feature provides useful and practical guidelines and suggestions for faculty that operationalize the legal, professional, and ethical principles discussed in the chapter.

Because the fundamental legal, professional, and ethical concepts and principles governing faculty in higher education environments are unlikely to change, students and faculty can use this book as a resource on a variety of issues. Faculty in education environments who understand and are knowledgeable of the professional, legal, and ethical dimensions governing their roles and responsibilities are now fully equipped to address many of the issues they will encounter.

Mable H. Smith

Acknowledgments

A special thanks is extended to my colleagues and friends who supported me throughout this endeavor. I would also like to acknowledge Susan Tweed, doctoral student in the College of Health Sciences at Old Dominion University, for her research assistance and helpful comments and Dr. Yvonne D. McKoy for her helpful and valued input, comments, and suggestions. The reviewers' comments and suggestions were helpful, appreciated, and incorporated into the final outcome. I truly appreciate the vision and encouragement for the book from Margaret Zuccarini, senior acquisitions editor; the support, constructive comments, and directive guidance from Helen Kogut, managing editor; the assistance of Quincy McDonald, senior acquisitions editor; and Marie Rim, editorial assistant. A special and sincere gratitude is extended to my co-contributors, Dr. Yvonne D. McKoy, associate professor at Xavier University, and Dr. Richardean Benjamin, chair, school of nursing at Old Dominion University. Finally, I would like to acknowledge the support and understanding of my daughters, Nakia Smith and Renee Smith, and my mother, Ms. Mamie Coefield.

Contents

The Legal, Professional, and Ethical Dimensions of Higher Education

1

The Legal Rights of Students

INTRODUCTION

Faculty members may have to assign a failing grade to students for poor academic or clinical performance or assist administrators in dismissing students for misconduct. Great caution must be exercised to protect the sanctity of the educational process while balancing the legal rights of students. Faculty have a legal and an ethical duty to make fair, unbiased, and systematic decisions related to students' progression toward graduation. An understanding of the legal framework within which these actions must occur is essential to minimize potential negative consequences and protect oneself in the event of a lawsuit. This chapter focuses on the processes and procedures faculty should use to protect the legal rights of students.

Randy Byrd was a third-semester nursing student with a grade point average (GPA) of 3.6 on a 4.0 scale. He received an "A" grade in all first-year nursing courses. At the beginning of the third semester, students are required to meet with their faculty advisor to plan future learning experiences based on the student goals. During the interview, Randy told his advisor, Dr. Terrell, that he did not plan to practice nursing, but wanted the degree to become a nurse-attorney. He also indicated that he was getting a dual degree in nursing and biology in case he decided to go to medical school. Dr. Terrell told Randy that he was wasting the faculty's time and taking a seat away from a student who wished to practice as a registered nurse. She strongly encouraged him to drop nursing and pursue another major. Surprised by the remark, Randy refused to withdraw from the program. He stated that he was learning a lot in the program and would use the information in a nonclinical way. Dr. Terrell then stated the advising process was useless because it was based on the student's career goals in clinical practice.

During the second half of the third semester, Randy rotated to geriatrics didactic and clinical practice taught by Dr. Terrell. He received a 96 on test 1, a 97 on test 2, a 50 on test 3, and an 84 in clinical practice. The tests and clinical grades each counted 25 percent toward the final grade. The first two tests contained 100 four-item multiple-choice questions. The third test contained five essay questions. Students must pass each test and clinical with a grade of 80. For test security purposes, Dr. Terrell did not review the tests nor provide students with their test scores until the end of the rotation. Randy was advised that he could not progress to the next level and must wait a year until the course was offered again.

Randy protested his grade orally and in writing to the undergraduate program director (UGD) and asked to review the third test. Dr. Terrell denied his request. In his protest papers, Randy provided evidence that during her eight-year tenure at the university, Dr. Terrell had never given an essay test. In addition, the course syllabus indicated that there would be three multiple-choice tests and Dr. Terrell did not tell any of the students that the third test would be in an essay format. Fifteen percent of the students failed the essay test. A committee appointed by the UGD to review the test, the test grid with answers, and Randy's test upheld the grade of 50. He unsuccessfully appealed to the dean and the University Student Grievance Committee. Randy initiated legal action alleging violation of procedural and substantive due process and breach of contract.

CRITICAL THINKING QUESTIONS

1. Discuss whether Randy's due process rights were violated.
2. What is the likelihood of the Court ruling in favor of Randy?
3. Does Randy have a valid argument for breach of contract? Support your answer.
4. What reasons, if any, would necessitate a professor changing the format of an exam?

DUE PROCESS

Students initiate legal action against educational institutions for a number of reasons, including breach of contract, due process violations, and discrimination. With few exceptions, courts will not intervene in faculty members' evaluation of the academic or clinical performance of their students. Applying the principle of judicial deference, courts examining cases concerning faculty's evaluation of students usually uphold the faculty's decision if there was an adherence to standard academic norms and the procedures used were fair and reasonable.

Students are protected from state actions that infringe on or deprive them of their property or liberty interests. The Due Process Clause of the Fourteenth Amendment of the United States Constitution reads,

> " *No person shall make or enforce any law which shall abridge the privileges or immunities of citizens of the United States; nor shall any State deprive any person of life, liberty, or property, without due process of law; nor deny to any person within its jurisdiction the equal protection of the laws.* " [1]

Once the student establishes or the Court assumes the existence of a property or liberty interest, the student is then entitled to due process as a matter of law.

Liberty Interest

A liberty interest is violated when a faculty member's action damages the student's standing in his profession or community or imposes a stigma or disability that precludes or interferes with other educational or employment opportunities. The case of *Greenhill v Bailey*[2] illustrates facts sufficient to establish a liberty interest. In *Greenhill,* a medical school notified the Association of American Medical Colleges that Bailey was dismissed for "lack of intellectual capacity and insufficient course preparation." This information was available to all other medical schools. Ruling in favor of Bailey, the Court found that language pertaining to "alleged deficiency in intellectual ability . . . would potentially stigmatize his future as a medical student elsewhere."[3] To avoid an infringement on Bailey's liberty interest, the reason provided for his dismissal should have focused on performance rather than intellectual abilities.

Property Interest

State law creates property interests. However, federal constitutional law determines whether the property interest rises to the level of a constitutionally protected interest. Students asserting a violation of property rights must first establish that they have a legitimate claim of entitlement to the property claimed. In higher education, the claim of entitlement is usually the academic degree.

In *Gaspar v Bruton,*[4] a forty-four-year-old student was pursuing practical nurse training in a vocational-technical program. After completing more than two-thirds of the program, she was dismissed for poor clinical performance. Prior to the dismissal, Gaspar was on probation for two months due to clinical deficiencies. She was informed that she would be dismissed if her performance did not improve. When it did not, she was notified of the dismissal in a conference with some of her instructors and the superintendent. Subsequently, she was offered a second conference and an opportunity to question other faculty members who had participated in the dismissal decision. The dismissal decision was upheld.

Gaspar's lawsuit against the university alleged that she was unlawfully deprived of an education, which is an infringement of her property right. Based on the infringement, she should have been accorded due process that consisted of the right to confront and cross-examine witnesses, to challenge the evidence supporting her dismissal, and to present evidence in her defense. The Court held that Gasper was entitled to due process based on a property interest in her education, especially since she had paid for enrollment and attendance in the program. However, expanding on an earlier decision that high school students' entitlement to public education is a property interest,[5] the Court rejected Gasper's assertion of the type of due process that applied to her case. As discussed below, all that is required to satisfy academic due process requirements is that the student be made aware, prior to termination, of his or her failure or impending failure to meet the academic standards.

TYPES OF DUE PROCESS

The types of due process that must be afforded students vary depending on whether the matter involves an academic decision or a disciplinary action. In cases involving academic decisions, students are only entitled to notice of their academic deficiencies, the resulting consequences, and suggestions for improvement. In contrast, students facing disciplinary proceedings are entitled to notice of the charges, the nature and type of evidence on which the charges are based, the opportunity to cross-examine witnesses, and to present evidence.

Academic Due Process

Academic due process relates to decisions and actions regarding students' academic issues and performance. An evaluation of academic due process looks at the process used to inform students of their academic standing and the basis of the decision. Two cases decided by the U.S. Supreme Court form the basis of the legal framework for analysis of academic due process as applied to higher education institutions in academic matters. The *Board of Curators of the University of Missouri v Horowitz*[6] addressed procedural due process, which is the fairness of the procedures used in the academic decision. The case of *Regents of the University of Michigan v Ewing*[7] addressed substantive due process, which looks at the basis for the academic decision.

Procedural Due Process

Students attending public colleges and universities are entitled to feedback regarding their academic performance before receiving a final failing grade. Faculty should incorporate a process in their curriculum that informs students of the grading criteria, notifies them of their impending failure, and provides recommendations for improvement. Failure to provide this information to students can lead to lawsuits alleging a violation of the student's procedural due process rights.

The following case outlines the factors involved in adhering to procedural due process mandates. In *Board of Curators of the University of Missouri v Horowitz*,[8] a medical student in her final year of a clinical residency was dismissed from the program. Her overall clinical performance showed patterns of below-average performance in clinical settings. In addition, she had deficiencies in interpersonal relations, attendance, and personal appearance. After the first year, the Council on Evaluation, a committee composed of faculty and students, recommended that Horowitz advance to the second and final year on probationary status. However, her clinical performance remained unsatisfactory and the council recommended delaying graduation and proposed dismissal from the program unless her performance showed radical improvement. Horowitz appealed the decision and was allowed to spend a substantial amount of time with seven practicing physicians. Of the seven, three recommended probation, delaying her graduation, and continuing her on probationary status; two recommended immediate dismissal; and two recommended graduation. Based on these evaluations, the council upheld its previous decision. Subsequently, Horowitz was dismissed from the program after receiving two more negative evaluations.

Horowitz initiated legal action alleging that the university deprived her of a liberty interest by "substantiating impairing her opportunities to continue her medical education or to return to employment in a medically related field."[9] Assuming the existence of a liberty or property interest, the U.S. Supreme Court addressed the issue of what due process procedures must be provided to students at a state educational institution whose dismissal may infringe on a property or liberty interest. Horowitz was provided notice of the faculties' dissatisfaction with her clinical performance and the consequences of her clinical deficiencies. Ruling in favor of the university, the Court held that Horowitz had received more due process than required by the Fourteenth Amendment. The Court further ruled that the school went beyond constitutional requirements by affording her an evaluation by independent physicians. Although clinical evaluation may be more subjective than the evaluation of classroom performance, due process requirements are the same because they are both academic evaluations. The Court noted:

- *It is well to bear in mind that respondent was attending a medical school where competence in clinical courses is as much of a prerequisite to graduation as satisfactory grades in other courses.*
- *Respondent was dismissed because she was as deficient in her clinical work as she was proficient in the "booklearning" portion of the curriculum.*
- *Evaluation of her performance in the former area is no less an "academic" judgment because it involves observation of her skills and techniques in actual conditions of practice, rather than assigning a grade to her written answers on an essay question.*[10]

In addition to the legal decision, the Court enunciated several legal principles that are of importance to faculty in higher educational institutions (see Box 1.1).

Substantive Due Process

The U.S. Constitution creates substantive due process rights, which examine the ultimate basis for the decision. Faculty members are held to a standard of fairness and impartiality in their relationship with students. They cannot arbitrarily and capriciously deal with students. Therefore, a decision to dismiss a student or limit his or her academic progression must reflect a careful and deliberate evaluation of the student's overall performance.

Box 1.1

Important Legal Principles Related to Due Process

- Courts evaluating due process violations will not engage in an evaluation of a student's academic performance.
- "University faculty have a wide range of discretion in making judgments as to the academic performance of students and their progression towards graduations."[46]
- "The determination whether to dismiss a student for academic reasons requires an expert evaluation of cumulative information and is not readily adapted to the procedural tools of judicial or administrative decision making."[47]
- Academic evaluations of a student will not be subject to the traditional judicial fact-finding procedures used in court and disciplinary proceedings.[48]

Courts, in reviewing cases alleging a violation of substantive due process rights, look at the fundamental basis for the negative academic decision.

The following case explores the nature of substantive due process. In *Regents of the University of Michigan v Ewing,* a medical student was enrolled in a six-year program that offered a joint undergraduate and medical degree. Ewing had academic and personal difficulties during the first four years in the program including marginal passing grades, incomplete assignments, and makeup examinations. After successfully completing the first four years, students must pass a written test administered by the National Board of Medical Examiners. Ewing failed five of the seven subjects on his examination and received the lowest score in the history of the program. After reviewing Ewing's entire academic record, the Promotion and Review Committee dismissed him from the program. The committee reaffirmed its decision after Ewing was given the opportunity to explain why his test score was not reflective of his academic abilities. Ewing's request to retake the exam was denied. He appealed the decision and presented his case to the Executive Committee, who upheld Ewing's dismissal from the program.

Ewing's claim against the university was predicated on the loss of a property interest in his continued enrollment and a violation of his substantive due process rights in that the decision to dismiss him was arbitrary and capricious. To establish a substantive due process violation, the student must show that the dismissal decision was arbitrary and capricious, that there was no rational basis for the decision, or that the decision was motivated by ill will or bad faith unrelated to academic performance. Courts look to determine if there was a substantial departure from academic norms to suggest that the faculty did not actually exercise professional judgment. Ewing presented statistical evidence that other students were routinely allowed to retake the exam. The Court ruled that the decision to dismiss Ewing, which was based on an evaluation of Ewing's entire academic career, was made with conscientious and careful deliberation.

Like *Horowitz,* the Court in *Ewing* enunciated several legal principles applicable to faculty in higher education institutions. First, "When judges are asked to review the substance of a genuinely academic decision such as this one, they should show great respect for the faculty's professional judgment."[11] The Court also noted the need to analyze actions in terms of expense. "Admittedly, it may well have been unwise to deny Ewing a second chance. Permission to retake the test might have saved the University the expense of this litigation and conceivably might have demonstrated that the members of the Promotion and Review Board misjudged Ewing's fitness for the medical profession."[12]

Legal principles derived from *Horowitz* and *Ewing* provide the foundation for deciding cases in which students initiate legal action against higher education institutions alleging violation of academic due process. Academic due process requires faculty members to provide students notice of their academic deficiencies and the associated consequences. In many instances, faculty members can provide further protection by providing students with suggestions to improve their performance and a time frame in which to make improvements.

Making careful and deliberate decisions regarding students' progress or lack thereof is the fundamental basis for establishing substantive due process. The case of *Richmond v Fowlkes*[13] illustrates careful and deliberate decisions and extensive due process in addressing a student's academic difficulties. The process and procedures used by faculty and administrators exceeded the articulated legal requirements. Richmond completed five of an eight-semester pharmacy program. During the spring semester of his junior year, Richmond received two negative noncognitive evaluations for sleeping in class, inappropriate comments during class, failure of basic examinations, and lack of preparation for class. Noncognitive evaluations address components of professional role development that are considered relevant for future pharmacists. In response to Richmond's academic performance, the following sequence of events occurred:

1. The associate dean notified Richmond of the evaluations and requested a letter explaining his behavior.
2. The Scholastic Committee reviewed the response and notified Richmond in writing that he was on probation and that another negative evaluation would result in his dismissal from the program.
3. The associate dean suspended Richmond from further clinical rotations pending committee review after he received another negative noncognitive evaluation for tardiness, unexplained absences, belligerent behavior, argumentative responses, and inadequate preparation.
4. The Scholastic Committee informed Richmond orally and in writing of the committee meeting/hearing and that he could appear in person, answer questions, and submit statements on his behalf.
5. Richmond appeared at the hearing and submitted personal references and answered questions.
6. The committee sent Richmond a letter notifying him of the recommended suspension, with a plan for its removal and his ultimate graduation. The letter requested Richmond to review the proposed plan and submit his own plan with the stipulation that his plan must incorporate selected items the committee considered essential.
7. The committee revised the plan submitted by Richmond and returned it to him for his signature. The committee dismissed Richmond from the program because he refused to sign and return the plan by the deadline date.

Richmond then initiated a lawsuit alleging that the committee rejection of his plan was arbitrary and capricious in violation of his substantive due process rights. Finding no violation, the Court ruled that the committee's plan to (1) require Richmond to be evaluated by a psychologist from an approved list as opposed to a self-selected psychologist, (2) limit his geographical practice options, and (3) require him to restart his fourth year of study to ensure professional development reflected careful and deliberate alternatives as opposed to outright dismissal.

Richmond also argued that his due process rights were violated because the associate dean was biased against him. As evidence, Richmond offered only his speculation and his mother's opinion that the associate dean was biased because he kept a log of his interactions with Richmond, asked faculty members to submit to him any negative evaluation of Richmond, and attended the meetings of the committee that decided the outcome. Rejecting this argument, the Court noted that the associate dean kept a computerized log of interactions with all students who attended meetings with him and their family members.[14] His attendance at committee meetings did not establish bias because the associate dean did not vote in the committee's deliberations and decision. Further, the Court noted that the content of evaluations were within the wide discretion of the faculty; therefore, a negative noncognitive evaluation could not be attributed to the associate dean.[15]

The concept of substantive due process involves the issue of fundamental fairness. Courts must balance their involvement in higher education with protecting the rights of students. As a general policy, "a student's challenge to a particular grade or other academic determination relating to a genuine substantive evaluation of the student's academic capabilities is beyond the scope of judicial review."[16] The quest for knowledge and truth cannot flourish in an environment with rigid oversight by judicial officials; however, as discussed later in the chapter, students must be afforded some safeguards against arbitrary and capricious behavior by faculty and administrations.[17]

Disciplinary Due Process

Issues involving academic dishonesty and the fairness and adherence to the procedural process are within the realm of judicial knowledge. Colleges and universities have rules and regulations governing students' conduct and behavior and procedures that will be implemented if students violate the rules and regulations. Academic dishonesty, such as cheating, plagiarism, lying, stealing, and falsification of records, poses great concern for faculty because of the connection between students' academic integrity and their future professional behaviors.[18] Students who cheat in school are more likely to cover up mistakes in the work environment or breach professional standards. Therefore, faculty must take every breach of academic integrity seriously by holding the student accountable for his or her behavior.

Disciplinary actions are invoked anytime a student violates the law or a school regulation by engaging in a prohibited or an illegal activity. The university's handbook for students and more specifically college and departmental handbooks should outline the process to be followed in disciplinary actions. The determination of whether a student is guilty of violating policy or the honor code is a question of fact to be decided by the appropriate committee or council. Students facing disciplinary actions must be afforded more due process than required for academic actions. Courts have found that, unlike academic decisions, which require professional judgments and evaluations, disciplinary determinations are more susceptible to traditional fact finding and thus more adaptable to the courts' fact-finding procedures.[19]

Handling Disciplinary Issues

The process used to handle disciplinary issues is usually outlined in the institution's policies and procedures and varies among institutions. Some institutions require that all breaches of academic integrity be reported to the hearing officers, while others allow the faculty to handle the matter, either internally or through referral to the institution's disciplinary representative. For example, if a student is caught cheating, the faculty member can make the student repeat the assignment, give the student an "F" on the assignment, assign an "F" for the entire course, or refer the issue to the appropriate college or university committee. The latter is usually preferred when additional information is needed to support the charges, such as when students do not readily admit to cheating and the faculty member did not directly witness the cheating incident. If the student disagrees with the faculty-designated consequence, the faculty member should refer the matter to the appropriate committee and allow someone else to implement the required process. This is time saving for the faculty and allows for an independent review and determination for the student.

Personnel who have knowledge of due process mandates usually handle cases involving disciplinary actions at the college or university level. Once a complaint is received, the hearing officer conducts an investigation and notifies the student of the complaint. "The notice should contain a statement of the specific charges and grounds, which, if proven, would justify [the disciplinary action] under the regulations of the board of education."[20] The hearing officer may request to meet with the student to discuss the allegations or ask the student to provide a written response. At the meeting or after reviewing the student's response, the matter may be resolved with both parties agreeing to the disposition. If the student does not agree with the decision, he or she can request a hearing. "A hearing which gives the board or the administrative authorities of the college an opportunity to hear both sides in considerable detail is best suited to protect the rights of all involved."[21] The procedures followed must comply with disciplinary due process requirements. In disciplinary proceedings, the accused student must be informed of the charges against him or her and the evidence on which the charges are based, and be given the opportunity to address the charges and present evidence and witnesses to support his or her case.

Courts are hesitant to intervene in disciplinary matters involving cheating if the appropriate procedures were followed. In *Papachristou v University of Tennessee*,[22] a student opened his test booklet and started reading the examination before the professor gave the class permission to begin. He closed his booklet after realizing that other students had their booklets closed. After time was called, the majority of the class stopped and formed a line to turn in their exams. However, a couple of students, including Papachristou, continued to work on the examination, in violation of the honor code. The hearing officer entered an order dismissing the charges; however, the university chancellor reversed the decision and found that Papachristou had violated the honor code. Specifically, the student was familiar with the honor code, the class was told not to begin the examination until so instructed, and the class was aware of when the examination ended. On appeal, the Court upheld the chancellor's decision.

Procedure for Disciplinary Hearings

A typical hearing for disciplinary matters usually follows a process similar to the one described below:

1. The accuser, often though the hearing officer, presents the charges made against the student.
2. The accuser presents evidence to support the allegation(s). The evidence may include witnesses, documents, reports, and other supporting data.

3. The accused student is allowed to question or cross-examine the witnesses and challenge the evidence presented.
4. After the accuser presents his or her evidence, the accused student can call witnesses and present evidence to rebut the accusations.
5. The accuser is given the opportunity to question and cross-examine witnesses for the accused student and to challenge any evidence.
6. Committee or panel members can ask questions of the witnesses and about the evidence.
7. Both sides can present a summary statement of the evidence and explain why the committee should (or should not) rule in the accused student's favor.
8. The parties are dismissed and the committee deliberates to render a decision based on the evidence.
9. The decision is presented to the hearing officer, who will notify the accused student of the decision.
10. The accused student may be given the opportunity to appeal an unfavorable decision of the committee to an Appeals Committee or to an authorized and designated administrator. Either may uphold or reverse the original decision.
11. The adminstrator or the university president is usually empowered to make the final decision.

The consequences of disciplinary actions against a student can have long-term consequences, ranging from the notation of academic dishonesty on his or her transcript to expulsion from the university. Students who have undergone disciplinary actions may encounter difficulty finding quality jobs or transferring to other educational institutions. Therefore, courts will more readily review cases asserting violation of due process rights in disciplinary proceedings.

For example, in *Donohue v Baker*,[23] the Court found that the university violated a student's due process rights by not allowing the accused student to cross-examine his accuser, in violation of its own policies. A female student accused Donohue of dating violence. Because of the sensitive nature of the charges and the emotional impact on the alleged victim, Donohue could only address the panel. The Court noted that cross-examination was essential in this case because the only evidence in front of the panel were the statements of both parties. Since the case was essentially one of credibility and the consequence of expulsion was severe, Donohue should have been afforded the right to confront his accuser.

Unique Cases

Faculty members may encounter cases that are difficult to classify as either academic or disciplinary. Many of these cases involve unique fact patterns that have not been previously addressed or fall outside of articulated policies. For example, a student was dismissed from a nursing program for failing to regularly attend classes, submit a state-required physical examination report, and inform school officials that he had attended another nursing program.[24] Although these reasons are nonacademic, they do not fit within the category of misconduct to warrant a disciplinary due process hearing. Academic due process would require the student to be given notice of an impending failure, informed of its consequences, or provided suggestions for improvement. As indicated in the case facts, this process is not applicable to this situation. Disciplinary due process mandates that students be given details about the charges or allegations, provided the opportunity to cross-examine witnesses, and allowed to present evidence on their behalf. Similarly, this process does not succinctly fit within the case facts. Since this situation involved a unique fact pattern, providing more due process than required would prevent future allegations of due process violations. [25]

ACADEMIC DEFERENCE

The practice of judicial deference to academic decisions (academic deference) is rather extensively applied in cases involving educational institutions. Courts have consistently ruled in favor of the university on academic issues. Legal principles derived from cases addressing the concept of academic deference are identified in Box 1.2.

Exception to the Principle of Academic Deference

Students are usually protected from arbitrary and capricious behavior by faculty and administrations. The case of *Sylvester v Texas Southern University*[26] demonstrates facts sufficient for the court to subject an academic decision to judicial scrutiny because of the major departure from accepted academic norms. Texas Southern University (TSU) had a policy allowing for committee review of students' grades upon written review. The Dean's office would then notify the student of the committee's review. The student could not appeal a grade after graduation. Sylvester ranked first in her law class at TSU. She received a "D" in wills and trust class, which dropped her ranking to third place. The associate dean did not respond to her grade protest. Sylvester continued to protest her grade throughout her third and final year of law school, but did not receive any responses. Before graduation, she approached the wills and trust professor, who informed her that her examination had been lost. She therefore initiated a lawsuit against the law school seeking a temporary restraining order (TRO) to stop the graduation ceremony and a permanent injunction against the university's imposition of the graduation deadline, claiming that TSU had violated her constitutional rights to due process by denying her review of her examination. The judge denied the motion for the TRO, but scheduled a status conference for a later date to allow the parties the opportunity to correct the problems.

Box 1.2

Legal Principles Related to Academic Deference

- Courts will show great respect for the faculty's professional judgment.
- Courts will only override a faculty member's academic decision when it is a substantial departure from accepted academic norms.
- Every student is different; therefore, courts are reluctant to engage in a student comparison process.
- Courts do not want to become involved in examining the basis of students' grades and assessing the credibility of faculty.
- Academic due process requires that faculty give students notice of the academic deficiencies and the consequences of failure to correct the deficiencies.
- Academic decisions regarding students' performance must be careful and deliberate.

The series of events described below formed the basis for the Court's decision to override its usual practice of academic deference to college and university officials.

- At the conference, TSU produced the examination but the professor was not present. Therefore, the Court ordered the dean to schedule a meeting with the professor so the student could review her examination.
- At the meeting, the professor did not produce an answer key or any comparable evaluation method by which Sylvester could judge her performance. The judge then ruled that the professor was to provide Sylvester with a written explanation of the correct answers to the disputed exam and how her answer deviated from the model answer. In addition, the professor was to attend all future court meetings.
- The professor failed to attend the next meeting. The judge ordered a committee review of Sylvester's exam, using the other students' answers as a comparison.
- The committee met, dismissed all student members, conducted a cursory review without an answer key, and generated a report concluding that they found no inconsistencies. One abstaining committee member wrote in a dissent report that the professor still had not furnished a complete answer key by which the committee could adequately review the exam and that the chairperson had reconstituted the committee. In the answer key, the professor had simply provided a "yes" answer to one of the questions. The Court issued an order for the professor's arrest and chastised the committee for the inadequacy of its review, noting that "no student could have received a perfect score for answering 'yes' to an essay question."
- The Court ordered TSU to change Sylvester's grade to a "Pass" and to file a certified corrected copy of her transcript. Consequently, she was named covaledictorian, sharing the rank with the student who had taken her place.

Courts are very reluctant to judicially impose a grade to a student. However, faculty and/or administrators who demonstrate bad faith or arbitrary and capricious behaviors and violate a student's constitutionally protected rights invite court intervention to protect the student.

CONTRACT

In addition to violations of due process, students initiating lawsuits against colleges and universities often assert a breach of contract claim. This is especially true of students attending private educational institutions because the Fourteenth Amendment due process protection does not extend to private institutions. Numerous courts have ruled that the relationship between the university and student is contractual in nature.[27] A contract is an agreement between two or more individuals to perform or refrain from performing a certain thing. Basic contract law contains the elements of competent individuals, an offer, mutual acceptance, and consideration.[28] A legal binding contract is based on consideration, which involves the payment of money, performance of some act, or abstention from doing something that one has a legal right to do. The contract, either written or oral, identifies the actual agreement between the parties; therefore, the terms must be clear, unambiguous, and definite.

A contract is established when students apply for admission, pay the required consideration or money, and are considered for admission. The university has an obligation to evaluate the applicant according to its published standards.[29] Once accepted for admission, the university agrees to provide the student an education that meets a predetermined program of study and goal (degree, certification, continuing education) if the student abides by the rules and regulations, pays tuition, maintains satisfactory academic grades, and completes the program of study. The student accepts the offer by attending the university and providing the necessary consideration, which is usually tuition and fees. Additional terms of the contract are found in student handbooks, university catalogs, course syllabi, or other statements of university policy. Once a contract is established, the university cannot arbitrarily disregard contractually imposed duties. In *People ex rel. Cecil v Bellevue Hospital Medical College*,[30] the college refused to allow a student who had completed all the curriculum requirements to take the examination and receive a medical degree. The college would not provide a reason for its actions, but insisted that it had "the right arbitrarily, without any cause, to refuse the [student] his examination and degree."[31] Rejecting this position, the Court refused to allow the college to arbitrarily and without cause withhold the medical degree from the student.

> • *The circulars of the respondent indicate the terms upon which students will be received, and the rights which they were to acquire by reason of their compliance with the rules and regulations of the college in respect to qualifications, conduct, etc.*
> • *When a student matriculates under such circumstances, it is a contract between the college and himself that, if he complies with the terms therein prescribed, he shall have the degree, which is the end to be obtained.*
> • *This corporation cannot take the money of a student, allow him to remain and waste his time (because it would be a waste of time if he cannot get a degree), and then arbitrarily refuse, when he has completed his term of study, to confer upon him that which they have promised.*[32]

The Court refused to allow such a "a willful violation of the duties that the college had assumed."[33]

Breach of Contract

To prevail on a breach of contract claim, a student must establish the existence of a legally binding contract, that he or she fulfilled all the contractual obligations, that the college or university failed to perform its contractual obligations without legal cause, and that the student suffered a detriment or damages as a result of the contractual breach. An aggrieved student can be judicially awarded a degree, seek an injunction against the breaching party's actions, obtain monetary damages, or seek specific performance of the contractual terms. In *University of Texas Health Science Center at Houston v Babb*,[34] the court granted a temporary injunction to a nursing student that allowed her to resume classes and complete the degree requirements. Babb entered the nursing program under the admission, progression, and graduation requirements outlined in the 1978–1979 catalog, which indicated that students who fall below a 2.0 GPA would be placed on scholastic probation. Another catalog provision read as follows: "A student may obtain a degree from the School of Nursing according to the requirements in the catalog under which he enters the School, or the catalog governing any subsequent year in which he is registered in the School, provided that he completes the work for the degree within six years of the date of the catalog."[35] Based on the advice of her counselor, Babb withdrew from the program because she was failing a twelve-hour course and reentered the program under a different catalog. The new catalog terms related to progression in the nursing program had a "no more than two Ds requirement" that was not included in the initial catalog under which Babb entered the program. Babb was dismissed from the program after making two Ds. Upholding the injunction, the Court noted the expressed promise in the 1978–1979 catalog to allow the student to continue under the entrance catalog.

Many institutions have inserted "disclaimer" language in their catalogs. This language reads that the information contained in catalogs, bulletins, and other printed materials is not intended to create a contract between the student and the university. Courts have generally ruled that expressed disclaimers are effective in avoiding a binding contract. Likewise, a reservation of rights clause, which acknowledges the university's right to make changes in its policies, procedures, catalogs, handbooks, and academic curricula, allows the institution to make changes whenever needed to fulfill and properly exercise its educational responsibilities and objectives.

Academic Modifications

The case of *University of Mississippi v Hughes*[36] reinforces the ability of a university to modify degree requirements as needed to adhere to changes in the professional environment. Hughes was dismissed from medical school when he failed the United States Medical Licensing Examination (USMLE) Step 1 after three attempts in accordance with university guidelines. The USMLE was not required when Hughes enrolled in the program. When Hughes was beginning his sophomore year, the School of Medicine adopted the recommendation of the Curriculum Committee to require students to pass the examination for promotion to the junior year. The rationale for the change was to ensure that students who graduated from the medical school would be qualified to enter residency training in Mississippi. The Federation of State Medical Boards and the National Board of Medical Examiners require students to pass the USMLE to be licensed. Similarly, the State Board of Medical Licensure required students to pass Steps 1 and 2 of the USMLE to enter residency training in Mississippi.

The issue was whether changing the standards required to progress in medical school resulted in a breach of contract. Hughes argued that according to his contract with the university, he was to receive his medical degree if he adhered to and satisfied the terms of the catalog at the time of his enrollment. Because the USMLE requirement was not in place when he enrolled, Hughes contended that the university breached the contract by requiring him to pass the USMLE to progress to the next level. He had complied with the conditions outlined by the university when he enrolled and was entitled to pursue his degree. The Court rejected the university's argument that no contractual relationship existed with Hughes. However, the Court noted that implicit in this contract was the university's right to modify its educational requirements, if the changes were not arbitrary and capricious.[37] To rule otherwise would unnecessarily interfere in the university's discretion to manage its academic affairs.[38] Effecting changes that align with standards in the professional community is not arbitrary and capricious.

Although courts have been very pro-university in terms of giving deference to the disclaimer and reservation of rights language contained in catalogs, students asserting a breach of contract claim may have a valid theory. The doctrine of "contract of adhesions" recognizes that certain parties to a contract may not be on equal footing and therefore unable to effectively negotiate the terms or modify the contract. Contracts of adhesion are usually void or made invalid based on public policy. The handbook can be construed as a contract of adhesions because "the student was not a party to the formation of the contract and the relative bargaining position of the parties is unequal."[39]

In *Russell v Salve Regina College,*[40] the college dismissed Russell from the nursing program because of her obesity. After admission to the nursing program, Russell began to encounter problems based on her weight. She became the model for procedures involving obese patients and had to endure lectures and discussions regarding the need to lose weight. The faculty related these comments to expressions of concerns regarding Russell's health. The college handbook required each student to inform the clinical coordinator of health problems and reserved to the coordinator the discretion to determine whether a student's participation in clinical is contraindicated based on health reasons. Russell's academic performance was satisfactory except for one failing clinical grade that was attributed to her weight. In her junior year, Russell entered into a contract with the college agreeing to base her continued enrollment on losing an average of two pounds per week. Russell attended diet programs but was not successful in losing weight. Consequently, the coordinator dismissed Russell from the nursing program. She eventually obtained her degree from another nursing program.

A jury found in favor of Russell in her breach of contract claim against the college. Upholding the award of $44,000, the Court noted that the college's actions were based on the belief that Russell's weight was inappropriate, which is outside the realm of academic judgment. The weight-loss contract between Russell and the nursing program raised several issues of concern related to duress, coercion, her state of mind, and no ascertainable consideration for her promise.[41] Russell could only be barred from clinical practice if her obesity hindered satisfactory clinical performance. However, three days before her dismissal from the nursing program, the clinical supervisor gave Russell a very positive evaluation, writing that she looked and acted in a very professional manner and had good attendance and clinical performance. In addition, the supervisor wrote that she intended to offer her a position as a nurse. Russell had maintained the terms of the general academic contract, namely maintenance of good academic standing, payment of tuition and fees, and adherence to the rules and regulations. Thus, having fully performed her part of the contract, Russell was entitled to her degree and to damages that resulted from the arbitrary denial of her degree.

Oral Statements as Contracts

Students have brought lawsuits alleging breach of contract based on oral statements made by professors, advisors, and other university personnel. Courts will refrain from intervening when students have not met the academic requirements and the professors acted in good faith and with reasonable conduct. These principles are clearly enunciated in *Olsson v Board of Higher Education of the City of New York.*[42] The professor erroneously told students taking the comprehensive examination that they must pass three of five questions when in actuality students must score three out of a possible five points on four of the five questions. Olsson achieved the former but not the required score. However, over 50 percent of the students passed the exam despite the professor's erroneous statement. Olsson sued the institution based on the contract principle of estoppel, which prevents one party from reneging on a statement or promise if the other party has relied on it to his or her detriment. Specifically, Olsson asserted that the university should award him the MA because he relied on the professor's statement in budgeting his time and had achieved the stated grade. Rejecting this argument, the Court refused to apply the "diploma by estoppel" doctrine and grant Olsson a degree on the premise that the university breached its contractual obligation; therefore, the Court should judicially award him a degree.[43] This remedy is reserved for the most egregious of circumstances and will not be imposed where a less academically intrusive remedy is available. Olsson had been offered, but refused, an opportunity to retake the examination. Noting that Olsson was not academically qualified, the court emphasized the meaning of an academic degree.

- *When an educational institution issues a diploma to one of its students, it is, in effect, certifying to society that the student possesses all of the knowledge and skills that are required by his chosen discipline.*
- *In order for society to be able to have complete confidence in the credentials dispensed by academic institutions, it is essential that the decisions surrounding the issuance of these credentials be left to the sound judgment of the professional educators who monitor the progress of their students on a regular basis.*
- *Indeed, the value of these credentials from the point of view of society would be seriously undermined if the courts were to abandon their longstanding practice of restraint in this area and instead began to utilize traditional equitable estoppel principles as a basis for requiring institutions to confer diplomas upon those who have been deemed to be unqualified.*[44]

Although courts continue to maintain a judicial "hands-off" on cases involving academic decisions, where the issue involves students' academic qualifications and progression, faculty must continue to deal with students in good faith.

PROFESSIONAL DIMENSION

Faculty have significant discretion in evaluating the academic performance of students and making decisions regarding their progression toward meeting the requirements necessary for graduation. On issues involving students' academic performance, courts will usually defer to the professional judgment of the professors, unless the student can demonstrate that the professor was motivated by ill will or substantially deviated from accepted academic norms. Grievance and appeal procedures have been established to protect the legal rights of students. Faculty should respect the process and deal with students in a fair and professional manner to protect the integrity of the academic environment.

ETHICAL DIMENSION

Faculty should remain objective in their interactions with and evaluation of students. Subjective grading is unfair to students who have studied the materials in hopes of receiving a good grade. Bias, prejudice, and ill will must remain strangers to the academic environment. Students should be treated fairly and recognized as individuals with goals, values, and beliefs. It is not the educator's role to create a clone of him or herself. In situations involving appeals and grievances, faculty should remain objective, neutral, and fair. Justice requires that students be allowed to protect their interests in the educational arena. Faculty should not become defensive but view it as a welcomed process with procedures to address students' issues, concerns, or conduct. Information presented to support a faculty members' action should be factual and never fabricated.

Implications for Educators

- Courts are extremely reluctant to override the grade faculty assign to students.
- Students must be afforded due process in academic and disciplinary issues that negatively impede their progression and graduation.
- More due process is required in disciplinary proceedings. For cases that do not clearly fall under either the academic or disciplinary category, faculty should err on the side of providing more due process.
- Courts are more willing to review cases involving disciplinary due process than those involving academic due process.
- Faculty should follow the policy of their respective schools or colleges to address issues of cheating and other instances of academic dishonesty.
- Academic due process mandates that students are given notice of academic deficiencies, the consequences if improvements are not made, and suggestions for improvement.
- Faculty should remain objective and avoid negatively labeling students.

Strategies to Avoid Legal Problems

- Prepare a course syllabus that outlines course requirements and grading policies. Students should understand the course objectives and evaluation methods.
- Include a reservation of rights clause in the syllabus.
- Review the syllabus with students to prevent and clarify any misconceptions.
- Correct errors on the syllabus, both orally and in writing as soon as detected.
- Provide criteria for how each assignment will be graded.
- Clearly articulate the basis for a failing grade and for failing the course.
- Follow the guidelines provided in the course syllabus.
- Notify students throughout the course, or at least by midterm, of their potential for failing the course and provide suggestions for improvement.
- Avoid making "exceptions" for one or a few students. Treat all students equally.
- Inform students of the procedure for a grade appeal or refer them to the college/university handbook for information on grade appeals.
- Be objective in evaluating students. Avoid grading based on personal values and beliefs.
- Provide a factual basis for a student's failure or dismissal. Avoid subjective comments that negatively label a student.
- Provide immediate and frequent feedback on the students' clinical performance. This feedback should be based on daily clinical records of anecdotal notes of the student's clinical performance.
- Follow established policies and procedures for handling students' academic and disciplinary issues.
- In cases involving disciplinary issues, provide students with the appropriate due process, which consists of notice of the allegations, the opportunity to be heard, and the ability to cross-examine witnesses and present evidence in their defense.

RESPONSE TO CRITICAL THINKING QUESTIONS

1. Discuss whether Randy's due process rights were violated.

Randy probably cannot establish violations of his due process rights. To fulfill due process requirements, faculty members are required to give students notice of their academic deficiencies and the consequences thereof. Dr. Terrell's practice of not providing students with their progression status until the end of the course is not academically strong. Students should be given timely notice that they are failing, suggestions on how to improve, and the consequences of failing the course at midterm or earlier to allow the opportunity for improvement. However, since Randy had passed the first two examinations and the clinical rotation, a midterm status report would have been satisfactory. In addition, since Randy's failure of the course was based on a single test score, counseling him would not change the outcome. Finally, a committee appointed by the chair to review the test, the test grid, and Randy's answers upheld the failing grade. Randy will probably raise the following questions: Should students fail a course based on one failing test grade? Why was the format of the third test different from the first two tests? Why did Dr. Terrell give an essay test this semester? Was this a policy in all nursing courses? Why was he precluded from reviewing the test?

Courts are unlikely to examine the contents, comment on the format, or decide whether an examination has been fairly graded. The appropriate weight given to course assignments is outside the realm of judicial intervention. Faculty members decide how much weight to give each project, examination, or other assignment. Faculty can give unscheduled quizzes to test students' knowledge of course content, ascertain their preparedness for class, and monitor the class' performance. In *Bindrim v University of Montana*,[45] a student alleged that the university breached its contract by adding a function examination as a component of the course and by requiring additional courses after he was advised that no additional courses were needed. Ruling for the university, the court held that Bindrim had not completed the conditions precedent to obtaining his degree. He failed the course by not taking the function examination and did not complete his program of study. In addition, the university catalog contained a reservation of rights clause that allowed them to change instruction and alter course content. Thus, Randy's concern regarding the weight given to one examination is not a judicially strong argument, especially since 85 percent of the students in the class successfully passed the examination.

2. What is the likelihood of the Court ruling in favor of Randy?

To prevail in this case, Randy must show that his assigned failing grade was motivated by bad faith or ill will unrelated to academic decisions or that the grading process used was such a substantial departure from accepted academic norms as to demonstrate that Dr. Terrell did not exercise professional judgment. Randy will probably rely heavily on the statement that Dr. Terrell made during his advising encounter to show bias and ill will. Although courts will probably view this as speculation and insufficient to show bias, the belief that Randy was wasting the faculty's time and taking a seat away from a student who wished to practice as a registered nurse represented Dr. Terrell's personal belief and should have never been stated to Randy. However, the statement, combined with her strongly encouraging Randy to withdraw from the nursing program, is

CHAPTER 1   The Legal Rights of Students

probably not enough to show bias. There is no evidence that Dr. Terrell treated Randy any differently from other students. As stated in the Richmond case, bias must be based on evidence and not speculation and conjecture.

3. Does Randy have a valid argument for breach of contract? Support your answer.

Randy will assert a breach of contract claim based on language contained in the syllabus that identified three multiple-choice examinations and because the professor did not notify the class of any changes in the examination format. Courts will not examine projects and examination formats. In *Harris v Alder School of Professional Psychology*,[46] two doctoral students who failed their qualifying examination initiated a lawsuit alleging that the examination was invalid to assess their knowledge of basic foundation courses in psychology. Rejecting this argument, the Court refused to engage in a judicial determination of course content and subject matter. The determination of whether to assign a passing grade is made by school officials. Randy's claim is premised on a court ruling that the professor could not change a test format or that the test was invalid. Courts will not review the adequacy of examinations to determine validity. The essay examination was given to the entire class. Regardless of the format, students were required to demonstrate knowledge of the subject matter, geriatric nursing. Courts will not intervene to make the professor give a multiple-choice examination or assign Randy a passing grade.

4. What reasons, if any, would necessitate a professor changing the format of an exam?

A strong reason for changing the format of an exam is when a breach of test security has occurred. One possible scenario is presented below. Dr. Terrell indicated she changed the test format because the evening before the examination, she received a call from an anonymous source informing her that several students had a copy of her examination. The source correctly identified the questions on the examination but refused to divulge any additional information. Because of the tight time schedule, Dr. Terrell could not develop another multiple-choice test, nor could she cancel the exam. Using lecture notes and the assigned readings, Dr. Terrell developed an essay test, which essentially measured the students' knowledge of the content. The dean of nursing was aware and approved of the change.

The Office of Student Services was notified and initiated an investigation into the breach of the honor code. Dr. Terrell was asked not to discuss the matter until the investigation was completed. After several students were disciplined for their role in taking and distributing the exam, the class was notified of the reason for the change in the exam format. Requests from students for another multiple-choice test were denied. Grievances filed by students were dismissed as having "no merit."

ANNOTATED BIBLIOGRAPHY

Steinberg v Chicago Medical School, 354 NE2d 586 (1976).
A student applied for admission to a private medical school and submitted the $15 application fee. The student sued the school, alleging it evaluated students for admission on standards other than those published in the bulletin. Specifically, applicants were evaluated according to their relationship to the school's faculty members and board of trustees or based on their ability to make money pledges to the school. Held for the applicant: Steinberg and the school had an enforceable contract; therefore,

the school had an obligation to judge his application according to the stated criteria. The school's obligation was stated in the bulletin and by accepting his application fee, the school had to fulfill its promises.

Aronson v North Park College, 418 NE2d 776 (1981).

A student enrolled in a private college was dismissed after she refused to comply with psychological counseling for a chronic paranoid condition that was considered a serious detriment to herself and others. Held for college: No breach of contract exists where a student signed an admission form that read: "if my application for admission is accepted, I agree to abide by all regulations of the institution and respect its tradition" and the college catalog contained a provision that read, "The institution reserves the right to dismiss at any time a student who in its judgment is undesirable and whose continuation in the school is detrimental to himself or his fellow students."

DeMarco v University of Health Science Chicago Medical School, 352 NE2d 356 (1976).

A student enrolled in a private college had completed all but the last six weeks of medical school. After learning that the student had failed to acknowledge that he had attended another medical school, the college recommended that if the student entered and was honorably discharged from the military, he could be allowed to complete the program. The school later refused to readmit him unless he pledged a contribution to the college. Held for the student: The school breached its contract with the student because the student did not have an obligation to pledge a contribution.

Morfit v University of South Florida, 794So 2d 655 (Fla App 2 Dist 2001).

Subjects in a research project accused Morfit of misconduct. The dean of student judicial services sent Morfit a letter detailing the charges and placed him on immediate suspension. At the hearing, the only evidence present was a report filed by a security officer who had interviewed one witness. Held for the student: Morfit's due process rights were violated because he was deprived of the opportunity to confront and cross-examine his accusers, which is an essential component in disciplinary judicial hearings. The university must follow its own policies and procedures.

Powell v Cooper, 622 NW2d 265 (Wis 2001).

A student was prevented from enrolling in the practicum component of her program of study because she refused to disclose her manic-depressive condition to the site supervisor. Consequently, she was unable to complete the program. Her academic advisor was aware of her condition on admission and assured her that the condition would not interfere with completing the program. Held for student: The faculty's action violated the student's due process rights and was arbitrary and capricious. The student had a constitutionally protected property interest in continuing her graduate studies.

Smith v Rector and Visitors of Univ of Virginia, 115 F Supp 2d 680 (WD Va 2000).

Smith, a student at UVA, was convicted of assault and battery for punching another student in the face, causing him severe facial injuries. He served 21 days in jail, attended anger management, served 400 hours of community service, and paid all related medical expenses. The student initiated disciplinary charges against Smith with the University's Judicial Committee (UJC), a student-run disciplinary body charged with handling complaints about student violations of the university's standard of conduct. The initial hearing was scheduled for February 1998, but was rescheduled until November 1998 pending resolution of the criminal matters. The day before the scheduled hearing, Smith and his father met with Mr. Harmon, vice-president for student affairs, to request a continuance. Smith alleged that his request was granted and contacted the student defense representative to inform the UJC chairperson that the hearing had been continued. Harmon alleges that he did not agree to a continuance. The hearing was conducted as planned, without Smith and against the protests of the defense representative. The UJC found Smith guilty and recommended his expulsion from the university. Smith appealed the decision and the university's Judicial Review Board (JRB) set aside the UJC's decision and remanded the case for a new hearing. A new panel hearing was scheduled for February 1999, but was postponed when the UJC's chairperson recused herself. The UJC then determined that it could not timely hear the case and referred it to Harmon, who appointed a committee composed of faculty, administrators, and students. At the hearing, after hearing Smith's evidence and witnesses, the committee recommended two semesters of suspension and community service. The recommendation was forwarded to the university president, who modified the sentence to two years of suspension, community service, and participation in an anger and alcohol abuse program. He then deferred final judgment pending an appeal of his decision to the JRB. However, the JRB denied Smith's appeal. Held for Smith: Smith had been deprived of notice and an opportunity to be heard at the November 1998 hearing and thus his due process rights had been violated. A student facing disciplinary action that could result in suspension or expulsion is entitled to some type of notice. The Court rejected the university's argument that any alleged violation of Smith's constitutional rights was irrelevant since the panel's decision was set aside and Smith was not harmed.

NOTES

1 U.S. Constitution: Fourteenth Amendment. Available from http://caselaw.lp.findlaw.com/data/constitution/amendment14/index/html.
2 *Greenhill v Bailey,* 519 F2d 5 (8th Cir 1975).
3 *Bailey* at *9.*
4 *Gaspar v Bruton,* 513 F3s 843 (10th Cir 1975).
5 *Goss v Lopez,* 419 U.S. 565 (1975).
6 *Board of Curators of the University of Missouri v Horowitz,* 435 U.S. 78 (1978).
7 *Regents of the University of Michigan v Ewing,* 474 U.S. 214 (1985).
8 *Horowitz.*
9 *Horowitz* at 82.
10 *Horowitz* at 95.
11 *Ewing* at 225.
12 *Ewing* at 227.
13 *Richmond v Fowlkes,* 228 F3d 854 (8th Cir 2000).
14 *Richmond.*
15 *Richmond.*
16 *Susan M. v New York Law School,* 556 N.E.2d 1104 (1990).
17 *Susan M. v New York Law School,* 544 N.Y.S.2d 829 (NY App Div 1989).
18 K. Gaberson. Academic dishonesty among nursing students. *Nursing Forum* 32, no. 3 (1997): 14–21.
19 W. Kaplin, & B. Lee. A legal guide for student affairs professionals (3rd ed.). San Francisco: Jossey-Bass Publishers, 1997.
20 *Dixon v Alabama State Board of Education,* 294 F2d 150 (5th Cir 1961).
21 *Dixon* at 159.
22 *Papachristou v University of Tennessee,* 29 SW3d 487 (Tenn Ct App 2000).
23 *Donohue v Baker,* 976 F Supp 136 (NDNY 1997).
24 *Brookins v Bonnell,* 362 F Supp 379 (1973).
25 *Brookins.*
26 *Sylvester v Texas Southern University,* 957 F Supp 944 (SD Tex 1997).
27 R. Cherry, & J. Geary. The college catalog as a contract. *Journal of Law & Education* 21, no. 1 (1992): 1–33.
28 Kaplin & Lee. *A legal guide for student affairs professionals.*
29 *Steinberg v Chicago Medical School,* 354 NE2d 586 (1976).
30 *People ex rel cecil v Bellevue Hospital Medical College,* 14 NYS 490 (NY Sup Ct), aff'd 28 NE 253 (1891).
31. *People ex rel cecil* at 490.
32. *People ex rel cecil* at 490.
33. *People ex rel cecil* at 490.
34 *University of Texas Health Science Center at Houston v Babb,* 646 SW2d 502 (1982).
35 *Babb* at 503.
36 *University of Mississippi v Hughes,* 765 So 2d 528 (Miss 2000).
37 *Hughes* at 535.
38 *Hughes.*
39 Cherry & Geary. The college catalog as a contract.
40 *Russell v Salve Regina College,* 890 F2d 484 (1st Cir 1989).
41 *Russell v Salve Regina College,* 649 F Supp 391 (DRI 1986).
42 *Olsson v Board of Higher Education of the City of New York,* 402 NE2d 373 (Mass 2000).
43 *Olsson.*
44 *Olsson* at 1153.
45 *Bindrim v University of Montana,* 766 P2d 861 (Mont 1988).
46 *Harris v Alder School of Professional Psychology,* 723 NE2d 717 (Ill App 1 Dist 1999).

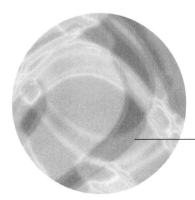

The Legal Rights of Faculty: Academic Freedom

2

INTRODUCTION

Speech is often provocative and challenging.[1] It may infuriate, ignite prejudices, highlight preconceptions, and evoke profound unsettling effects as it presses for acceptance of its substance.[2] That is why freedom of speech, though not absolute, is nevertheless protected against censorship or punishment.[3] In education environments, academic freedom has found its niche under the auspices of the First Amendment to the U.S. Constitution. Academic freedom is a fluid concept. Its foundation is firm, but its interpretation and meaning is varied. This chapter explores academic freedom as the foundation of the legal rights of faculty in higher education environments.

June Pedyt has been employed as an assistant professor of nursing and health education in a tenure-track position at Casey University for five years. She teaches courses in basic concepts of health, leadership, and ethics to students in nursing and health education. She has consistently maintained above-average to excellent student evaluations, has a consistent record of scholarship, and is on numerous university and college committees, including the faculty senate. June is a staunch anti-abortion advocate and an active member of the independent party. During the annual address to the faculty senate, the university president addressed the senators' concerns regarding administrative-imposed constraints on academic freedom and reiterated his positions on academic freedom for students and faculty. He stated, "students must be taught that women should have the right to an abortion, that minority students shall have access to an education, education is the gateway to achievement and success, and this university will continue to engage in the scholarly pursuit and dissemination of knowledge." June immediately questioned the president regarding the appropriateness of teaching students to become "pro-abortion." The meeting quickly became a debate between anti- and pro-abortionists. The president clarified his statement to mean that students must be taught the issues surrounding both positions and formulate their own opinions. After the meeting, he called June aside and said, "Never again challenge me in public. Remember, I give the final approval for everything."

The next semester, June assigned her leadership students to research and write a paper on whether the president's remarks on abortion were appropriate and to identify topics that are inappropriate for leaders in health care and educational institutions to discuss during professional presentations. Two students who were pro-abortion and pro-president asked for an alternate assignment because it conflicted with their values. June refused and the students filed a complaint with the dean. Another student wrote an excellent paper regarding the president's abortion comments and asked June to assist her in editing the paper for submission to the university paper commentary section. The student acknowledged June's assistance, guidance, and knowledge in the published article, which questioned the integrity and sincerity of the president as a leader. The article had a divisive effect on the campus. Opponents of abortion organized a march to the president's office to protest his stand on abortion. Proponents of abortion organized to counter with a supportive march. The groups also planned and executed a march to the offices of their state representatives. June participated in the latter, but not the former march. At the march, a local reporter interviewed June regarding her position as the local president of the anti-abortion chapter and the president's pro-abortion statements. June refused to comment on the president's statement due to her university position. The next day, an article in the local newspaper read, "Local professor in conflict with university president over women rights." It also contained statements from an anonymous source indicating that the president and his administration had eroded academic freedom and many faculty members had their lectures censored or were punished for taking positions contrary to that of the president.

The dean informed June during a called meeting that her contract would not be renewed because of budgetary constraints and student complaints against her not allowing an alternate assignment. The dean stated that other faculty members would teach June's courses, but no other information was provided. After exhausting all administrative remedies, June filed a lawsuit, alleging violation of her First Amendment rights of speech, assembly, and organizational membership.

CRITICAL THINKING QUESTIONS

1. Should June have provided students with an alternate assignment?
2. Did June's speech involve issues of public concern?
3. Were June's actions disruptive to the university?
4. What is the probability of June prevailing in her lawsuit against the university for violation of her First Amendment rights?

DEFINITION OF ACADEMIC FREEDOM

The concept of academic freedom refers to the rights faculty have to teach their subject matter, engage in research, speak on matters of public concern, and provide service to others without unnecessary interference from administrators. Specially, academic freedom allows educational institutions to pursue their goals without interference from external entities and allows faculty within educational environments to discover, disseminate, and advance knowledge without interference from administrators and governing boards.[4] The American Association of University Professors' (AAUP) 1940 statement on academic freedom provides the foundation for academic customs and norms in colleges and universities. The statement, which has been widely endorsed by numerous professional and education institutions, reads:

" • *Teachers are entitled to full freedom in research and in the publication of the results subject to the adequate performance of their other academic duties.*

• *Teachers are entitled to freedom in the classroom in discussing their subject, but they should be careful not to introduce into their teaching controversial matter that has no relation to their subject.*

• *College and university teachers are citizens, members of a learned profession, and officers of an educational institution. When they speak or write as citizens, they should be free from institutional censorship or discipline, but their special position in the community imposes special obligations. As scholars and educational officers, they should remember that the public may judge their profession and their institution by their utterances. Hence they should at all times be accurate, should exercise appropriate restraint, should show respect for the opinions of others, and should make every effort to indicate that they are not speaking for the institution.*"[5]

DEVELOPMENTAL STAGES OF ACADEMIC FREEDOM

As a framework, academic freedom has undergone a rocky and currently unstable developmental process. The first stage of development was to identify the fundamental basis of its existence. Academic freedom found its niche in the First Amendment to the U.S. Constitution, which reads, "Congress shall make no law respecting an establishment of religion, or prohibiting the free exercise thereof; or abridging the freedom of speech, or of the press;

or the right of the people peaceably to assemble, and to petition the Government for a redress of grievance."[6] This amendment is the fundamental basis for the free exchange of ideas in a democratic society. Especially important is the protections provided under this amendment to teachers at all levels of education. The U.S. Supreme Court has protected and enforced teachers' rights to freedom of expression, thought, inquiry, and association under this amendment. Although not specifically identified in the U.S. Constitution, numerous legal decisions have upheld faculty members' right to academic freedom under the auspices of the First Amendment. Teachers have the freedom to advocate for truth, challenge the status quo, introduce controversial issues, and pursue knowledge. Faculty must foster in students open-mindedness, sensitivity, critical inquiry, accountability, and responsibility necessary to become informed productive citizens. They should not be restrained by fear of retaliation by administrators who may have different opinions. Academic freedom does not apply to faculty in private colleges and universities, unless they have enough state involvement as to render them state actors. For example, if private colleges receive state funding or state contracts, they may be subject to constitutional standards. This topic is discussed in detail in Chapter 3.

Protection of Academic Freedom: Legal Cases

Although clearly stated, the boundaries of academic freedom have and continue to be judicially tested, yielding varied and sometimes conflicting results. In essence, courts have been generous in affording academic freedom to faculty; however, faculty should understand the cases that provide the foundation for an analysis of their employment rights. Two early cases provide the analytical framework for decisions related to academic freedom in government or educational institutions. Both cases exemplify the respect courts have for faculty as producers and disseminators of knowledge.

Sweezy v New Hampshire. In *Sweezy v New Hampshire,*[7] a legislative act made subversive organizations unlawful and subversive persons ineligible for employment by the state. The attorney general was empowered to investigate violations of the act and initiate criminal prosecutions when necessary. Sweezy was summoned to appear before the attorney general on two separate occasions to testify about his past conduct and associations with certain groups. During the last appearance, Sweezy refused to answer questions related to his knowledge of the Progressive Party and about a lecture he gave to a group of university students, invoking First Amendment protection. Although Sweezy was not a faculty member at the university, the U.S. Supreme Court extended him academic freedom and articulated several important legal principles regarding the importance of free speech in educational institutions:

- *Scholarship cannot flourish in an atmosphere of suspicion and distrust.*
- *Teachers and students must always remain free to inquire, to study and to evaluate, to gain new maturity and understanding; otherwise our civilization will stagnate and die.*
- *To impose any strait jacket upon the intellectual leaders in our colleges and universities would imperil the future of our Nation.*[8]

In an era where there was generalized fear of the effect dissent groups could have on our country, the court emphasized that governmental actions cannot curtail the freedoms that are essential for the survival of the nation in the pursuit of the truth. The Court's message was clear—academic freedom will be protected under the auspices of the First Amendment.

Keyishian v Board of Regents. Ten years later, in *Keyishian v Board of Regents,*[9] the Court refused to uphold a policy that required faculty to sign a certificate that they were not Communists and if involved in a subversive group, they would communicate such to the university president. This requirement had the effect of preventing or limiting a faculty member's statements and/or associations. Faculty could not, without fear of retaliation or termination, be a member of a subversive group or educate students on or advocate for certain groups. The Court found the plan unconstitutional because it curtailed or chilled "the exercise of vital First Amendment rights"[10] by teachers:

- *Our nation is deeply committed to safeguarding academic freedom, which is of transcendent value to teachers and all of us.*
- *Freedom is a special concern of the First Amendment, which does not tolerate laws that cast a pall of orthodoxy over the classroom.*
- *The classroom is peculiarly the "market place of ideas."*[11]

Faculty must be given the four essential freedoms, "to determine for itself on academic grounds who may teach, what may be taught, how it shall be taught, and who may be admitted to study."[12] They must be allowed to challenge existing perspectives, seek truths, reject and modify beliefs upon which traditions are built, and examine the very essence of our existence and civilization. Faculty in colleges and universities cannot fulfill the missions of higher educational institutions if they are forced to become instrumentalities of the state.

The Limits of Academic Freedom: Legal Cases

Once the U.S. Supreme Court articulated its protection of academic freedom under the First Amendment, the next stage involved the identification of limits on free speech in higher education and governmental environments. Courts could not give faculty unrestricted control to say and do whatever they pleased under the guise of the First Amendment's protection of speech because to do so would leave employers helpless to control the employment environment.

A series of cases discussed later describe the analysis process that courts apply to balance the protection of employee's protected speech with employer's need to operate an efficient work environment. The analysis process incorporates identifying speech involving matters of public concern, balancing the rights of employers with those of employees, and determining protections afforded to employees to avoid violations of their rights.

Distinguishing Matters of Public Concern

The case of *Pickering v Board of Education*[13] distinguishes matters that are of concern to the public from those that are personal. Pickering, a high school teacher, was fired because he wrote a letter to the local newspaper criticizing the board's allocation of resources from a previous bond and accusing the superintendent of attempting to prevent teachers from speaking out against the issue. Prior to Pickering's letter, the superintendent and a teacher's organization had published articles in support of the tax increase. The lower court found no free-speech violation because Pickering's letter contained numerous false statements, unjustifiably impugned the reputation of school administrators and the board, and was detrimental to the interests of the school system.[14] Rejecting this finding, the Supreme Court ruled that teachers do not "relinquish their First Amendment rights they would otherwise enjoy as citizens to comment on matters of public interest in connection with the operation of the public schools in which they work."[15] Nevertheless, the government as an employer recognizes that the speech of its employees may be different from that of general citizens. Therefore, Pickering requires an analysis of the "balance between the interests of the teacher, as a citizen, in commenting upon matters of public concern and the interest of the state, as an employer, in promoting the efficiency of the public services it performs through its employees."[16] The issue of funding for school districts is a matter of public concern. Although Pickering's letter contained erroneous statements, they were not made in reckless disregard for the truth. The Court found that free speech outweighed the employer's interest, since the letter neither disrupted the daily operations of the school nor impeded Pickering's performance of his duties. The core value of the Free Speech Clause of the First Amendment is the "public interest in having free and unhindered debate on matters of public concern."[17] The simple threat of dismissal based on one's speech is enough to prohibit free speech on matters of public concerns.

Courts have articulated an analytic framework to use when reviewing cases alleging violations of rights guaranteed under the Free Speech Clause of the First Amendment (Box 2.1). This framework can be used to minimize or prevent infringements on free speech of governmental employees and academic freedom of faculty.

Matters related to academic quality and integrity, finances, discrimination, sexual harassment, and wrongdoings or breaches of the public trust by administrators are of concern to the public. In contrast, issues related to personal grievances or internal employment problems are not matters of public concern. In examining the context of the speech, one must answer the question, "Is the employee's speech made in the context of his role

---

Box 2.1

Analytical Framework Used in Examining Right to Free Speech

- Courts look at the content, context, and form of the speech to determine if it is a matter of public concern.
- If the speech is not a matter of public concern, then no violation of rights has occurred and further analysis is unnecessary.
- If the speech is a matter of public concern, courts will review the facts to determine if the speech interferes with the employee's performance of his duties or impedes the efficient operation of the employment environment.
- If the speech does not interfere with the work environment, courts will then determine if it was a substantial reason for the adverse employment decision. If the answer is yes, but the employer would have made the same decision even in the absence of the protected speech, the court will rule in favor of the employer.
- If the speech does not interfere with the work environment and the employer had no other basis for the adverse employment decision, courts will rule in favor of the employee.

as an employee or as a citizen?" The former may not be protected speech, unless it relates to a matter of public concern. For example, a professor's comments on grading policies, reduction in faculty, and student enrollment are matters of public concern of educational standards and academic policy.[18]

Balancing Employer and Employee Rights

The employer's interest in maintaining an efficient work environment is balanced with the employee's right to speak out on matters related to public concern. Factors germane to this analysis include "whether an employee's comments meaningfully:

- interfere with the performance of his or her duties or with the employer's general operations,
- undermine a legitimate goal or mission of the employer, create disharmony among coworkers,
- undercut an immediate supervisor's discipline over the employee, or
- destroy the relationship of loyalty and trust required of confidential employees."[19]

As the following case will illustrate, if the protected speech interferes with the work environment, courts will rule in favor of the employer.[20]

Myers, an assistant district attorney, was upset over being transferred to another division. She developed and circulated a survey at work related to office morale, the need for a grievance committee, previous transfers, feeling pressured to work in political campaigns, and employees' confidence in several supervisors. Connick learned of the survey and terminated Myers for refusal to accept the transfer. In addition, he objected to the questions regarding confidence in supervisors and whether employees felt pressured to work in political campaigns, labeling the distribution of the questionnaire as insubordination. The question—feeling pressured to work in political campaigns—related to a matter of public concern, because "official pressure upon employees to work for political candidates not of the worker's own choice constitutes a coercion of belief in violation of fundamental constitutional rights."[21] The Court, in balancing the interests of the state as an employer with the rights of the employee to speak on matters of public concern, looked at the intent of Myers's actions. Noting that her mission was to gather information to support her personal stance, whether than to promote efficiency in the office, the court ruled in favor of the employer. As an employer, the government has wide latitude and discretion in maintaining efficiency and managing its personnel and internal affairs; it is not required to keep an employee who is disruptive to and negatively affects the morale, harmony, and efficient operation of the office. A greater degree of deference is given employers when close working relationships are imperative to fulfilling employment-related missions and goals.[22]

Determining Protections Provided to Employees

Although the First Amendment creates a strong presumption against punishing innocent people, employers are only required to implement reasonable safeguards to avoid free speech violations. In *Waters v Churchill*,[23] a nurse was terminated from her position because of statements she allegedly made to another employee criticizing the obstetrics unit and her supervisors. If true, the speech was unprotected because it related to internal grievance, discouraged people from working in the unit and undermined management's authority. Churchill denied the allegations, stating she had criticized the supervisor's cross-training policy and the negative effect it had on patient care, which are issues related to matters of public concern. The head of clinical obstetrics and another nurse corroborated Churchill's version, but were not interviewed by administrators prior to her termination. Ruling for Churchill, the court noted that she had produced enough evidence to create an issue as to whether the hospital's actual motive for firing her was based on speech related to matters of public concern.

Employers should not base adverse employment decisions on minimum or no evidence when strong evidence is available. The possibility of inadvertently punishing an employee for exercising her First Amendment rights mandates the use of reasonable care in adverse employment actions.

ACADEMIC FREEDOM IN PUBLICATIONS

Faculty members enjoy considerable freedom in their publication endeavors. Administrators neither require faculty to obtain permission to publish nor approve their topics. Publications are usually viewed as speech and afforded constitutional protection. As the following case illustrates, faculty cannot be punished or subjected to negative treatment because of the beliefs they express in print.

Dr. Levin, a tenured professor, published several writings that contained controversial and denigrating comments about the intelligence and social characteristics of African Americans.[24] African American students had not complained that the professor subjected them to unfair or unequal treatment in class. However, based on negative responses about the writings, the dean, over the objections of the chairperson, created an alternate or shadow section of Dr. Levin's class and allowed students to transfer out of his class. At a press conference, the university president stated that Levin's comments were offensive and had no place at the college. He also appointed an ad hoc committee to determine if Levin's views affected his teaching abilities and to ascertain when extracurricular speech went beyond conduct unbecoming of a faculty. Ruling in favor of Professor Levin, the court noted that the administration had subjected Levin to negative treatment based solely on the expression of his constitutionally protected speech. The creation of the shadow classes greatly reduced his class size and, fearing termination, Levin declined at least 20 speaking or writing opportunities. These actions violated Levin's First Amendment rights.

Publications designed to impede the efficient operations of the work environment may not find protection under the First Amendment. Publications are considered disruptive when they are based on personal vendettas and internal grievances. For example, in *Maples v Martin*,[25] faculty members who were displeased with and critical of the departmental chairperson published a review that identified faculty involvement in decision making, low faculty morale, and "weaknesses in the curriculum, inadequate facilities, low faculty-to-school ratio and students' poor performance on the professional licensing examination."[26] A copy of the review was sent to the department's accrediting agency who determined that most of the content in the review was unrelated to accreditation criteria. The visiting team from the accrediting agency labeled the review as "academic terrorism" to discredit the chairperson and concluded that the long-standing infighting within the department was seriously disrupting the efficiency of the educational process in the mechanical engineering department and affecting other departments within the college. Based on the accreditation team's findings, the university president transferred several mechanical engineering faculty to other engineering programs within the college. The transferred faculty retained their salary, rank, and tenure. Although faculty motives were sincere in try-ing to maintain a quality program and the review contained constitutionally protected materials, it interfered with the efficient operation of the department. The review was pub-lished just prior to the accreditation visit, faculty attempted to bring students into the con-troversy, and the accrediting team counseled the department that immediate correction was required. The administrative actions did not violate the faculty members' First Amendment rights because of the negative effect their actions had on the education environment.

ACADEMIC FREEDOM IN CLASSROOM ACTIVITIES

Teaching

The AAUP's 1940 policy statement reaffirms the rights of faculty to academic freedom in the classroom as long as the content is related to the subject matter. This policy statement has been incorporated into policies on academic freedom adopted by numerous institutions of higher education and has provided guidance to courts confronted with issues related to academic freedom. Faculty members are usually given leeway to determine the appropriate teaching methods for their content and development of assignments to fulfill course objec-tives. Course content, teaching methods, learning exercises, and examination methods related to the subject matter are usually outside the realm of judicial analysis.

Analysis of Protected Content

The determination of whether or not content taught in a course is protected speech is based on the nature of the content in relation to course goals, objectives, and learning assign-ments. As illustrated in the following case, content offensive to some students may be allowed in order to foster intellectual discourse and promote learning.

In *Hardy v Jefferson Community College*[27] the college refused to offer teaching assign-ments to an instructor who used certain words in his class discussion. Hardy, who was hired as an adjunct instructor in 1995, taught the course Introduction to Interpersonal Communi-cation. During his standard lecture on language and social constructivism, students were asked to examine how language is used to marginalize minorities and other oppressed groups and to provide examples of such language. Students identified several terms, including "nigger," "bitch," "faggot," "girl," and "lady." They found the class discussion academically and philosophically challenging. An African American student objected to the use of the terms "nigger" and "bitch" and complained to Hardy, administrators, and a community civil-rights activist. She believed such language directly contradicted the instructor's policy, as outlined on the class syllabus that "there would be no abusive (i.e. sex-ist, racist, otherwise derogatory) language in discussion."[28]

Although Hardy apologized to the student for any discomfort, the student took the matter to the local civil-rights activist, who met with college administrators and demanded corrective actions. Hardy met with the assistant dean and attempted to explain that the words were used "as illustrations of highly, offensive, powerful language and were not used in an 'abusive' manner"[29] and asked how he could rectify the situation. The assistant dean did not address Hardy's question, but informed him that a prominent member of the African American community had threatened to negatively affect the school's enrollment unless the college corrected the situation. Hardy was later informed that the situation had been corrected and not offered any more teaching assignments.

Hardy initiated a lawsuit alleging a number of claims, including retaliation for exercising his free speech and academic freedom rights in violation of the First Amendment. The college argued that the use of racially vulgar words did not have constitutional protection. Acknowledging that classroom instruction will often fall within the Supreme Court's conception of "public concern," the court ruled that Hardy's speech was protected because it was germane to the classroom discussion and did not exceed the context of the topic. Teachers should formulate stimulating ideas and topics that teach students the "process of rational discourse that allows them to participate meaningfully in public debate," which is an essential component of becoming a responsible citizen.[30]

The college also asserted that its interests in controlling the curriculum, including the pedagogical methods of the faculty and in maintaining an efficient, nondisruptive academic environment, outweighed Hardy's free-speech rights. Rejecting this argument, the court noted that:

- *Only one of nine African-American students objected to the language.*
- *Hardy's teaching evaluations were positive.*
- *The lectures did not impede the performance of Hardy's duties.*
- *Administrators' fear that the civil rights activist involvement would interfere with the regular operation of the college was unfounded.*

Administrators' desire to avoid the unpleasantness that accompanies controversial topics is not sufficient to erode the First Amendment rights of teachers. In assessing the constitutionality of classroom speech, faculty members should ask three questions:

1. Does the subject matter have an educational foundation?
2. Is the speech germane to the course content?
3. Will the speech have a disruptive impact on the efficiency and operation of the college?

If the answer to the first two questions is yes, the speech is protected from censor unless the university can show a disruptive impact, sufficient to override First Amendment Protection.

Analysis of Unprotected Content

Courts will protect the needs of administrators in a higher education institution in order to promote an environment conducive to student learning. Faculty cannot use their classrooms to present potentially offensive content that is unrelated to course goals and objectives or that can be presented in a more neutral manner.

The case of *Bonnell v Lorenzo*[31] applies the analysis questions listed above and highlights the principle that academic freedom is not a license to say and do as one pleases in the classroom. Bonnell, a teacher of English Language and Literature at the community college, was terminated after 21 years for his classroom language and for violating disciplinary mandates. In February 1998, Bonnell was informed of a complaint against him for his classroom use of the words "fuck," "cunt," and "pussy," which were viewed as degrading to women. Bonnell responded that the words were used to highlight attitudes that depicted women as sexual objects. The meeting was followed by a memorandum to Bonnell that stated that those words might be the basis of a sexual harassment claim, unless they were germane to the classroom discussion of subject-matter content. Eight months later, another student filed a complaint of sexual harassment based on Bonnell's classroom speech stating, "Some of the stories that were required reading revealed sexual innuendoes and implications. This should have been dealt with in a professional and appropriate manner, yet Mr. Bonnell displayed a lack of maturity, sensitivity, and responsibility, by taking advantage of the conversations to express his own sexual experiences."[32] The student requested that Bonnell be dismissed from the college. Bonnell removed the student's name from the complaint, posted a copy on the bulletin board and distributed it to students in his class. Consequently, administrators warned Bonnell to cease distribution of the complaint because it was confidential. Bonnell continued to distribute the complaint and wrote a satirical apology essay to faculty members. He was later suspended for the use of vulgar and obscene language in the classroom. Despite the warning, Bonnell provided a copy of the complaint and apology to the local television station and informed his students of his suspension. Bonnell was suspended with pay for distributing a copy of the complaint and apology to the local media. He was subsequently suspended for four months without pay for insubordination, breach of confidentiality, disruption of the educational process, and retaliation. The district court granted Bonnell's motion for preliminary injunction and he returned to his teaching responsibilities. Shortly after his return, another student was offended by Bonnell's profanity and offensive language and demanded a full tuition refund. The college appealed the district court's ruling that allowed Bonnell to escape the suspension and continue teaching.

To determine whether Bonnell's speech, apology, and classroom language addressed matters of public concern, the court examined the context, form, and content of the statement and written materials. The content of the sexual harassment complaint against him was a matter of public concern as were allegations of racial discrimination and abuse. Likewise the context and the form of the speech was a matter of public concern because "other students attending and planning to attend the College certainly would be interested in learning the nature of the sexual harassment complaint."[33] Although both the complaint and apology were protected under the First Amendment, the offensive language used in the classroom was not germane to the subject content and therefore was not constitutionally protected.

Because some of Bonnell's speech was protected, the court analyzed the impact of the speech on the education environment. The college contended that their interest in disciplining a faculty member that engages in activities that threaten their federal funding, such as sexual harassment, outweighs any constitutional protection. Ruling in favor of the college, the Court held that "colleges and universities are legally required to maintain a hostile-free learning environment and must strive to create policies which serve that purpose."[34] A faculty cannot create an environment that compromises "a student's right to learn in a hostile-free environment."[35] In the era of concern over lawsuits alleging sexual harassment, administrators sometimes walk a tightrope in trying to balance faculty members' rights to academic freedom with students' rights to learn in a hostile-free environment.

Curriculum Decisions

The faculty, as scholars and experts, are in the best position to determine the learning needs of students. Students cannot challenge a professor's learning assignments as contrary to their personal or moral beliefs.[36] For example, a nursing student cannot challenge a clinical assignment that is an essential part of the curriculum because he or she objects to the faculty or some other aspect of the assignment. However, the curriculum committee or departmental chairperson can impose limits on faculty rights. In Edwards V. California, a professor objected to the department determining the syllabus that would be used in his course.[37] The department had approved an earlier version of the syllabus, but Edwards used an unapproved syllabus that addressed the issues he wanted to teach. The department chair also cancelled the book ordered by Edwards to be used in the course. The Supreme Court left intact the federal court's ruling that "a public university professor does not have a First Amendment right to decide what will be taught in the classroom."[38] was allowed to stand.

Policies regarding the selection process of textbooks and course materials will vary among higher education institutions. Nevertheless, faculty should have input and remain involved in the decision-making process.

Internet

The Internet is a forum for the expression of ideas. Universities provide services and hardware that allow access by both students and professors. Many faculty members maintain web pages that depict and highlight their professional interests and research endeavors. Principles that apply to speaking and writing also apply to faculty's electronic communications. Any communications made through university-owned and -operated equipment should adhere to the university's policies and regulations. Some institutions may restrict the use of cyberspace communications to those having a valid educational purpose, while others may require a disclaimer that the faculty member's communications do not reflect the views of the institution. The AAUP statement on academic freedom and electronic communications provides guidance. "While expression in cyberspace is obviously different in important ways from print or oral expression . . . such factors do not appear to justify alteration or dilution of basic principles of academic freedom and free inquiry within the academic community."[39]

However, a recent decision curtailed academic freedom in cyberspace. In *Urofsky v Gilmore*,[40] several professors initiated a lawsuit challenging a Virginia statute that restricted state employees from accessing sexually explicit material on computers owned or leased by the state except to the extent required in conjunction with a bona fide, agency-approved research project or other undertaking.[41] Permission to access the material could be given by the appropriate department head. The professors alleged that the statute interfered with their academic endeavors. For example, one professor indicated that he did not assign an online research project on indecency because he feared that he would be unable to verify the students' work. Another complained he was restricted in his ability to access sexually explicit poetry in connection with his study of Victorian poets. None of the professors had requested or was denied permission to access materials. Ruling for the university, the court held that the Constitution protects the academic freedom of a professor against dismissal for the exercise of Free Amendment rights; however, academic freedom inheres in the university and not the individual professor. Therefore, the state can require "its employees to undertake the responsibilities of their positions in a specified way."[42] Critics of this decision argue that this case ignores the essences of academic freedom and its inherent rights and duties, using the following arguments:

• Faculty members should have the right to pursue chosen research topics and to present their professional views without the imposition or threat of institutional penalty for the political, religious, or ideological tendencies of their scholarship, but are subject to fair professional evaluation by peers and appropriate institutional officers.

- Faculty members have the right to teach without the imposition or threat of institutional penalty for the political, religious, or ideological tendencies of their work, subject to their duties to satisfy reasonable education objectives and to respect the dignity of their students.
- Faculty members may exercise the rights of citizens to speak on matters of public concern and to organize with others for political ends without imposition or threat of institutional penalty, subject to their academic duty to clarify the distinction between advocacy and scholarship.
- Faculty members have the right to express views on the educational policies and institutional priorities of their schools without the imposition or threat of institutional penalty, subject to duties to respect colleagues and to protect the school from external misunderstandings.[43]

By refusing to hear the case of *Urofsky v Gilmore,*[44] the Supreme Court did not provide the necessary and needed guidance to faculty and administrators on issues related to the impact of technology and technological advances on academic freedom.

Grading

Although faculty members' grading policies have withstood student challenges, they have received mixed outcomes against department or university policies. Colleges and universities develop grading policies to ensure consistency in the processing and reporting of grades. Professors must follow their institution's grading policies and procedures, including grading scale, submission of grades for review, and filing of grades on or before the deadline. Courts have not extended First Amendment protection to professors who refuse to comply with their institution's grading policies. Professor Wozniak[45] refused to comply with the university's requirement to grade on a prescribed curve and to submit his materials for review. Consequently, he was stripped of his professorial responsibilities but kept his rank and salary. The Court upheld the premise that colleges and universities have the institutional authority to promulgate regulations related to the grading process.

Although educational institutions can engage in a reasonable review of a faculty member's assignment of grades, professors cannot be pressured to change a grade that represents the true evaluation of a student's performance. Courts differ in what protection, if any, faculty have in the assignment of grades. In *Parate v Isibor,*[46] a professor's contract was not renewed because he refused to change a student's grade. The Court found a First Amendment violation because the assignment of a grade is a symbolic communication designed to send a message to the student. In contrast, the Court refused to extend First Amendment protection to a tenured professor who refused to change a student's grade from an "F" to an incomplete because the student missed 12 out of 15 classes. The Court ruled that "a public university professor does not have a First Amendment right to expression via the school's grade assignment procedures" because the assignment of grades is subsumed under the university's freedom to determine how a course is taught."[47] Faculty members evaluate students based on established criteria and assign grades accordingly. Once grades are assigned, students may challenge their grades according to the grade appeal process. Grades should not be overturned unless students can show bias and unfairness in the grading process.

Teaching Methods and Styles

Faculty are the foundation of colleges and universities. Students are the consumers of the knowledge, service, and scholarly endeavors of teachers. The student-teacher relationship is unique. Teaching involves imparting knowledge, challenging conventional ideas, promoting critical thinking, and evaluating the acquisition of acquired or learned knowledge. Faculty members are evaluated on their knowledge and presentation of the subject matter, their involvement with students, availability for consultation and feedback, and appropriateness of assigned learning activities. By tradition, most administrators allow faculty members to determine how the subject matter will be taught. For example, the department chairperson, in consultation with the curriculum committee, will approve the program of studies for specific majors. Colleagues in the discipline determine what will be taught and who will teach it. Although the vice president for academic affairs gives final approval, great deference is given to the collective wisdom of faculty in the disciplines.

Little constraints are imposed on faculty in the classroom. Faculty are socialized to teach in a professional and respectful manner. When alerted to a problem, administrators should engage in a peer-review process to evaluate the situation and provide constructive feedback to the faculty, if needed. The advent of distance learning provides a ready means of evaluation because the faculty members' lectures, classroom presentation, and demeanor are audiotaped. Online courses, likewise, provide a fixed medium that is amenable to ready review.

Conflicts arise when a faculty's teaching style is inconsistent with the accepted traditions of the institution or fails to meet the learning needs of students. Administrators must address the concerns and fulfill the educational needs of their tuition-paying student-consumers. Similarly, they must respect the theoretical basis and parameters of academic freedom. These conflicts have feuled and continue to fuel legal controversy over the boundaries of faculty versus institutional academic freedom. For example, Professor Cohen utilized a teaching style where he took the devil's-advocate role in controversial topics and assigned provocative essays. One student was offended by Cohen's use of profanity, sexual innuendoes, and the assignment to write an essay defining pornography. After her request for an alternate assignment was refused, she stopped attending class and received a failing grade. The president and Grievance Committee found that Cohen had violated the sexual harassment policy. On appeal, the court found that the imposition of discipline against Cohen violated his First Amendment rights because the university's sexual harassment policy was unconstitutionally vague. The Court did not, however, rule on Cohen's teaching style; therefore, several questions and concerns were not addressed. For example, how can students be taught to confront their biases and prejudices, expand their tolerance, and learn to respectfully disagree with others in a scholarly manner if, when uncomfortable, they can simply not participate? How can a professor promote a free exchange of ideas if he cannot invoke controversial topics and issues? When does a controversial topic become sexual harassment?

Administrators can require faculty to utilize teaching methodology appropriate to the type of students admitted into the university. The pedagogical teaching style of the professor must be consistent with the needs of the students. In *Hetrick v Martin,*[48] a professor was dismissed because her pedagogical style and philosophy were inconsistent with the needs of the students and the university's goals. Students had restrictive backgrounds that required teachers to use more basic, fundamental, and conventional teaching styles. Hetrick assigned independent and out-of-class work to "teach them how to think." In addition, she did not cover the required class content nor did she develop a sense of camaraderie with her colleagues. Ruling in favor of the university, the court noted that the First Amendment does not require the university to keep in its employment a teacher whose teaching style is inconsistent with that prescribed by the university. Similarly, academic freedom does not mandate that a university tolerate any "manner of teaching method the teacher may choose to employ."[49]

Courts have had to balance the freedom of educational institutions with the academic freedom of faculty. Although faculty members enjoy a certain amount of academic freedom in the classroom, courts have imposed limitations. Each faculty is a member of the educational team and not the team; therefore, he or she must consider and incorporate, to the extent possible, norms of the department. However, because faculty are expected to be innovative and creative, they must move beyond norms and tradition. Creativity and innovation are welcomed if grounded in a valid educational purpose.

Evaluation

Another major issue for faculty is the adequate evaluation of their teaching abilities. University policies and procedures require an evaluation of how well faculty perform their academic duties. Faculty members must adhere to institution-developed or -approved evaluation methods. Many faculty criticize standardized evaluation methods as not reflective of their true teaching abilities. An analysis of data related to students' evaluation of faculty provides administrators with information on how well the faculty member is at performing one aspect of his or her academic responsibilities. Courts have upheld the principle that poor performance of teaching can be the basis for dismissal because it is considered an essential component of a faculty's duties. For example, a professor who frequently left his class unattended and assigned independent work for students to foster their autonomy and independence was denied tenure.[50] He alleged that his teaching methods were protected speech under the First Amendment and that student evaluations should not be the primary method to evaluate his teaching effectiveness. The university prevailed because academic freedom cannot be used as a shield to insulate faculty from evaluation and because he was an ineffective teacher as evidenced by his teaching evaluations and peer review of his portfolio.

ACADEMIC FREEDOM IN EXTRAMURAL ACTIVITIES

Consulting

Faculty members engage in extramural activities away from the work environment that may directly relate to their academic interest and expertise. Faculty are often sought by private industry, attorneys, and other interest groups for their knowledge of and expertise in their selected fields. These activities fulfill the service and/or scholarly components of a faculty member's role and directly benefit the institution by showcasing its community of scholars. The public-relations office of many educational institutions is instrumental in broadcasting and publishing the scholarly endeavors of its faculty members even when the speech or activity involves a controversial subject matter.

The case of *Hoover v Morale*[51] illustrates that administrators cannot arbitrarily impede the consulting activities of its faculty. A state statute and university policy prohibited faculty members from serving as expert witnesses against the state but allowed them to serve as experts for the state. The Court rejected the argument that the expert witness's speech is commercial because of the compensation and thus entitled to less constitutional protection. Applying the balancing analysis discussed in the *Pickering* case, the faculty member's testimony related to the addictive nature of nicotine and its health consequences was a matter of public concern. Therefore a ban on serving as an expert witness was effectively curtailing speech. The Court rejected the university's conflict of interest argument, noting that the university allowed faculty to serve as experts for the state but not against the state. "The notion that the State may silence the testimony of state employees simply because that testimony is contrary to the interests of the State in litigation or otherwise, is antithetical to the protection extended by the First Amendment."[52]

The AAUP 1940 statement provides guidance to faculty members engaging in extramural activities.

> "*When [faculty] speak or write as citizens, they should be free from institutional censorship or discipline, but their special position in the community imposes special obligations. As scholars and educational officers, they should remember that the public may judge their profession and their institution by their utterances. Hence they should at all times be accurate, should exercise appropriate restraint, should show respect for the opinions of others, and should make every effort to indicate that they are not speaking for the institution.*" [53]

It is not uncommon for the media and others to reference a professor by his or her title and place of employment. An example is a newspaper publication that reads, "a professor of nursing at XYZ University advocates against a law that allows mothers to abandon their newborn babies at hospitals without facing criminal charges." Although the professor was speaking in her role as vice president of the group, Association for Responsible Citizens, the media associated her with the university. Therefore faculty must remember that their extramural activities may be directly linked with the university. Administrators may peruse the extramural activities of faculty to determine the impact, if any, on the university. For example, a tenured professor of black studies brought an action against the university after he was demoted from his position as chairperson based on the content of an off-campus speech.[54] Administrators feared that the derogatory comments about Jews would be disruptive to the operations of the school. Although no disruption occurred, the court found no violation because the action was based on a reasonable belief of disruption to the efficient operations of the college. The professor also did not have First Amendment protection in his position as chairperson, which is an "At-will" administrative position.

Freedom of Association

The First Amendment guarantee of "the right of the people peaceably to assemble" extends to faculty members in colleges and universities. Although not specifically stated, the freedom of association is incorporated into the freedom of speech and assembly. Early case law[55] extended protection from arbitrary discipline and retaliation to faculty based on their associations and protests. In *Selzer v Fleisher,* a faculty member who specialized in psychopolitics was denied tenure based on his association with the CIA.[56] He contacted the CIA to request access to data for his research on the psychology of Nazi leaders and agreed to be "debriefed" after a European research trip. Prior to his association, committees in the department and school enthusiastically recommended him for promotion and tenure. These committees voted against his promotion after his association with the CIA became known. Selzer proved that his association was a substantial motivating factor in the denial of tenure. The college failed to prove that the same decision would have been the same without the association. Freedom of association, like other aspects of faculty speech, has constitutional protection unless the association becomes disruptive to and impedes the efficient operation of the education environment.

Freedom of Assembly

The primary focus in cases related to assembly is on the manner of expression and not the content, since content-based restrictions usually violate the First Amendment. Protection will not extend to faculty members whose activities are disruptive and clearly unprofessional. In *Adamian v Jacobsen,*[57] a tenured professor participated in a demonstration that went beyond the march approved by the university. Adamian and others tried to disrupt a ceremony by stopping a motorcade carrying ceremony officials, making loud noises, and confronting another group. The court found that Adamian could be disciplined under a university code requiring faculty to utilize appropriate restraint and show respect for others, which was consistent with the AAUP's guideline focusing on manner of expression rather than the content of expression. Similarly, in *Megill v Board of Regents*[58] a professor was denied tenure because his actions were not consistent with standards required by the university system. At an off-campus academic panel discussion on student dissent, Megill twice disrupted the meeting by making remarks described by the chancellor of the state university system as ranting, unrelated to the presentation, and offensive due to slang and profanity. At an on-campus meeting that was opened to the public, Megill yelled out, upon the arrival of certain guests, that the administrative spies had arrived. The court upheld the denial of tenure based on Megill's lack of character and intellectual responsibility needed for a tenured professor. Although Megill had a right to protest, the manner in which it was implemented was inconsistent with respect and professionalism in the academic community.

PROFESSIONAL DIMENSION

Constant conflict within a department or college can have detrimental effects on faculty, students, and administrators and convey a negative image to the general public. Administrators can take actions to promote harmony, ensure long-term stability, and avert future disruptions. In many institutions, faculty are held in high esteem and administrators usually defer to their (faculty) expertise on issues concerning the curriculum, content, grading, textbooks, teaching methodology, and evaluation. This deference should be disregarded, however, if academic decisions impede the efficient operation of the educational institution. Faculty must likewise show respect for administrators and develop a relationship that allows for discussion and resolution of problems. They should avoid getting into personality battles with administrators and use clearly established procedures to resolve differences. Internal grievance procedures are in place for faculty to address issues and concerns. Faculty should not incorporate students and external entities into their grievances on university issues. Likewise, faculty should not utilize their classrooms to broadcast their displeasure with the governance system, unless it directly relates to the subject matter. Faculty and administrators should resolve differences in a professional and amicable manner.

ETHICAL DIMENSION

Professors are charged with the production and dissemination of knowledge. In the fulfillment of these roles, faculty must consider what is right, wrong, good, or bad. Many of faculty's views or perspectives related to students and colleagues are obtained from the socializations process into the faculty role and interactions, observations, and communications with other faculty and mentors. Likewise, their personal values, beliefs, goals, hopes, biases, and prejudices also impact their professional beliefs and actions. For example, a faculty member should assign grades based on established criteria, but may be confronted with the dilemma of passing a student who did not achieve a passing grade. It is highly unlikely that anyone would discover that a faculty member added points to a student's grade. Ethics, however, would mandate that faculty are honest in the grading process and treat all students equally and fairly. Similarly, ethics would mandate that faculty members related course content to articulated goals & objectives and not fulfillment of personal needs or desires. In extramural activities, faculty should avoid conflict of interest situations and acceptance of responsibilities that impede the fulfillment of their responsibilities to the academic community. Because of the freedoms provided faculty in higher education environments, they must consider ethics in the performance of the duties and responsibilities.

Implications for Educators

- The First Amendment provides broad protection for faculty speaking on matters related to their subject matter.
- Faculty do not have to restrain from assigning or discussing controversial topics.
- Faculty are expected to produce and disseminate knowledge.
- Administrators cannot engage in actions that curtail or limit faculty's speech on matters related to public concerns.
- Faculty members' response to administrators' actions and employment decisions are more likely to be classified as internal grievances, which are unprotected speech.
- Faculty should refrain from actions that distract employees from the focus of their employment-related duties.
- Faculty have the right to freedom of association with groups, organizations, and political parties.

- Clearly understand that academic freedom does not give faculty the broad freedom to do as they please.
- Have an educational foundation for all academic endeavors. The case law on academic freedom is varied and inconsistent; therefore, it is important for faculty to act within an established framework.
- Ensure that your activities do not disrupt academic endeavors. Faculty have the right to peaceful assembly, protest, demonstrate, or march, as long as it doesn't interfere with the operation of the institution or disrupt the academic process.
- Understand the academic norms in the discipline. Discuss with administrators, such as deans, the provost, and even the university president, the university's philosophy of and position on academic freedom.
- Know and follow the correct procedure to handle internal grievances.
- Differentiate between matters of public concern and internal grievances. When one reacts to a situation or decision, it is more likely a personal matter.
- Differentiate between advocacy and undermining. Faculty promote and advocate for change by clearly identifying the problem and the basis for requesting the change.
- Review and follow the policies on the use of university-owned and -operated equipment. If you feel the policies infringe on academic freedom, address it in the appropriate forum, such as the faculty senate or other faculty advocate group.
- Post a disclaimer if required by your institution on web pages. Otherwise, clearly differentiate between personal and academic use according to policy.
- Understand the university's policies on Internet use and any limitations.

Strategies to Avoid Legal Problems

RESPONSE TO CRITICAL THINKING QUESTIONS

1. Should June have provided the students with an alternate assignment?

June did not violate her teaching responsibilities by not allowing the two students to do a different project. The assignment of learning exercises and papers are designed to fulfill the course objectives. By enrolling in colleges and universities, students agree to do all assignments necessary to complete their programs of studies. Learning is a process that involves recognizing, embracing, and appreciating different perspectives. Society is not comprised of clones. Therefore, one goal of higher education is to prepare students to become responsible citizens in a multifaceted and multicultural society. This goal cannot be achieved if students are allowed to mandate different assignments, simply because they are uncomfortable with the content or topic. Because no allegations were made that June's teaching style and methodology were ineffective or inconsistent with the standards of the university, little evidence exists on this issue to support disciplinary or adverse employment actions.

2. Did June's speech involve issues of public concern?

Participation in debates on political or societal issues can be viewed as matters of public concern. Since the *Roe v Wade* decision, abortion as a topic is a matter that has been and continues to be a highly contested issue. It is a source of campus, community, society, and political debate. Because internal policy and grievance issues may not be viewed as matters of public concern, the president's remarks to the faculty senate and June's response may not be protected speech. However, issues related to restrictions of academic freedom of faculty and students are issues of public concern. June's participation in a march against abortion is protected expression and assembly.

3. Were June's actions disruptive to the university?

No evidence exists that June's actions impeded the performance of her academic responsibilities or disrupted the efficient operation of the university. She used the situation to develop an appropriate learning activity for her leadership students. Faculty should deviate from the textbook and incorporate current events in their syllabi. Both assignments have an educational foundation. Abortion is an appropriate topic for ethics students and analysis of leaders' remarks are appropriate for students in leadership. June did not comment publicly on the president's comments and she refused to discuss internal university matters with the reporter. Her actions cannot be characterized as disruptive to the university.

4. What is the probability of June prevailing in her lawsuit against the university for violation of her First Amendment rights?

Faculty members do not relinquish their rights as citizens once they become members of the academic community. They are free to associate with their chosen political organization and march against or for societal issues. No incidents occurred during the march that reflected negatively on the university. To avoid the appearance of impropriety, June did not participate in the campus march nor did she address the reporter's questions. June, as did other faculty-senators, had the right to challenge or take issue with the president's comments. The president's remarks to June may be true, but they were totally inappropriate. They had a chilling effect on her participation in protected assembly and her speech. June must prove that the local and campus newspaper articles and her statements were the primary motive behind the nonrenewal of her contract. If the university cannot disprove these reasons or show the same employment decision absent the protected speech and assembly, June will probably prevail in her lawsuit.

ANNOTATED BIBLIOGRAPHY

Aumiller v University of Delaware, 434 FSupp1273 (1977).

A lecturer brought an action against the university alleging violation of rights of freedom of expression and association. Aumiller, a homosexual, published several articles in the newspaper and gave interviews on the topic of homosexuality. He also lived with two students who were homosexual, but their relationship was house sharing/economic. Aumiller did not have a relationship with the students nor were they in any of the classes he taught. Held for Aumiller: The university violated his rights to free association and expression by refusing to renew his contracts based on his public statements and writings.

Hollister v Tuttle, 210 F3d 1033 (9th Cir 2000).

A tenured professor of English alleged that he was denied promotion and tenure for his stand against nontraditional, feminist-orientation courses and feminist criticism of male writers in American literature. Hollister alleged that as a result of his speech, his course offerings were reduced, his promotion to full professor was opposed and delayed, and his pay merits and raises were affected. Held for Hollister on the issues of promotion and pay increases as retaliation for protected speech:

The lifeblood of a college is free inquiry and free speech. However, administrators can determine composition of search committees and the number of units assigned to an academic course. The proper length of a course is an academic decision.

Gearhart v Haynes, 201 F3d 646 (5th Cir 2000), cert denied, 531 U.S. 1014 (2000).

As director of RICIS, Gearhart was hired to diversify and increase funding sources. She unsuccessfully advocated that the excessive amount of discretionary funds retained by the university be reallocated to the research program. Two years later, she was terminated for failing to secure new funding sources. Gearhart alleged she was fired because of her complaints regarding the allocation of funding. Held for the university: No First Amendment violation occurred because Gearhart was speaking in her role as an employee and not a citizen on matters of public concern.

Clinger v New Mexico Highlands University, Board of Regents, 215 P3d 1162 (10th Cir 2000).

Clinger advocated in front of the faculty senate for a no-confidence vote in four board members, criticized the university president for accepting the position, and criticized the proposed academic reorganization of the university because it conflicted with the BOR policy manual and faculty handbook. Clinger's application for tenure was later denied. Held for the university: Speech concerning personal disputes or internal grievances is not a matter of public concern. The First Amendment protects speech that exposes improper government operations or questions the integrity of government officials. Clinger's speech involved an internal matter related to the selection of a president.

Gardetto v Mason, 100 F3d 803 (10th Cir 1996).

Gardetto publicly opposed the reduction in force (RIF) proposed by the president. Held for Gardetto: Gardetto's speech challenged the integrity and alleged misrepresentations of a public official and was thus a matter of public concern. The RIF was a matter of public concern because it involved expenditures of public funds. The no-confidence vote implicated broader concerns about the president's possible misrepresentation of his educational status, lack of integrity and leadership, and decline in enrollment.

Power v Summers

Trustees authorized a catch-up salary raise for the faculty that was allocated as discretionary funds and based on merit. Power received only $400 although enough money was appropriated for $1,000. He alleged that the low amount was based on faculty members' comments regarding faculty salaries. The defendants conceded that merit-based raises were used to reward faculty who were combating dissension; however, Power's salary rose relative to the average salary in their division. Held for Power: A one-time raise had lasting effects because it was added to base salary. Anything that deters free speech is actionable.

Vega v Miller, 273 F3d 460 (2nd Cir 2001).

A professor at a public institution engaged prefreshman students in a clustering exercise, in which students would select a topic and identify words related to that topic. The students select "sex" as the topic and proceeded to identify words related to sex and relationships. The students became extreme with the exercise and started to identify words such as "fist fucking," "eating girls out," and "penis." The professor wrote the words on the board and did not attempt to curtail the students' words. None of the students or their parents complained about the exercise. Later, administrators became aware of the activity and terminated Vega for a topic related to sex and allowing sexually explicit language in the classroom. Held for the university: The vulgarities permitted in the "classroom were not part of an etymological exploration."

Lovelace v Southeastern Massachusetts University, 793 F2d 419 (1st Cir 1986).

Professor Lovelace alleged she was denied a contract because she refused to inflate grades or lower academic expectations in response to students' complaints that the course was too hard and the homework too time consuming. The dean consulted with the faculty regarding the student complaints and sent a memo that suggested that upgrading of the course was warranted and reflected receptivity to Lovelace's concerns. Held for the university: Constitutional protection would not be extended to a faculty's grading policy that conflicted with university's standards. The university defines its educational mission and decides the types of students it admits. Therefore, course content, grading policy, and homework loads must be consistent with the mission of the university.

Kruger v Cressy, 2000 US App Lexis 67 (1st Cir 2000).

Professor alleged she was removed as chairperson because of her opposition to a restructuring plan. Held for the university: A significant amount of time had elapsed between her opposition and her removal. In addition, her record contained serious and consistent student complaints about her conduct.

NOTES

1 *Terminiello v City of Chicago,* 337 US 1 (1949).
2 *Terminiello.*
3 *Terminiello.*
4 W. Kaplin, & B. Lee, *The Law of Higher Education* (3rd ed.) (San Francisco: Jossey-Bass Publishers, 1995).
5 AAUP, 1940 Statement of Principles on Academic Freedom and Tenure. Available at: http://www.aaup.org/ statements/Redbook/1940stat.htm.
6 U.S. Constitution. Available at; http://caselaw.lp.findlaw.com/data/constitution/amendments.html.
7 *Sweezy v New Hampshire,* 354 US 234 (1957).
8 *Sweezy* at 250.
9 *Keyishian v Board of Regents,* 385 US 589 (1967).
10 *Keyishian* at 603.
11 *Keyishian* at 603.
12 Sweezy at 263.
13 *Pickering v Board of Education,* 391 US 563 (1968).
14 *Pickering.*
15 *Pickering* at 568.
16 *Pickering* at 568.
17 *Pickering* at 572.
18 *Johnson v Lincoln,* 776 F2d 443 (3rd Cir 1985).
19 *Johnson* at 569–70.
20 *Myers V. Connick* 461 US 138 (1983).
21 *Connick* at 149.
22 *Connick.*
23 *Walters v Churchill,* 513 US 804 (1994).
24 *Levin v Harleston,* 966 F2d 85 (2nd Cir 1992).
25 *Maples v Martin,* 858 F2d 1546 (11th Cir 1988).
26 *Maples* at 1549.
27 *Hardy v Jefferson Community College,* 260 F3d 671 (6th Cir 2001), cert. denied, 122 S. Ct. 1436 (2002).
28 *Hardy* at 673.
29 *Hardy* at 675.
30 *Hardy* at 679.
31 *Bonnell v Lorenzo,* 241 F3d 800 (6th Cir 2001).
32 *Bonnell* at 805.
33 *Bonnell* at 813.
34 *Bonnell* at 823.
35 *Bonnell.*
36 *Axson-Flynn v Johnson,* 151 FSupp 2d 1326 (D Utah 2001).
37 *Edwards v California University of Pennsylvania,* 156 F3d 488 (3rd Cir 1998), cert. denied, 525 US 1143 (1999).
38 *Edwards.*
39 AAUP, Academic Freedom and Electronic Communications. Available at: http://www.aaup.org/statements/ archives/reports/pre2000/Statelec.htm
40 *Urofsky v Gilmore,* 219 F3d 401 (4th Cir 2000), cert. denied, 531 US 1070 (2001).
41 *Urofsky.*
42 *Urofsky* at 409.
43 P. Byrne, Academic Freedom without Tenure? New Pathways Working Paper No. 5, *American Association of Higher Education,* 6 (1997), as cited in P. Byrne, Academic Freedom of Part-Time Faculty. *Journal of College and University Law,* 27, no. 3 (2001), 583–593.
44 *Urofsky.*
45 *Wozniak v Conry,* 236 F3d 888 (7th Cir), cert. denied, 121 S Ct 2243 (2001).
46 *Parate v Isibor,* 868 F2d 821 (6th Cir 1986).
47 *Parate* at 824.
48 *Hetrick v Martin,* 480 F2d 705 (6th Cir 1973).
49 *Hetrick* at 707.
50 *Hetrick.*
51 *Hoover v Morule,* 164 F3d 221 (5th Cir 1998).
52 *Hoover* at 226.
53 AAUP's 1940 Statement of Principles on Academic Freedom and Tenure. Available at: http:// www.aaup.org/ statements/Redbook/1940stat.htm.
54 *Jeffries v Harleston,* 52 F3d 9 (2nd Cir 1995).
55 See *Sweezy* and *Keyishian.*
56 *Selzer v Fleisher,* 629 F2d 809 (1980).
57 *Adamian v Jacobsen,* 523 F2d 929 (1975).
58 *Megill v Board of Regents,* 541 F2d 1073 (5th Cir 1976).

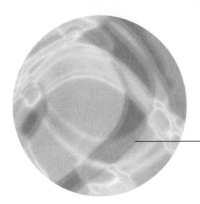

3

Faculty Protection Against Lawsuits

MABLE H. SMITH WITH CONTRIBUTIONS
BY YVONNE D. McKOY

"Qualified immunity protects all but the plainly incompetent or those who knowingly violate the law."[1]

INTRODUCTION

Faculty members in public colleges and universities who try to sue their institution may encounter a challenging and significant legal barrier, immunity. Likewise, these faculty can assert the strong affirmative defense of immunity to provide them protection against lawsuits by students and colleagues. In essence, faculty members can perform their academic duties and responsibilities without needless fear of lawsuits from students and colleagues. The protection provided by the immunity doctrine can be penetrated under certain circumstances. This chapter explores the concept of sovereign immunity and its scope of protection against lawsuits for faculty in higher education environments.

Dr. Johnson, a 12-year tenured professor, was forced to take a medical leave of absence based on his addiction to pain medication and alcohol. He had suffered several broken bones 18 months earlier in a motor vehicle accident that killed his wife and only child. Although he fully recovered from his physical injuries, he started to drink heavily and abused pain pills to help him sleep. After several incidents involving missed classes, verbally berating two faculty members, and reporting to work smelling of alcohol, Dr. Cannon, the university president, placed him on a three-month medical leave. Dr. Johnson underwent a substance abuse evaluation, treatment, and counseling. Prior to the accident, he never consumed alcohol or abused drugs. His therapist focused on therapeutic methods to handle his grief and concluded that Dr. Johnson was at minimal risk for repeat abuse of alcohol. After his return to work, he received excellent teaching evaluations, published four articles, and volunteered at the boys club. There were no further negative incidents.

Eight months after he returned to work, the department chair took a deanship position at another university. Dr. Johns, a fellow colleague, whom Dr. Johnson had berated, became the interim chair. He immediately assigned Dr. Johnson to teach night and early morning classes, came to his classes unannounced, criticized his teaching performance, which resulted in negative evaluations, and assigned him to more department and university committees. Dr. Johnson discussed these incidents with Dr. Kisly, the dean of the college, who responded, "You are lucky to have a job." The next day, Dr. Johns came to his office and stated, "Things will get harder for you now. It's a new day around here and no one sympathizes with you." He also demanded an explanation on why Jean Braun, an honor student, received a "C" in his class. Dr. Johnson explained that Jean made grades of 70 and 74 on two multiple-choice examinations and that only five of the 42 students in his class had made below an 86 on these examinations. Dr. Johns responded, "Perhaps your exams are invalid."

Two months later, Dr. Johnson was asked to cover a mandatory clinical orientation for an ill colleague. At the orientation, Jean told the director of nursing, the charge nurse, and two staff nurses, "You better lock up your drugs, because Dr. Johnson is a drug addict." The director informed Dr. Johnson of Jean's comments and requested he talk with the student about professionalism. Jean became very upset after Dr. Johnson asked her about the comments and replied, "You are indeed a drunk and everyone should know." He told her to leave the orientation. Consequently, Jean could not complete her clinical training and received an incomplete in the course. She complained to Dr. Johns and added that she had smelled alcohol on Dr. Johnson's breath. Consequently, Dr. Johnson was placed on immediate paid suspension, with only library and e-mail privileges. He filed an appeal with the Drs. Kisly and Cannon. Dean Kisly's attempt to rescind the suspension was overruled by Dr. Cannon.

Several days later, Dr. Johnson received an e-mail from Dr. Kisly's secretary that was intended for Dr. Johns. The attachment included a copy of the college's budget, which contained numerous discrepancies, omissions, and falsifications. In addition, there was evidence that the university had engaged in illegal contracting activities. He

scenario continues on page 46

reviewed the report with a colleague, who made a copy without his knowledge or approval. The next day, a reporter who was investigating the illegal activities identified in the report contacted Dr. Johnson who refused to comment. He decided to resign after the president gave him the option of resigning or being terminated.

Dr. Johnson brought a lawsuit against the university and against the president, dean, and chair in their official and individual capacity for monetary damages based on retaliatory discharge and harassment in violation of his First Amendment rights. All defendants raised the affirmative defense of sovereign and qualified immunity. Jean brought a lawsuit against Dr. Johnson in his individual and official capacity under Section 1983, alleging violation of her substantive and procedural due process rights. Dr. Johnson asserted the affirmative defense of qualified immunity.

CRITICAL THINKING QUESTIONS

1. How does the doctrine of qualified immunity apply to faculty and administrators in colleges and universities?
2. What is the probability that Dr. Johnson will win his lawsuit against the university? The president? The dean? The chair?
3. What is the probability that Jean will win her lawsuit against Dr. Johnson?

THE ELEVENTH AMENDMENT

The doctrine of *immunity* has its roots in the common law belief that the "king can do no wrong" and therefore courts could not enforce judgments against him.[1] Its American counterpart, *sovereign immunity,* protects the sovereignty of the states (Box 3.1). When the Constitution was ratified, it was believed that the states were protected under sovereign immunity from private lawsuits. However, in 1793, the U.S. Supreme Court, under Article III of the Constitution, allowed a private citizen from South Carolina to sue the state of Georgia without its consent.[2] To prevent future occurrences, the Eleventh Amendment was ratified.

The Eleventh Amendment to the U.S. Constitution reads,

> "*The Judicial power of the United States shall not be construed to extend to any suit in law or equity, commenced or prosecuted against one of the United States by Citizens of another State, or by Citizens or Subjects of any Foreign State.*"[3]

Federal courts normally have the authority to hear civil cases involving persons from different states (subject-matter jurisdiction). This amendment basically deprives federal courts of the subject-matter jurisdiction or authority to hear lawsuits brought against the states by citizens of another state or any foreign states. For example, a professor from State X tries to sue CDE University located in state Y in federal court. Because the Eleventh Amendment deprives federal courts of the subject-matter jurisdiction or the authority to hear and decide these types of cases, the professor is prevented from suing

Definitions of Key Legal Terms

Immunity	A legal exemption from law-suits that are granted to certain individuals.
Sovereign Immunity	The government's immunity from being sued and the state's immunity from being sued in federal court by the state's own citizens.[33]
Absolute Immunity	A complete exemption from all civil liability without limits.[34]
Qualified Immunity (Limited Immunity)	Immunity from civil liability for state employees or public officials in the performance of their discretionary duties that are done in good faith and do not violate established rights.[35]
Declaratory Judgment	A judgment that establishes the legal rights or obligations of the parties to resolve a dispute about a legal right. It does not award any damages.[36]
Discretionary Function	"A deed involving an exercise of personal judgment and con-science,"[37] or in the discretion of the decision maker. An example would include decisions made by administrators in the daily operation of the university or by professors in the classroom to promote the teaching-learning process.

State Y in federal court, unless he can find an exclusion. Exclusions will be discussed later in the chapter.

The U.S. Supreme Court later interpreted and extended the Eleventh Amendment to prevent citizens from suing their home state in federal courts based on the immunity doctrine, which protects the government from being sued, unless the state has waived or given up its immunity.[4] Immunity is designed to prevent federal courts or the judiciary from interfering in the states' operations and functions. Whereas, the Eleventh Amendment protects states from the federal judiciary by stripping them of subject-matter jurisdiction or their ability to hear such cases, the doctrine of sovereign immunity protects states from its own citizens. Thus, faculty members will encounter a strong barrier in their attempts to sue their employing institution. As an arm of the state, colleges and universities enjoy immunity or protection from certain types of lawsuits.

The Eleventh Amendment is designed to protect the financial stability and integrity of the states. Any obligation of colleges and universities to pay monetary damages to faculty and/or students would create major burdens and threaten the financial stability of the institution and the state, which would negatively impact their continued existence.[5] Therefore, any lawsuit against a public institution that must be paid out of public funds of the state's treasury, such as monetary damages, interests, costs, and other monetary categories, is barred. A lawsuit seeking damages against state officials, such as faculty members in their official capacity, is viewed as a lawsuit against the state because the defendant faculty will look to the state to defend against the lawsuit and pay the awarded damages. If a student sues a faculty member and wins, he or she will look to the state, or university as the employing agency, to pay the awarded amount.

TYPES OF IMMUNITY

The level and type of immunity provided to state entities and officials depend on their position and function. *Absolute immunity* provides complete protection from lawsuits for the "President of the United States, legislators carrying out their legislative functions, and judges carrying out their judicial functions."[6] In contrast, state agencies, such as public colleges and universities and their governing boards, are protected from lawsuits under the doctrine of *qualified* or *limited immunity* (Box 3.1). Liability for state entities and employees is dependent on the particular circumstances or facts. Qualified immunity protects government employees from liability for discretionary duties performed in good faith in the scope of their employment. It "shields [public employees]/officials from undue interference with their duties and from threats of liability that could threaten to disable the official's performance."[7] The premise underlying the doctrine is that fear of lawsuits can negatively impact an employee in the performance of his or her duties and can sometimes impede decision making in situations where decisions are needed and required. Public employees cannot effectively perform their duties if they are constantly worried about being sued. Imagine the impact on the preparation of a lecture or presentation if the professor is worried that he or she may be sued if someone is offended by its content.

EXCLUSIONS FROM IMMUNITY

There are several ways to penetrate the immunity shield. The first is the type of relief sought by the plaintiff (Box 3.2). Lawsuits against state officials are allowed if they seek a court order to prevent an action (injunctive relief); an order to establish the legal rights of the parties (declaratory relief); or an order that compels state officials to comply with federal laws to remedy an ongoing violation

Box 3.2

Factors Affecting Immunity

1. Type of relief
2. Behavior and conduct of faculty
3. Waiver of sovereign immunity

Table 3.1

Types of Relief

TYPES OF RELIEF	DEFINITION	LEGAL OUTCOME	EXAMPLE
Injunctive Relief	A court order commanding an action or prohibiting the continuation of an action.	Usually permitted	Students bring a lawsuit against the College of Nursing seeking an injunction to prevent its faculty and administrator from using race as a factor in its admission process.
Declaratory Relief	A court order that declares the legal rights of the parties.	Usually permitted	A professor brings a lawsuit requesting the court to declare that under the university policy, she is entitled to ownership of the computer program she developed.
Prospective Relief	Refers to future actions or conduct; an action that becomes effective or operative in the future.[38]	Usually permitted	Students sue, requesting that the university provide reasonable testing accommodations for students with learning disabilities.
Retroactive Relief	Refers to things past or a prior time. A request to provide relief for something that happened in the past.	Usually barred	An assistant professor denied tenure sues the university seeking reinstatement to her original position and back pay at an associate professor's level.

(prospective relief). These types of relief *are* permitted under the Eleventh Amendment.[8] In contrast, retroactive relief, which is based on past violations of one's legal rights, is barred (Table 3.1).

The case of *Dvorak v Wright State University*[9] illustrates the types of relief allowed by the courts. Dvorak, a lesbian, caucasian assistant professor, was denied tenure after 6 years of employment. She sued several administrators and faculty members based on the numerous discrepancies and deviations she encountered in the tenure process. She alleged that her heterosexual colleagues who were engaged in sexual relationships with students were not threatened, their tenure criteria scores were given more weight and value, and that

African Americans and male colleagues with similar or lesser scores were awarded tenure. She sued, seeking:[10]

1. A declaration that the defendants' (president, board of trustees, dean, chair, and some faculty members) conduct violated her rights
2. An injunction prohibiting the defendants from engaging in such conduct
3. An injunction requiring the defendants to reinstate her to an associate's professor position with tenure

The Court ruled that a declaration or formal legal announcement that her rights had been violated is in essence a request for retrospective relief because it is based on a past conduct, which is barred by sovereign immunity. The injunction to prohibit faculty and administrators from engaging in future behavior and conduct that violates her constitutional rights (freedom of association and religion, right to privacy, due process, and equal protection) was permitted because it is prospective. However, the request for reinstatement, promotion, and tenure was barred because it is retroactive and compensatory and has financial implications for the university that directly impact the state's treasury. In conclusion, courts will provide relief to end ongoing violations of one's statutory and constitutional rights, especially when the relief directly ends the violations of the law.[11] This type of relief is provided by injunctions, which prohibit the defendants from engaging in conduct that violates another person's legal or constitutional rights. An injunction prohibiting continuing conduct is a claim for prospective relief and is allowed under the Eleventh Amendment.

In *Hamil v Vertrees*,[12] the Court provided relief because the administrators' conduct was a continuing and ongoing violation. Hamil, a white female, attended a predominately black university to obtain a master's of education degree in school counseling. After successfully completing the didactic component, she was required to complete a 300-hour clinical practicum. After completing the required hours, the department chair indicated that Hamil had completed only 279 of the required hours and was not eligible for graduation. She met with and followed the recommendations of the chair for completing the remaining 21 hours. However, the chair again denied Hamil a degree, because she worked under a vocational rather than a school counselor and she needed to spend more time with students. Hamil then obtained approval from the chair to perform another 21 hours under a different counselor. After completing the hours, the chair refused to provide the counselor with the necessary evaluation forms and refused to certify Hamil for graduation. Attempts to appeal the chair's decision at the various academic levels and to the board of trustees were unsuccessful. Hamil then sued the board of trustees, vice president for academic affairs, the dean, and the chair in their official and individual capacity, alleging violations of her constitutional rights and a state law claim of breach of contract. She sought compensatory and punitive damages for violation of her federal rights and a *declaratory judgment* ordering the defendants to issue her degree (Box 3.1). Applying the Eleventh Amendment, the Court dismissed the lawsuit against the board of trustees and university employees who were sued in their official capacity for compensatory and punitive damages. However, the Court refused to dismiss Hamil's lawsuit against the administrators, who were sued in their official capacity, because their actions or omissions violated Hamil's right "to be free from arbitrary state action and to equal protection under the law guaranteed by the Fourteenth Amendment to the Constitution of the United States."[13] The Court ruled that the administrators, as state employers, *can* be sued in their official capacity for declaratory relief when there is an ongoing violation of federal law. Hamil continued to be deprived of her degree, which she would have received if the defendants had not violated her constitutional rights.

Behavior of State Employees

As inferred in *Hamil,* the second way to penetrate the shield of immunity is based on the behavior of the public officials (Box 3.2). The Eleventh Amendment does not protect public employees who intentionally and recklessly infringe on the rights of others. Faculty or administrators who violate federal law and infringe on constitutionally protected rights of others can be individually liable for their acts or omissions. The Supreme Court has ruled that when a state employee, under the color or authority of state law, acts in a manner that violates "the Federal Constitution, he comes into conflict with the superior authority of that Constitution, and he is in that case stripped of his official or representative character and is subjected in his person to the consequences of his individual conduct."[14] As state employees, faculty fulfilling their duties and responsibilities are acting under the auspices of the state authority or color of the law. Their misbehavior or improper conduct while in the faculty role can erode the shield of protection provided under the immunity doctrine and make them individually liable for their wrongdoings. For example, in the case discussed earlier, Hamil asserted that the administrators' act of withholding her degree was based on personal vendetta, prejudice, ill-will, and bad faith, factors that are unrelated to her academic performance. Immunity does not protect such conduct.

Legal Basis: Section 1983 of the Civil Rights Act

Faculty and administrators in public colleges and universities are working under the color or authority of state law and are protected from lawsuits seeking compensatory, monetary, and retroactive relief. However, they can be sued in their official capacity, as faculty, to stop an ongoing violation of one's protected legal rights as well as in their individual capacity for compensatory and monetary damages for engaging in unprotected conduct. Nevertheless, a faculty member who feels that a university official did him or her wrong can sue under Section 1983 of the Civil Rights Act,[15] which allows for legal and equitable remedies against:

> "*every person who, under color of any statute, ordinance, regulation, custom ... of any State ... subjects, or causes to be subjected, any citizen of the United States or other person within the jurisdiction thereof to the deprivation of any rights, privileges, or immunities secured by the Constitution and laws, shall be liable to the party injured in an action at law, ... or other proper proceeding for redress.*" [16]

Faculty must show that an administrator deprived him or her of a constitutionally guaranteed right or law. The administrator can then be sued for damages in his or her individual capacity for the actions performed "under the color of the law." Because the employer (higher education institution) is not a party to the lawsuit, it cannot be held liable for the faculty member's actions. Cases brought under Section 1983 are decided on a case-by-case basis. University officials must show that they had a reasonable and good-faith basis for the decision or action that caused harm to another individual.[17] The concept of "good faith" balances the conduct of faculty and administrators with the established law. Therefore, courts analyze the case facts to determine whether the faculty member or administrator was performing *discretionary functions* and whether the applicable law was clearly established at the time of the violation,[18] such that the faculty member knew or should have known that he or she was violating the constitutional rights of another person[19] (Box 3.1). The contours of the law must be so clearly established that a reasonable person would know that he or she is violating the law.[20] Supreme Court cases, cases in the particular circuit, or an abundance of cases from other courts that addressed the issue provide the basis for identifying clearly established law.[21]

The case of *Harris v District Board of Trustees of Polk Community College*[22] addresses the "discretionary function" requirement. The plaintiffs, employees of the college, were terminated after numerous unsuccessful attempts to get administrators to address the alleged irregularities and deviations from established law and policy within the criminal justice department, some of which violated state statutes and regulations. Due to inaction by college administrators, the plaintiffs delivered a memorandum that detailed the violations to the Florida Department of Law Enforcement, who initiated an investigation. College administrators immediately terminated one employee, subjected another to unmerited criticism, verbal harassment, unwarranted searches of his diary and personal papers, and negative performance evaluations prior to termination. A third employee resigned after being subjected to similar negative treatment. The administrators then published statements in the local newspaper that the former employees were responsible for the violations and eventually terminated.

The former employees brought a lawsuit under Section 1983 seeking relief for violation of their First Amendment rights of free speech. To substantiate their claim, they had to prove three elements:

1. College administrators acted under the authority or color of state law.
2. The administrators deprived the employees of their First Amendment rights.
3. The employees' rights were protected by the U.S. Constitution.

The first element was easily established because the college is a state entity and the president of the university was acting in her official capacity as president. Second, the administrators infringed on the former employees' First Amendment rights by subjecting them to negative treatment because of their speech. Finally, the allegations of wrongdoings by the college that were contained in the memorandum were matters of public concern and thus protected by the First Amendment.

The president then asserted the affirmative defense of qualified immunity, which if proven, would provide her a strong defense against liability. If the president could show that she was acting within the scope of her discretionary authority when the allegedly wrongful activities occurred, the burden is then shifted back to the former employees to establish that the president did not act in good faith. This is accomplished by showing that the president's actions violated clearly established constitutional law and/or that she intended to cause harm to the employees regardless of the state of the law at the time of the conduct. Rejecting the application of qualified immunity, the Court ruled that the president failed to establish the first element of the test for using the defense of qualified immunity, which is acting within the scope of one's discretionary authority. The president was aware of the contents of the memorandum because in an exit interview she referred to it as a negative factor contributing to the employees' termination. Thus, the retaliatory discharge for the employees' whistleblowing activity, which was ratified by the president, was outside the scope of her discretionary duties.

Because the university president could not establish the first element of the analysis process, the Court did not engage in further analysis. However, if the president had successfully established the "scope of authority" requirement, the former employee must have then shown that the president acted in bad faith. In the *Hamil* case discussed earlier, the Court addressed the "good faith" element. The Court found that the administrators did not violate a clearly established constitutional right that a reasonable person would know. Because the U.S. Supreme Court has not specifically addressed the issue of whether a student's enrollment in a postsecondary education program is a protected property interest, the constitutional right was not clearly established at the time of the administrators' conduct. Although Hamil was consistently denied her degree, she could not show that the administrators acted in bad faith, because she could not establish the clear existence of the law.

Waiver of Sovereign Immunity

The third way to penetrate the shield of sovereign immunity is based on congressional enacted legislation that abrogates or eradicates the Eleventh Amendment (Box 3.2). Congress has the power to abrogate the sovereign immunity of the states pursuant to the Section 5 of the Fourteenth Amendment that reads, "Congress shall have the power to enforce, by appropriate legislation the provisions of this Article."[23] To abrogate the states' immunity, Congress must:[24]

1. Unequivocally express its intent to do so
2. Act pursuant to a constitutional provision granting it that power.

Faculty should be aware that a purported congressional waiver of immunity does not ensure success in their abilities to initiate lawsuits against education administrators or erode their protection from lawsuits by students. In *Sims v University of Cincinnati*,[25] the university and union had a collective bargaining agreement that reserved to the university the right to terminate any employee who without approval accepts other employment while out on any authorized leave. Sims was terminated because she was involved in catering activities without authorization while out on a paid medical leave. She filed a lawsuit against the university alleging that her termination was a violation of the Family Medical Leave Act (FMLA).[26] FMLA authorizes employees to sue employers who violate the act for damages and equitable relief.[27] Thus, the first element of the test, that Congress had unequivocally authorized state employees to sue, was met.

The Court then addressed the second element of whether Congress, in enacting FMLA, acted under a constitutional provision authorizing it to abrogate the states' immunity. The analysis process is detailed and involved examining the constitutional foundation and legislative history of the act (see Box 3.3). The Court found that Congress did not have the authority to abrogate or waive the state's immunity; therefore, Sims could not proceed with her lawsuit, because the immunity doctrine provided a shield for the state against lawsuits alleging FMLA violations.

Analysis Process Used by the Courts

FMLA's constitutional foundation is in the Equal Protection Clause of the Fourteenth Amendment, which provides, "No state shall make or enforce any law which shall abridge the privileges or immunities of citizens of the United States; nor shall any State deprive any person of life, liberty, or property, without due process of law." The Supreme Court held that "legislation is plainly adopted to enforcing the Equal Protection Clause where there is congruence and proportionality between the injury to be prevented or remedied and the means adopted to that end."[39] To do this, courts look at the legislative history of the act to determine what wrongs Congress was trying to prevent. An analysis of FMLA's legislative history revealed that Congress was not acting to correct a pattern of discrimination, but rather was formulating social legislation. FMLA is an affirmation obligation on the part of the state to provide an employee with leave from employment in given circumstances. There is a dichotomy between the coverage under FMLA and the Fourteenth Amendment. The former applies to all covered employees; whereas the latter allows employers to formulate gender specific policies in some circumstances. Thus, the provisions in FMLA exceed the requirements in the Fourteenth Amendment. Because the legislation is not corrective, Congress cannot enact broad preventive legislation if a significant pattern of discrimination has not been identified. FMLA failed the congruence and proportionality test and therefore was not a valid exercise of Congress's power under Section 5 of the Fourteenth Amendment. Consequently, Congress's purported abrogation or elimination of the states' immunity was accordingly invalid.[40]

IMMUNITY IN PRIVATE COLLEGES AND UNIVERSITIES

Faculty in private institutions of higher learning encounter a different type of barrier when trying to sue their employing institution. Private colleges and universities, unlike their public counterparts, cannot rely on the defense of immunity to shield them from lawsuits nor can they rely on constitutional provisions or mandates for protection. The Constitution, which applies to governmental entities, does not apply to private institutions. These institutions have no obligation to adhere to constitutional mandates; therefore, they can take actions and make decisions without consideration of the constitutional protections afforded to officials in public institutions. For example, private institutions can terminate an employee without affording him due process and can infringe on an employee's First Amendment right to free speech.

Faculty or other plaintiffs suing private institutions often rely on Section 1983 as the basis of institutional liability. However, the "under color or authority of state law" element excludes private entities. Therefore, plaintiffs must establish "state action," which would trigger constitutional protection of individual rights. Five material factors are considered to establish state action:

1. "the degree to which the private organization is dependent on governmental aid;
2. the extent and intrusiveness of the governmental regulatory scheme;

3. whether the scheme connotes government approval of the activity or whether the assistance is merely provided to all without such connation;
4. the extent to which the organization serves a public function or acts as a surrogate for the State;
5. whether the organization has legitimate claims to recognition as a private organization in associational or other constitutional terms."[28]

As the following cases illustrate, these factors are considered in combination and no one factor is conclusive as to establish state action.

In *Wahba v New York University*,[29] the Court ruled that receipt of a federal grant did not create a partnership or joint venture between the private institution and the government. Wahba, a research associate professor, agreed to speak at a symposium and submitted a manuscript. He was rebuked for submitting the manuscript without adding the name of Dr. Ochoa, the principal investigator. Dr. Ochoa demanded that Wahba inform the editors that experiments conducted after the manuscript had been submitted necessitated the withholding of its publication. Wahba refused, was removed from the project, and informed that his contract would not be renewed. The Court ruled that the relationship established by the grant did not sufficiently involve the government to invoke constitutional protections; the receipt of public financial assistance was not enough to invoke the "state action" doctrine.

Likewise, no state action was established in *Rendall-Baker v Kohn*,[30] where a private educational institution contracted with a school district to provide private education to high school students with special needs. The private institution received 90% of its budget from federal and state funding sources and had to adhere to public school standards. The court refused to find state action because the legislative enactment did not establish these education services as exclusive to the state.

Conversely, in *Brentwood Academy v Tennessee Secondary School Athletic Association*,[31] the Court found state action based on the extensive entanglement between the state and the structure of the private educational institution. Numerous factors existed to transform the private institution into state action, including:

• There would not be an association without the public schools, which represented 84% of its membership.
• The association's employees could join the state's retirement system.
• State board members sat ex officio on the association's governing boards.
• The association provided an integral element of public schooling.

Faculty members in private colleges and universities who are attempting to sue their educational institutions under a state action doctrine must establish a combination of the factors discussed here.

PROFESSIONAL DIMENSION

Educational officials, as state employees, are afforded legal protection against lawsuits because they act for the benefit of the state and the general public at large. Faculty members who are attempting to sue their employer should seek injunctive or prospective relief and ascertain whether the state has waived its immunity. Likewise, faculty members in public colleges and universities have a shield of protection against lawsuits from disgruntled and unhappy students. They can perform their educational-related duties without fear of lawsuits because the immunity afforded the educational institution also extends to its faculty members. However, this immunity also creates a barrier to faculty who have been aggrieved by administrators or colleagues in their institution. To avoid eradicating the exclusions that allow students and colleagues to bring lawsuits, such as misconduct, faculty should not mistreat students and should remain, at all times, professional and sincere in their interactions with students. Faculty employed by private educational institutions cannot rely on constitutional-mandated protections unless they can establish state action. Similarly, they cannot rely on the immunity shield to protect them against lawsuits from students. The employing institution cannot assert the affirmative defense of immunity to avoid lawsuits by faculty.

Faculty should remain current on court decisions related to the rights of students and faculty in higher education. Courts apply the "know or should have known" standard in determining the existence of a constitutional violation. Therefore, if courts in your area or the U.S. Supreme Court have ruled on the issue, you are expected to know how it impacts education. To remain current, faculty should consult with the university legal counsel and/or research educational law bulletins and resources in their library.

ETHICAL DIMENSION

"Do unto others as you would have them do unto you" is the rule that should governs all interactions with students. Administrators and faculty should incorporate this into their everyday practice. Although the law provides faculty a degree of protection from lawsuits, they should treat students with respect and be honest and fair in their dealings with them. Likewise, administrators should practice the same in their interactions with faculty.

- State entities and officials enjoy varying degrees of immunity against lawsuits.
- Faculty members should review their state's statutes and policies related to sovereign immunity.
- Lawsuits against state employees in their official capacities are viewed as against the state and therefore barred by the doctrine of sovereign immunity.
- Faculty members should always act in good faith and have a reasonable basis for their actions and behaviors. Evil, harmful, and vindictive actions are outside the bounds of discretionary duties and thus not protected under the immunity doctrine.
- Sovereign immunity is a strong shield against lawsuits by students if faculty acted within their official capacity.
- Faculty members can be sued in their individual capacity and held personally liable for violations of another's constitutional rights.
- Immunity is a strong defense against lawsuits; however, several exclusions exist that allow faculty- and/or student-initiated lawsuits.
- Courts are hesitant to bring private educational institutions under the doctrine of state action for litigation purposes.

Implications for Educators

**Strategies
to Avoid
Legal
Problems**

- Review your state's statutes and policies related to sovereign immunity.
- Always act in good faith and have a reasonable basis for your actions and behaviors. Evil, harmful, and vindictive actions are outside the bounds of discretionary duties and thus not protected under the immunity doctrine.
- Sovereign immunity is a strong shield against lawsuits by students if faculty acted within their official capacity.
- Understand the realm of constitutionally protected rights. Faculty members can be sued in their individual capacity and held personally liable for violations of another's constitutional rights.
- Remain current on court decisions related to the rights of students and faculty in higher education. Courts apply the "know or should have known" standard in determining the existence of a constitutional violation. Therefore, if courts in your area or the U.S. Supreme Court have ruled on the issue, you are expected to know how it impacts education.
- Consult with the university's attorney or request a seminar designed to understand how the law affects you in your faculty role.
- Remember, "Qualified immunity protects all but the plainly incompetent or those who knowingly violate the law."[32]

RESPONSE TO CRITICAL THINKING QUESTIONS

1. **How does the doctrine of qualified immunity apply to faculty and administrators in colleges and universities?**

   The doctrine of qualified immunity shields faculty members performing their educational duties from liability for civil damages if their actions and behaviors do not violate a clearly established statutory or constitutional right that a reasonable person would know or should know. It allows faculty members to perform their duties without fear of lawsuits, monetary liability for assigning failing grades, and the performance of other discretionary duties.

2. **What is the probability that Dr. Johnson will win his lawsuit against the university? The president? The dean? The chair?**

   Dr. Johnson's lawsuit against the university will probably be dismissed because a lawsuit brought against the state or one of its agencies is barred by the Eleventh Amendment. The university is an agency of the state for liability purposes.

   The lawsuit against the administrators, Drs. Cannon, Kisly, and Johns in their official capacity for monetary and compensatory damages is barred because it is viewed as a lawsuit against the state, because any award of damages would be paid by the state. Therefore the Eleventh Amendment will prevent Dr. Johnson from obtaining monetary and compensatory damages under Section 1983.

   However, the lawsuit against Drs. Cannon, Kisly, and Johns in their official capacity, if for declaratory or injunctive relief, has a better prognosis. This type of relief is permitted under the Eleventh Amendment because it is an ongoing violation and the remedy does not affect the state's treasury. The Court may grant a declaration that the actions of the administrators violated Dr. Johnson's Fourteenth Amendment rights to due process and his First Amendment rights to free speech.

In response to the lawsuit against them in their official capacities under Section 1983, Drs. Cannon, Kisly, and Johns asserted the affirmative defense of qualified immunity. This defense evokes a different type of analysis. Their behaviors and actions extended beyond the boundaries of discretionary duties. Dr. Johnson's forced resignation violated his due process rights because he was deprived of a property interest. The law is well established that a tenured professor has a property interest in continued employment. The Supreme Court has made numerous decisions related to the due process rights of tenured professors. Likewise, case law establishes that a professor has a protected First Amendment right to speak out on matters of public concern and should not be subjected to harassment or retaliatory discharge for exercising his protected rights. The publication of the documents outlining the university's illegal financial dealings was a major impetus in the forced resignation of Dr. Johnson. Therefore, the administrators should have known that their actions and behaviors violated Dr. Johnson's clearly established constitutional rights.

3. **What is the probability that Jean will win her lawsuit against Dr. Johnson?**

Jean's lawsuit against Dr. Johnson will probably be dismissed. Dr. Johnson was acting in his official capacity at all times. To overcome qualified immunity, the student must show substantial violation of procedural and due process rights. The Supreme Court has never directly held that a student has a property right in continued enrollment in academic programs. Therefore, the law is not clearly established supporting her claim to a property interest. Likewise, Jean's case against Dr. Johnson in his individual capacity is weak. There was no violation of the student's constitutional rights. Dr. Johnson is shielded from personal liability because his actions were in his official capacity and Jean's evidence does not support a deprivation of any rights.

ANNOTATED BIBLIOGRAPHY

Saville v Houston County HealthCare Authority, 852 FSupp 1512 (MD Ala 1994).

A faculty member relied on the qualified immunity as a defense against a student's lawsuit. Saville was enrolled in a nurse anesthesia program. She alleged that Shanks, her clinical instructor, made inappropriate sexual comments to her, suggested that she was a lesbian in front of her supervisors and grabbed her buttocks in front of others. Shanks received a written disciplinary warning for the latter incident. Although no further incidents occurred, Saville stated that Shanks retaliated against her by downgrading her clinical evaluations. She ultimately failed out of the program. Shanks argued that the immunity doctrine shielded him from "personal liability for money damages for actions taken in good faith pursuant to their discretionary authority." Held: Mixed decision. The Court ruled that Shanks was entitled to qualified immunity on the charge of sexual harassment but no immunity on the charge of intentionally harassing Saville because of her sex.

Dvorak v Wright State University, 1997 US Dist Lexis 23804 (WD Ohio 1997).

Dvorak, assistant of religion, sued the university, board of trustee, and numerous administrators and faculty after she was denied tenure. Three years after she was hired, the department chair received an anonymous letter indicating that Dvorak was involved in a same-sex relationship with a student. The chair confronted Dvorak in her home and informed her that if the allegations were true, she would be terminated. Subsequently, the dean of the college informed her that if the allegations were true, she had demonstrated poor professional judgment, which would be weighed in the tenure process. The news of Dvorak's sexual orientation circulated throughout the college and university. Several months later, the department excluded her from a conference on African American religion, although this was her scholarly focus. Dvorak withdrew her first bid for tenure after the college denied her request. Her request to review her tenure file was denied because it had been destroyed. In her second bid for tenure, numerous discrepancies emerged. Materials in her tenure file were highlighted to focus on the negative aspects of the review, committee members were directly contacted, and others were lobbied against her asserting racism and lesbianism. Another defendant issued a minority report criticizing Dvorak's scholarship and attempted to have the report considered during the tenure proceedings. The four-tiered tenure process allowed the university president to override the recommendation of the university tenure committee, who likewise could support or override the college committee's recommendation. Although Dvorak received a positive endorsement from the department and college committees, she did not get the required two-thirds vote at the university level. The president refused to override the university's committee recommendation. Dvorak was denied tenure. Held for Dvorak: The lawsuit against the defendants in their individual capacity is allowed, because the allegations included violations of racism, sexism, and unequal treatment in regard to the promotion and tenure process.

Ex Parte Craft, 727 So2d 55 (Ala 1999).

Trussel and Craft applied for the position of dean of instruction. The president appointed Trussell to the position. A year later, the president retired and Craft was approved as interim president, effective June 1, 1994. Nine months later, Craft sent Trussell a letter dated March 24, 1995, relieving him of his deanship responsibilities and placing him on administrative leave with full pay and benefits, effective March 27, 1995. He was required to clean out his office during business hours with staff, faculty, and students present rather than wait until the next week, which was spring break. Trussell received a response to his letter of complaint indicating that he was a noncontractual probationary employee and thus only entitled to 15 days notice of termination. Trussell had worked 35 of the 36 months probationary period. Held for the college: The college is a state institution of higher learning and is entitled to absolute immunity, as are state officials and employees in their official capacities and individually when the action is one against the state. Discretionary functions such as decisions not to renew contracts possess qualified immunity.

Ellis v Board of Governors, 466 NE2d 202 (1984).

A tenured professor at Northeastern Illinois University sued the Board of Governors of State Colleges and Universities alleging she was forced into early retirement and constructively dismissed because she was denied temporary disability. Ellis went to Sweden to participate in an educational research program and became ill. She applied for temporary disability, which required the certification of two doctors. The university physician would not certify her condition and unaware that two Swedish physicians could certify, she resigned after receiving a letter from the provost requiring her to return to work or be terminated. Ellis sued, seeking monetary damages and injunctive relief for her breach of employment rights. Held for the university: Although the state had abolished its sovereign immunity status, statutory law provided that the state could only be made a defendant or party to a lawsuit as specified in the Court of Claims Act. Thus, because plaintiff was seeking monetary relief, the Circuit Court did not have subject-matter jurisdiction.

McCartney v May, 50 SW3d 599 (Tex App Amarillo, 2001).

May, a tenured professor and chairman of the Opthalmology Department, was removed from his position by the dean of the Medical School and offered a 6-month associate dean of special projects position that did not include clinical responsibilities. The college's bylaws allowed the dean to remove a department chair without notice or a hearing but required a hearing for any actions that adversely affected clinical privileges. May was instructed not to speak with the faculty or staff in the department. He requested, but was not given, a hearing. May filed suit alleging substantive and procedural due process violations under Section 1983 against various administrators. The Court held that May could sue employees in their official capacity but could not sue an employee in his or her official capacity without naming an agency of the state as a defendant because it is still a claim against the state. Held for May: Only on the violation of his due process rights associated with the denial of his clinical privileges. The dean had immunity from the removal of chair because reassignment of a department chair is a discretionary duty.

Roach v University of Utah, 968 FSupp 1446 (D Utah 1997).

A graduate student dismissed from a clinical training program due to inappropriate sexual contact with a patient brought an action against the university and various administrators after he was dismissed from a second graduate program, in psychology, for misleading information on his application. The dean rescinded his admission effective immediately without notice or a hearing. On appeal, he was readmitted to the program on probation with conditions. He sued, alleging violations of his substantive and procedural due process rights. Held: The dean in psychology was not entitled to qualified immunity for alleged violations of the student's due process rights. The law on due process was well established at the time of the violation.

Crawford v Davis, 109 F3d 1281 (8th Cir 1997).

A student brought a lawsuit against university administrators alleging they mishandled her complaints of sexual harassment by a faculty member who was subsequently terminated. The administrators contended that Congress did not have the authority to abrogate their immunity under Section 5 of the EPC because Title IX was enacted pursuant to the Spending Clause. Held for the student: Title IX abrogated the states' immunity from suit and the remedial scheme in Title IX did not foreclose the use of Section 1983 to redress its violations. The student had a right to be free from discrimination against and harassment on the basis of sex.

Parker v State of Florida Board of Regents, 724 S02d 163 (Fla App 1 Dist 1998).

A professor and his wife were offered positions at another university. The dean countered with meeting all the terms, with the exception of Dr. Parker's salary, but promised that he would match the offered salary within 3 years. The provost told the dean that he would support his commitments. Dr. Parker sued for fraudulent misrepresentation and breach of contract when the dean failed to honor his promise. Held: Mixed outcome. Florida statute provides for sovereign immunity for "acts committed by governmental employees acting within the course and scope of employment which are committed in bad faith or with malicious purpose or in a manner exhibiting wanton and willful disregard of human rights." Ruling that bad faith is an element of fraud, the doctrine of sovereign immunity barred the claim for fraudulent misrepresentation. However immunity is not extended to breach of contract claims. Rejecting the argument that the dean did not have the authority to bind the university in contract, the Court noted that the dean had the authority to give discretionary monetary increases to faculty and the provost was supportive of the dean's efforts to retain Dr. Parker.

Trotter v Regents of University of New Mexico, 219 F3d 1179 (10th Cir 2000).

A student dismissed from the medical program for poor academic performance brought a lawsuit against the university and administrators for violations of her due process rights. Held for the university: To overcome qualified immunity, the student must show that the university violated a clearly established federal law when they dismissed her. She failed to identify any law that stated she had a property or liberty interest in continued enrollment in the medical school.

NOTES

1 *McCartney v May,* 50 SW3d 599 (Tex App-Amarillo 2001).
2 *Edelman v Jordan,* 415 US 651 (1974).
3 United States Constitution, Amend. 11. Available at http://supreme.lp.findlaw.com/constitution/amendment11/.
4 *Edelman v Jordan,* 415 US 651 (1974).
5 *Alden v Maine,* 527 US 706 (1999).
6 *Hafer v Melo,* 502 US 21 (1991).
7 *Harris v District Board of Trustees of Polk Community College,* 9 FSupp 2d 1319, 1326 (MD Fla 1998).
8 *Harris* at 755.
9 *Dvorak v Wright State University,* 1997 US Dist Lexis 23804 (WD Ohio 1997).
10 *Dvorak.*
11 *Dvorak.*
12 *Hamil v. Vertrees,* 2001 U.S. Dist Lexis 1634.
13 *Hamil.*
14 *Ex Parte Young,* 209 US 123, 159–60 (1908).
15 42 USC Section 1983.
16 Section 1983.
17 *Scheuer v Rhodes,* 416 US 232 (1974).
18 *Hamil.*
19 *Wood v Strickland,* 420 US 308 (1974).
20 *Anderson v Creighton,* 483 US 635 (1987).
21 *Harlow v Fitzgerald,* 457 US 800 (1982).
22 *Harris v District Board of Trustees of Polk Community College,* 9 FSupp 2d 1319 (1998).
23 US Const Amendment XIV.
24 *Seminole Tribe v Florida,* 517 US 44 (1996).
25 *Sims v University of Cincinnati,* 219 F3d 559 (6th Cir 2000).
26 29 USCA Section 2601 et seq.
27 Section 2617(a).
28 *Jackson v The Statler Foundation,* 496 F2d 623 (1973).
29 *Wahba v New York University,* 492 F2d 96 (1974).
30 *Rendall-Baker v Kohn,* 457 US 830 (1982).
31 *Brentwood Academy v Tennessee Secondary School Athletic Association,* 531 US 288 (2001).
32 *McCartney v May,* 50 SW3d 599 (Tex App-Amarillo 2001).
33 B. Garner, (Ed.). *Black's Law Dictionary* (7th ed.) (St. Paul, Minn.: West Group, 1999).
34 Garner, *Black's Law Dictionary.*
35 Garner, *Black's Law Dictionary,* p. 753.
36 J. Clapp, *Random House Webster's Dictionary of the Law* (New York: Random House, 2000).
37 Garner, *Black's Law Dictionary,* p. 479.
38 Garner, *Black's Law Dictionary,* p. 1238.
39 *City of Boerne v Flores,* 521 US 507, 524 (1997).
40 *Sims.*

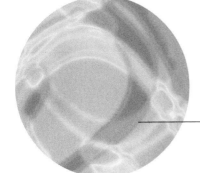

4

Faculty and the Employment Relationship

MABLE H. SMITH AND YVONNE D. MCKOY

INTRODUCTION

The decision to hire a particular faculty member is an investment for the university and has implications for teaching, research, and service. Faculty are essential to the institution's survival and successful achievement of its mission and goals. Indeed, essential functions of the university involve interpersonal contacts and interactions. Consequently, it is important that the institution recruit and retain the best-qualified faculty to promote academic excellence. This chapter addresses many issues faculty in higher education encounter in their employment relationship with the institution.

Kevin Guiso worked as an adjunct professor in the departments of nursing and social work and as a Sexual Assault Nurse Examiner (SANE) at the local children's hospital. Hoping to focus his career, Kevin applied, was interviewed, and was offered an assistant professor position in both departments. Although the salaries were comparable, the dean of nursing offered Kevin more benefits; assured him of a positive recommendation for tenure, a $1,500 a year travel allowance for two years, a reduced teaching and service load for two years; and offered him the opportunity to coauthor publications and grants for three years. In return, Kevin must immediately develop his research focus and receive good- to above-average teaching evaluations.

In contrast, the dean of social work offered Kevin a reduced teaching and service load for the first year and mentorship assistance throughout the probationary period. He reviewed the requirements for tenure with Kevin, emphasizing the rigorous nature of the process. The handbook also stated that teaching performance is a major component of the tenure review process, followed by scholarship. Tenure review is a multistep process with reviews at several levels, including the department, dean, college, university, and chancellor. A recommendation is provided at each level, with the chancellor making the final decision. After the interview, Kevin contacted the dean of nursing and relayed his concerns. She again assured Kevin that her recommendation for tenure would not be overturned. Based on these assurances, Kevin accepted the position of assistant professor of nursing.

During the first five years, Kevin's teaching and service assignments were above average for the department. On numerous occasions he complained to the dean, who assured him that he was progressing well toward tenure. His teaching evaluations from students remained at average. They complained that he was too hard and expected too much from them. Kevin pondered how some of the students had ever reached the upper division in college. Annual evaluations by the Promotion and Tenure Committee focused on his efforts from the past years, summarizing his teaching evaluations, research and scholarship efforts, and service commitments. The committee recommended an improvement in teaching performance, but praised the high standards he established for students.

Kevin's relationship with his colleagues was strained. Several faculty members resented his perfectionist attitude. Others praised him for the high standards he established. Six months prior to submitting his portfolio for tenure, Kevin overheard the assistant dean and chair of the university's promotion and tenure committee comment, "No male will ever get tenure in this department. He should have gone to the school of social work. Even the dean no longer wants him here. He thinks that he can just change our standards and requirements for students." A colleague and supporter warned Kevin to make sure he has "his ducks in a row" when he applied for tenure and "do not give them a reason to turn you down."

Kevin submitted his tenure portfolio 4 months early. He published five manuscripts, four in refereed journals, completed a research study, presented his research at a national conference, chaired three school committees, served on two university committees, and worked part time as a SANE nurse. His teaching evaluations were consistently average, with students' comments that were complimentary of his dedication and commitment but

scenario continues on page 64

critical of the poor relationship between course objectives, grading criteria, and lecture content. Numerous students commented that his teaching style did not promote learning.

Two weeks later, Kevin was diagnosed with colorectal cancer and required immediate surgery and follow-up chemotherapy and radiation. When he applied for medical leave, the dean commented, "Why can't you wait until the summer break? It is only four months away. You are taking leave at a critical time. This will affect your tenure recommendation." The university approved his leave under the Family Medical Leave Act (FMLA). A month later, he received notice that his application for tenure was denied based on inadequate teaching evaluations and inconsistent scholarship.

CRITICAL THINKING QUESTIONS

1. What mistakes, if any, did Kevin make during the interview and negotiations process?
2. What is the likelihood of Kevin prevailing on a breach of contract claim against the dean?
3. What is the likelihood of Kevin prevailing on a sex discrimination claim?
4. What remedies, if any, does Kevin have under the Family Medical and Leave Act (FMLA)?

THE ACADEMIC APPOINTMENT PROCESS

The academic appointment process involves defining and obtaining permission for the position, advertising, screening, selecting, interviewing, and hiring the best applicant. From an academic and administrative perspective, it is better to conduct a second search than to hire a weak candidate. When a faculty vacancy occurs, public higher education institutions must follow their established policies and procedures for advertising the position. The dean works closely with the provost and vice president for academic affairs to determine the type of appointment and corresponding salaries and benefits.

Search Committee

A search committee is then appointed to develop the job description, create the advertisement for the position, review applications, select qualified candidates, and invite them to campus for an interview. The committee:

- Meets with the director of equal opportunity to ensure compliance with federal and state law in the process.
- Develops the position description, which includes the type of position, department, qualifications, and an overview of the institution. The appropriate administrators and the director of equal employment opportunity (EEO) review the ad to ensure the language is correct, neutral, and nondiscriminatory.
- Designs the job announcement that will be advertised and mailed to potential candidates.
- Submits the job announcement to the appropriate administrator to be published in professional journals, magazines, and newspapers and on web pages appropriate to the specific discipline.

- Develops criteria upon which to evaluate each application.
- Determines questions to be asked during a preliminary telephone interview or to e-mail to selected candidates.
- Evaluates telephone or e-mail responses to screen out unqualified candidates and develop a short list of qualified candidates.
- Submits the short list of candidates who possess the required experience and educational credentials to the dean and EEO director, if required by institutional policy.
- Conducts reference checks on the selected candidates. At this point, the background reference checks are limited to those identified and listed by the applicant.
- Invites selected candidates to campus to interview with departmental faculty, the dean, and other appropriate administrators.
- Compiles the evaluation of candidates to determine the final candidate and submits the name(s) to the dean, who will formally recommend the candidate for appointment.
- Conducts final reference checks, which can extend beyond those listed by the applicant. Final candidates are informed that it is the policy of the institution to conduct an extensive background check on all prospective faculty members. However, faculty candidates can request that the committee refrain from obtaining references from certain individuals.

Interview

The candidate's on-campus interview is essential in the evaluation process. It allows the candidate the opportunity to evaluate the university and university personnel to evaluate the applicant. Prior to the interview, the search committee will send the candidate an agenda; information about the university, college, and department; and information on the geographical area. The agenda will usually include meetings with selected administrators, the search committee, and faculty; a tour of the campus; and a presentation by the faculty candidate. A set of core questions focusing on the candidate's education, qualifications, and professional experiences as they relate to the position will be asked of each candidate. Likewise, the candidate can and should ask questions of the committee. Faculty candidates should review all information and be prepared to ask questions related to student body; policies relating to student admission, retention, and graduation; academic freedom; tenure; faculty evaluation; promotion and dismissal; and expectations regarding and support for teaching, research, and service. Federal and state law prohibits certain questions from being asked during an employment interview. Table 4.1 contains a list of permissible and nonpermissible questions.

Offer

The candidate must investigate numerous factors about a university before accepting a position. It is important that the faculty member is able to accept the values of the educational institution. The case of *McEnroy v St. Meinrad School of Theology*[1] illustrates the need to clearly understand the ethics of the educational institution. Dr. McEnroy was terminated for signing her name to a letter that openly criticized the Pope's position on the ordination of women as priests. The Court upheld the termination as consistent with the Church's canon and school policies. The candidate should carefully consider the ethics of an organization, which is reflected in its mission and policy statements.

Permissible and Nonpermissible Interview Questions*

Table 4.1

SUBJECT	PERMISSIBLE INQUIRIES	NONPERMISSIBLE INQUIRIES
Name	Whether applicant has worked for the university under a different name. Whether any additional information relative to change of name or use of an assumed name or nick-name is necessary to enable a check on applicant's work and educational record.	Inquiries about the name that would indicate applicant's lineage, ancestry, national origin, or descent. Inquiries into previous name of applicant when it has been changed by court order, marriage, or otherwise.
Marital and family status	Whether applicant can meet specified work schedules or has activities, commitments, or responsibilities that may hinder the meeting of work attendance requirements. Inquiries as to a duration of stay on job or anticipated absences that are made to males and females alike.	Any inquiry indicating whether an applicant is single, divorced, engaged, or the like. Inquiries about num-ber and age of chil-dren. Any such ques-tion that directly or indirectly results in limitation of job oppor-tunity in any way.
Age	If a minor, require proof of age in the form of a work permit or certificate of age. Require proof of age by cer-tificate after being hired. Whether applicant meets the minimum age requirements as set by law; or statement that upon hire, proof of age must be submitted. If age is a legal requirement, whether applicant, if hired, can fur-nish proof of age; or state-ment that hiring is subject to verification of age.	Requirement that appli-cant state age or date of birth. Requirement that applicant produce proof of age in the form of a birth certifi-cate or baptismal record before hiring. (The Age Discrimina-tion in Employment Act of 1967 forbids dis-crimination against persons who are age 40 and older.)
Citizenship	If applicant is not a U.S. citizen, whether he or she has the legal right to remain permanently in the United States. Statement that if hired, applicant may be required to submit proof of citizenship. If not a citizen, whether applicant is pre-vented lawfully from becom-ing employed because of visa or immigration status.	Inquiry asking specifi-cally the nationality or racial or religious affili-ation of a school. Inquiry as to appli-cant's mother tongue or how foreign lan-guage ability was acquired.

Table 4.1

Permissible and Nonpermissible Interview Questions (continued)

SUBJECT	PERMISSIBLE INQUIRIES	NONPERMISSIBLE INQUIRIES
Education	Inquiry into applicant's academic, vocational, or professional education and schools attended. Inquiry into language skills such as reading, speaking, and writing foreign languages.	
Experience	Inquiry into applicant's work experience, including names and addresses of previous employers, dates of employment, reasons for leaving, and into other countries visited.	
Address or duration of residence	Inquiry as to applicant's address and place and length of current and previous addresses. Inquiry into how long applicant has been a resident of the state or city.	Specific inquiry into foreign addresses that would indicate national origin. Inquiry into names or relationship or persons with whom applicant resides. Whether applicant rents or owns a home.
Military record	Inquiry into type of education and experience in service as it related to a particular job, dates of service, branch of service.	Type of discharge Military service in any non-U.S. country.
Photograph	Statement that it may be required after hiring for identification.	Request of photograph before hiring. Requirement that applicant affix a photograph to his or her application. Request that the applicant, at his or her option, submit photograph. Requirement of photograph after interview but before hiring.
Disability	May ask about an applicant's ability to perform specific job functions. May ask applicants to describe or demonstrate how they would perform job tasks. Once a conditional job offer is made, disability-related questions and medical exam-	Inquiries about an applicant's physical and/or mental condition. Disability-related questions or request for medical examination prior to making a conditional job offer to the applicant.

Table continues on page 68

Permissible and Nonpermissible Interview Questions (continued)

Table 4.1

SUBJECT	PERMISSIBLE INQUIRIES	NONPERMISSIBLE INQUIRIES
Legal	inations are permissible if required of all employees in the job category. May ask if the applicant has pending felony criminal charges or has been convicted of a crime.	Inquiries about arrests that did not result in convictions.

*Reprinted with permission, ReNee Dunman, Director of Equal Employment Opportunity and Affirmative Action, Old Dominion University, Norfolk, Virginia.

The dean or designee will usually contact the candidate by telephone to inform him or her of the intent to make an offer, subject to the approval of the appropriate administrator and verification of academic credentials and degrees. The telephone call is followed with a written letter of offer, which outlines the position, academic rank, salary, benefits, and specific academic responsibilities. The faculty candidate should inquire about initial workload, committee assignments, research support and assistance, computer access, probationary period, type of employment, the tenure process, and other items that are essential for junior faculty. In many public educational institutions, neither the dean nor department chair has the legal authority to appoint faculty. This authority is usually vested in the governing board, chancellor, or president.

Hiring Procedures

University policies and procedures for hiring, promotion, reappointment, nonrenewal, and termination are commonly found in the faculty's handbook or manual. These documents are generally posted on the institution's web sites or made available upon request to persons seeking faculty appointment or immediately after selection for an on-campus interview. The policies and procedures for public institutions are usually systemwide as promulgated by the governing board or chancellor. Criteria used by the institution in the selection of the candidate and granting of a particular rank include the nature and extent of experience in teaching, research, and service; leadership abilities; and the potential growth of the individual. The institution and its accrediting bodies define the criteria used to appoint a faculty member to a selected rank and outline their academic responsibilities. For example, the accrediting body for nursing requires that anyone teaching in a nursing program holds a master's in nursing degree. Faculty members may be hired as in one of several ranks:

Instructors are individuals with a master's degree or its equivalent and/or extensive expertise and experience in a selected area and are qualified to perform the assigned duties. This position may be full or part time and is usually nontenure track.

Adjunct faculty are individuals with expertise and experience in a particular area and are hired on a part-time basis to teach, perform research, and engage in some other designated noninstructional service. Adjunct faculty are not eligible for tenure, but like instructors, are vital to the intellectual development and growth of students. Many adjunct professors are either retired or hold full-time positions in other institutions.

Assistant professors are faculty members with terminal degrees in their specialty or related area, experience in their practice area, and who may or may not have previous teaching experience. This is the entry-level tenure-track position in many institutions of higher learning.

Associate professors are faculty members who have a terminal degree in their specialty or related area, teaching experience for a specified number of years, and an established record of teaching, research, and service. Assistant professors granted tenure are usually promoted to the rank of associate professor. An experienced faculty member may be promoted to the rank of associate professor with or without tenure.

Professors are tenured faculty members with a terminal degree in their specialty or related area, have a specified number of years in the rank or associate professor and are nationally recognized for excellence in teaching, distinguished scholarship, and/or outstanding service to the institution, community, and profession.

According to the institution's appointment process, faculty are initially appointed to a position that is consistent with their prior teaching experience, educational credentials and qualifications, accomplishments, past performances, and scholarly and creative works. The academic dean or department chair should provide new faculty with specific information regarding his or her responsibilities in the classroom, to the institution, and in the area of scholarly endeavors. The department chair should also assist new faculty in getting acquainted with other faculty in the department and integrating the faculty into the rest of the institution.

Faculty members hired in nontenure-track positions may have to apply for a tenure-track position or request permission to have their position converted to tenure-track status. The policy on this procedure is institution specific, but usually requires the permission of the provost and vice president for academic affairs, the president, and/or the governing board. It is strongly recommended that young faculty members with no teaching experience and incomplete or undefined research agendas be hired into nontenure earning positions to allow for professional growth prior to starting the tenure clock.

An experienced faculty member who accepts employment at another institution can avoid restarting the tenure clock by bargaining for credit toward or a reduction in years to apply for tenure. This reduction results in a shortened probationary period and a quicker tenure decision date. These faculty should not assume that the criteria for tenure based on the reduction are different or that there is a set of new criteria. Faculty considering a reduction in tenure should negotiate for an "opt out" clause that allows them the opportunity to convert to the regular probationary period based on evaluations, recommendations, and/or unforeseen circumstances.

In *Trimble v Washington State University,*[2] a professor who was told he was "tenurable" applied for tenure after three years. His application was denied based on two year teaching evaluations of 3.5 and 2.7, respectively on a 5.0 scale, and no single authored publications. The Court ruled that the failure to discuss the downsides of credit toward tenure during pre-employment negotiation, such as lack of time to show teaching improvement, does not create a cause of action. Further, actual assurances of tenure will not preempt a written tenure system.

TYPE OF EMPLOYMENT

Employment-at-Will

The employment-at-will doctrine provides that the employee or the employer can terminate the employment relationship at any time for any or no reason. Administrators in higher education institutions are usually "at-will" employees. The two caveats to this doctrine are that institutions must follow their established procedures for terminating the employment relationship and an employer cannot terminate an employee for reasons that contravene public policy. The public policy exception provides job security to employees who refuse to commit employer-mandated unlawful acts, blow the whistle about an employer's illegal activities, or are the victims of statutory discrimination.

Contract

A contract transforms an employment-at-will relationship into a contractual one, which provides more job security. The terms of the contract will specify how and when an employee can be terminated and the length of the employment relationship. Courts will apply general principles of contract law to decide contractual issues. Table 4.2 contains general principles of contract law.

Faculty members in higher education are usually contractual employees. The terms and length of the contract will vary from one institution to another. Nontenure-track faculty, such as instructors and adjuncts, have a contract for 1 academic year. There is no obligation on the part of the university or faculty member to renew the contract. Tenure-track employees may work under a series of 1-year contracts or for selected time periods, such as two or three years.

Negotiations

Litigation can have negative consequences for all parties. To minimize the possibility of lawsuits alleging breach of contract, faculty members must ensure that the negotiations process is complete and put in writing before signing the contract for employment.

In *Lewis v Loyola University of Chicago*,[3] a professor sued the university for failure to fulfill pre-employment promises. The search committee had approached Dr. Lewis to consider a department chair's position. After several months of negotiations, the dean sent him a letter of offer, which contained the terms of the appointment. Dr. Lewis countered with questions and the negotiations continued. A second letter addressed Dr. Lewis's concerns and contained a statement that the dean would propose an early approval of tenure. The one-page letter of appointment incorporated the faculty handbook and outlined the teaching salary and administrative stipend. A year later, Dr. Lewis was appointed as a professor. However, the dean failed to submit Dr. Lewis's name for early tenure consideration, but promised that he would submit his name the following year. Seven months later, the dean resigned and returned to the faculty. The next month, Dr. Lewis received a letter relieving him of his chairperson position and informing him that his present contract as professor was terminal and would not be renewed. The Court held that the letters from the dean promising to recommend tenure were part of the contract.

The following case illustrates the principles that faculty must understand the complete context of any bargained for change, the need for written closure to an agreement, and that

Principles of Contract Law with Examples

PRINCIPLES	APPLICATION
A valid enforceable contract has three elements: offer, consideration, and acceptance. The acceptance must be the mirror image of the offer. Any change in the offer constitutes a counteroffer, which the offeror is free to reject.	The dean offered the candidate an assistant professor's position with a salary of $35,000. The candidate stated that she would take the position at a salary of $40,000. No contract exists unless the dean agrees to the candidate's salary demand.
The terms of the contract must be definite and complete. All preliminary negotiations and communications regarding the offer should be consistent with institutional policy and included in the final written agreement or contract to avoid broken promises and legal entanglements.	The dean should clearly identify the position, rank, salary, starting date, and academic responsibilities. He or she should reference and provide the candidate a copy of the institution's faculty handbook.
When the terms of a contract are clear and unambiguous, no *parol* (oral) evidence is allowed to vary the meaning of the terms.	Once a valid contract is signed, the faculty member will encounter difficulty trying to provide oral evidence of agreed upon terms that were not included in the contract.
When a contract is incomplete or does not reflect the understanding and complete agreement of the parties, additional evidence may be allowed to explain the terms of the agreement.	If the contract is not clear or has major gaps, such as no specified salary or position, oral and written evidence will be allowed to complete the contract.
A party may be obligated by a promise if he or she knew or should have known that another party would rely on it to his or her detriment.	To compete with employment offers from other institutions, the dean offered and the candidate accepted a position at a higher rank. The candidate then rejected the other offers. The candidate has relied on the dean's offer to his or her detriment (rejecting the other offers).
A promise made without consideration may nevertheless be enforced to prevent an injustice if it was reasonable for the promisor to expect and the promisee relied on the promise to his or her detriment.	The chair promised a junior faculty member release time to complete a research project that was essential for the third-year review. Relying on the promise, the faculty member focused on teaching and publications, rather than completing his research. No consideration was given for the promise (like teach

Table continues on page 72

Table 4.2

Principles of Contract Law with Examples (continued)

PRINCIPLES	APPLICATION
In the absence of expressed contractual terms, courts will imply a contract based on the actions of the parties to prevent a great benefit to one party at the expense of an injustice to the other party.	additional classes), but he relied on it to restructure his time and efforts toward the third-year review. Failure to give release time would create a detriment (inability to complete research project) to the faculty. A professor verbally hired a graduate student to conduct literature searches for his research. After completing all assigned duties, the professor denied entering into a contract with the student. The professor is enriched and the student has suffered an injustice.

oral promises are usually too vague and indefinite to create an enforceable contract. In *McJamerson v Grambling State University*,[4] a tenured professor serving in dual administrative and faculty positions was requested by the then university president to develop a new program. The proposal, which McJamerson accepted, required him to resign his 12-month administrative position, assume his full-time 9-month faculty position, and draft the proposal for the new program. If the proposal was rejected by the board, McJamerson would return to his previous administrative position or, if accepted, become director of the new program, an at-will unclassified position. Shortly after submitting the proposal, the president resigned. The new president rejected the proposal and refused to reappoint McJamerson to his previous administrative position. Ruling in favor of the university, the court ruled that McJamerson was not entitled to his previous position. Any reliance on the representations of the former president was unreasonable because he did not alter the at-will nature of the administrative position by providing him with a contract or any documentation of a new employment status. McJamerson's employment status must be viewed in the context of the employment-at-will doctrine, which allows a party to be terminated at any time for any or no reason. McJamerson did not have a written agreement with the former president that offered any employment security; therefore, the new president did not have to reappoint McJamerson.

Long-term Contracts

Employers faced with losing a valuable employee may offer certain benefits, including a promise of long-lasting employment. Courts are reluctant to accept as a contract promises of employment for life or for extended time periods. The person making such a promise must have the authority to bind the institution and must clearly delineate all terms. Otherwise, courts will view these promises as statements of friendly reassurances of employment. The contract may be enforceable if the person relied on the promises to his or her detriment. For example, in *Shebar v Sanyo Business System Corp.,*[5] an employee submitted his resignation to accept a position at another institution but rescinded it based on the promises of his current supervisors that he would not be fired. Several months later, his supervisors terminated him without giving him notice or a reason. The Court ruled that although the assurances of his supervisors did not create a contract for life, his reliance on the promise transformed the employment relationship from one of at-will to employment with termination only for cause.[6] Therefore, the employer had to articulate a reason for the termination and give the employee the opportunity to refute the reason.

Consideration

After an offer has been made and accepted, the contract must specify the consideration that is the basis for the contract. Consideration is the promise to do something that one is not legally obligated to do or to refrain from doing something that one has a right to do. For example, a nurse educator on a 9-month contract is not legally obligated to teach in the summer but may do so based on promises of additional pay or some other benefit. Similarly the same nurse educator may be asked to reject a summer clinical position at a local clinical agency and devote his or her time to the summer courses in return for a comparable salary.

The case of *Orem v Ivy Tech State College*[7] illustrates the importance of fully understanding the type and extent of consideration in relation to one's promises to act or refrain from acting. In *Orem,* an at-will employee filed several internal grievances against the university. In exchange for rescinding the grievances, he was offered and accepted a director's position as consideration for executing a release agreement to resolve the dispute. Five years later, after a reorganization, his position was eliminated. Orem sued, alleging that the release of his grievances transformed his employment-at-will status to one of termination for cause. The Court ruled that although Orem had given consideration, it did not include a job-security provision. The Court concluded that he had only bargained for the position. As a general principle of contract law, courts will not "inquire into the adequacy of consideration exchanged in a contract".[8]

Implied Contracts

In certain situations, in the absence of an expressed contract, courts will impose a contract by the law because of the behavior, conduct, or actions of the parties; the special nature of the relationship between them; or because one party would greatly benefit from the other without a contract.[9] This "implied contract" is deduced from:[10]

- The parties' acts, conduct and statements as a whole
- Whether there was a meeting of the minds on the agreement's essential elements
- The parties' intent to enter into a contract upon defined terms
- Whether one of the parties has relied in good faith upon the alleged contract

The application of an implied contract is illustrated in the following case. Dixon was an adjunct professor at the college for seven years when he was terminated two weeks prior to the start of fall classes, allegedly for failure to resolve a grade dispute.[11] At the end of the previous semester, Dixon was notified of the classes he would teach in the fall semester. Dixon was always hired on a semester-by-semester basis and usually signed his contract after classes had started. The contract contained a cancellation provision that allowed either party to cancel the agreement, before the first class session. The trial court ruled for the university on the basis of an employment-at-will relationship, where either party could terminate employment at any time for any or no reason without legal recourse. Affirming the outcome in favor of the university, the state's supreme court reversed the legal bases of the decision. Dixon had an implied contractual relationship with the college. The parties' actions and statements indicated there had been a meeting of the minds that Dixon would teach the fall courses on terms similar to previous semesters. The act of terminating him was unnecessary if no implied contract existed. However, explicit in the terms and conditions of the implied employment contract was the right to cancel provision, which allowed the university to cancel the contract prior to the first meeting of class.

Remedy for Breach of Contract

Courts must decide the correct remedy for faculty in breach of contract cases. A general principle is that courts will not award specific performance of a personal contract and therefore will not require colleges and universities to grant tenure.

> " *It would be intolerable for the courts to interject themselves and to require an educational institution to hire or maintain on its staff a professor or instructor whom it deem undesirable and did not wish to employ.*[12] "

A second principle regarding remedies is that courts will not give the aggrieved party more than he or she would have gotten under the contract. Appropriate remedies include the awarding of monetary damages[13] or a new tenure review.[14] The remedy for breach of contract is designed to make the person whole. The measure of damages in a breach of contract case is the monetary salary minus any amount earned or what should have been earned through reasonable efforts. For example, if a faculty member's contract was at $35,000 for a 1-year appointment and the education institution breached the contract, the faculty is entitled to that amount minus what he or she has already received.

TENURE PROCESS

The majority of public and private universities have tenure systems, which incorporate terms, procedures, and customary recommendations outlined in the 1940 American Association of University Professors'(AAUP's) Statement of Principles on Academic Freedom and Tenure.[15] Tenure is the assurance that a faculty member who has met the identified qualifications in numerous areas including research, scholarship, teaching, and experience can expect continued employment unless "cause for termination" is supported in a full and fair hearing that fulfills the mandates of due process.[16] The tenure process protects inexperienced or junior faculty during the period leading up to the application for tenure. The AAUP principles recommend a maximum probationary period not to exceed seven years of faculty service, with retention beyond that period to be with tenure. The presumption is that this will provide adequate time for probationary faculty to prove themselves and for their colleagues to observe, critically review, and evaluate their work performance.

Criteria for Tenure

An initial faculty appointment to a tenure-track position is based on a series of contracts for a specified time period with the expectation of continued employment until the third-year (or other specified time period) review. Throughout this time, the faculty is evaluated on growth in teaching, scholarship, and service, which are essential areas toward receiving tenure. For example, at the first review for reappointment, usually the second or third year, depending on the institution, the faculty member may be expected to demonstrate:[17]

- A clear indication of the development of teaching effectiveness
- Evidence of promise and direction in scholarship
- Evidence of participation in the work of the department and/or program

At the second review, the faculty is expected to have shown growth and productivity in the above areas by demonstrating:[18]

- Evidence of teaching effectiveness and involvement in advising of students and supervising student research [or projects]
- Early promise in scholarship coming to fruition and continuing, focused scholarly activities
- Manifest service to the department and beginning service to the college

At the final stage, the application for tenure, the faculty member should demonstrate:[19]

- Full teaching effectiveness in a wide range of courses and in advising and supervising students
- Research that has progressed beyond the stage of promise, achieved full fruition, publicly demonstrated and recognized
- Service to the department, college, university, community and profession

Some institutions have numerous other categories such as positive relationships with colleagues and demonstration of leadership abilities.

The weight given to each of these factors toward receiving tenure is institution specific. Some institutions will not grant tenure to a faculty member with below-average teaching evaluations, despite exemplary scholarship and service. Conversely, some institutions will grant tenure under these circumstances because they value research, grants, and other indices of scholarship. At the end of the designated time period, a comprehensive evaluation is conducted of the faculty member's teaching effectiveness, research agenda, scholarly publications, grant writing, and service to the educational institution, community, and profession. A faculty member who does not meet the educational institution's criteria for tenure is dismissed after the seventh year, hired into a nonteaching position or assumes a position of nontenurable rank, such as lecturer. This process is "vital to the integrity of the faculty personnel process. The requirement that so stark a judgment be made relatively early in the teacher's career provides the most reliable form of quality control."[20] A faculty member who meets the criteria is recommended for reappointment and tenure.

Evaluation for Tenure

During the probationary period, opportunities and provisions should be made for periodic review of a faculty member's performance with specific suggestions for improvement and recommendations for professional growth based on the tenure criteria. Tenure-track faculty members should expect extensive guidance, feedback, and support from their peers and colleagues. They should be informed of any special standards or practices adopted by their particular departments or schools that would affect the tenure decision. Guidelines on preparation of the tenure dossier should be provided to ensure that faculty submit information that would be helpful in the careful and considerate deliberation of their tenure application.

Tenure review is a multistep process. The schedule for this process is established by each institution and outlined in faculty manuals, handbooks, or other written policies. A faculty member submits his or her dossier containing information that establishes and supports the fulfillment of the published tenure criteria. The decision to recommend or not to recommend tenure is made after a thorough review of the candidate's dossier. The process usually starts at the departmental level with a review by the promotion and tenure (or similar) committee. The committee must consider the academic, professional, and future needs of the department. The evaluation should not include legally statutory and impermissible reasons that violate institutional criteria and principles and policies of academic freedom. The basis of the committee's recommendation should adhere to published criteria and standards. These standards should be applied consistently and fairly to each candidate to ensure an unbiased evaluation based on teaching performance, scholarship, service, and other defined criteria. The departmental committee forwards its recommendation to the chairperson, who reviews the material and makes a separate recommendation to the dean. The dean's review and recommendation is forwarded to the university review committee who evaluates the dossier and makes a recommendation to the provost and vice president of academic affairs. At each stage of the process, the previous recommendation can be declined or supported. The final tenure decision rests with the president or governing board.

The case of *Craine v Trinity College*[21] illustrates the importance of adhering to the AAUP's recommendation that probationary faculty be advised early in their appointment of the substantive criteria used in decisions affecting renewal and tenure. The midtenure evaluation should establish the faculty member's progress toward tenure. Failure to do so can create conflict and anger if tenure is later denied, which can result in litigation.

Craine was hired as an assistant professor into a tenure-track position that required an evaluation and recommendation for reappointment or nonrenewal after the second and fourth years. The final review required an award of tenure or dismissal. At the first review, the Appointment and Promotion (AP) Committee recommended reappointment and complimented Craine for her clear research agenda and "energy and commitment to teaching despite a more onerous course load than typically given to beginning instructors."[22] The second review also resulted in reappointment. The committee was required to review Craine's statement that outlined her teaching, research, and service agenda and "indicate as clearly as possible those areas to which she needed to address special attention before the next scheduled review."[23] The committee recommended that she devote her scholarly energies to original research projects, publish her research results, show evidence of teaching effectiveness, and continue her current efforts. At the third review, Craine was denied tenure because of weaknesses in research and scholarship, although the external reviews were positive. She sued, alleging that the university changed the tenure standard, which was a breach of contract. The Court analyzed the language stated in the faculty manual, which read, "a negative tenure decision would be based on the failure to meet standards of improvement . . . specified in the last letter of appointment."[24] Ruling in favor of Craine, the Court noted several discrepancies in the tenure-review process:

- *The committee charged with providing junior faculty with guidance was generally positive at the second review and vague about her deficiencies. "In an academic setting where research projects take place over the course of years, the warning signs that Craine would not meet the research standards should have been apparent at the fourth year."[25]*
- *The committee changed the standard from quality of work to quantity of work. The reason provided Craine for denying tenure was that she did not have an adequate number of publications. The language used in the second letter required "focused effort" by Craine, but did not require publication at the time of the tenure review. Therefore, quantity of publications was never recommended at the second review. Further, the letter sent to external reviewers required them to evaluate the quality of work more than its quantity.*
- *The feedback given to Craine was not clear and directed toward achieving the goal of tenure. "A clearer statement of expectations would have given Craine more guidance for planning the last two years before her tenure review and would have given her a chance to redirect all of her effort to address directly the committee's eventual concern with the quantity of her publications."[26]*

The quality and performance of each faculty member is crucial to the institution's success in achieving its mission; therefore, courts will defer decisions regarding academic tenure and promotion to the educational institution. However, as evident in Craine, courts expect institutions to follow the criteria specified in the faculty handbook. Faculty alleging that the university did not adhere to its published criteria or procedures in the tenure process leads to lawsuits.

Tenure and Promotion

Perhaps no other issue presents more discussion in higher education than issues related to tenure and promotion. The tenure process is an area that has increasingly been a cause for numerous lawsuits in the academic environment. The nature and purpose of tenure is to create an environment in which academic freedom is protected and the rights of faculty are ensured by the institution.[27] Embedded in the idea of tenure is a public demonstration by the institution and the faculty member's colleagues that the individual is valuable and essential to the quality and high standard of the institution. The historical basis for tenure is a reflection and presumption of competence and continuing service of faculty of academic institutions. Tenure is not a guarantee of lifetime employment for faculty; it simply provides full-time faculty with the guarantee that adequate procedures will be implemented to protect him or her from arbitrary and capricious termination after completion of a probationary period.

Post-tenure Review

Post-tenure review requires periodic performance evaluations of tenured faculty, similar to the pretenure process. The outcome of these reviews is used to determine if a tenured faculty member is retained in his or her position. Many institutions have adopted some form of posttenure review to address the problem of nonproductive tenured faculty. However, the procedures, time

Standards for Post-tenure Review

Box 4.1

1. Post-tenure review must ensure the protection of academic freedom as defined in the 1940 *Statement of Principles*. The application of its procedures, therefore, should not intrude on an individual faculty member's proper sphere of professional self-direction, nor should it be used as a subterfuge for effecting programmatic change. Such a review must not become the occasion for a wide-ranging "fishing expedition" in an attempt to dredge up negative evidence.

2. Post-tenure review must not be a reevaluation or revalidation of tenured status as defined in the 1940 *Statement*. In no case should posttenure review be used to shift the burden of proof from the institution's administration (to show cause why a tenured faculty member should be dismissed) to the individual faculty member (to show cause why he or she should be retained).

3. The written standards and criteria by which faculty members are evaluated in post-tenure review should be developed and periodically reviewed by the faculty. The faculty should also conduct the actual review process. The basic standard for appraisal should be whether the faculty member under review discharges conscientiously and with professional competence the duties appropriately associated with his or her position, not whether the faculty member meets the current standards for the award of tenure as those might have changed since the initial granting of tenure.

4. Post-tenure review should be developmental and supported by institutional resources for professional development or a change of professional direction. In the event that an institution decides to invest the time and resources required for comprehensive or "blanket" review, it should also offer tangible recognition to those faculty members who have demonstrated high or improved performance.

5. Post-tenure review should be flexible enough to acknowledge different expectations in different disciplines and changing expectations at different stages of faculty careers.

6. Except when faculty appeals procedures direct that files be available to aggrieved faculty members, the outcome of evaluations should be confidential, that is, confined to the appropriate college or university persons or bodies and the faculty member being evaluated, released otherwise only at the discretion or with the consent of the faculty member.

7. If the system of post-tenure review is supplemented, or supplanted, by the option of a formal development plan, that plan cannot be imposed on the faculty member unilaterally, but must be a product of mutual negotiation. It should respect academic freedom and professional self-direction, and it should be flexible enough to allow for subsequent alteration or even its own abandonment. The standard here should be that of good faith on both sides—a commitment to improvement by the faculty member and to the adequate support of that improvement by the institution—rather than the literal fulfillment of a set of nonnegotiable demands or rigid expectations, quantitative or otherwise.

8. A faculty member should have the right to comment in response to evaluations, and to challenge the findings and correct the record by appeal to an elected faculty grievance committee. He or she should have the same rights of comment and appeal concerning the manner in

Box 4.1

Standards for Post-tenure Review (continued)

which any individualized development plan is formulated, the plan's content, and any resulting evaluation.

9. In the event that recurring evaluations reveal continuing and persistent problems with a faculty member's performance that do not lend themselves to improvement after several efforts, and that call into question his or her ability to function in that position, then other possibilities, such as a mutually agreeable reassignment to other duties or separation, should be explored. If these are not practicable, or if no other solution acceptable to the parties can be found, then the administration should invoke peer consideration regarding any contemplated sanctions.

10. The standard for dismissal or other severe sanction remains that of adequate cause, and the mere fact of successive negative reviews does not in any way diminish the obligation of the institution to show such cause in a separate forum before an appropriately constituted hearing body of peers convened for that purpose. Evaluation records may be admissible but rebuttable as to accuracy. Even if they are accurate, the administration is still required to bear the burden of proof and demonstrate through an adversarial proceeding not only that the negative evaluations rest on fact, but also that the facts rise to the level of adequate cause for dismissal or other severe sanction. The faculty member must be afforded the full procedural safeguards set forth in the 1958 *Statement on Procedural Standards in Faculty Dismissal Proceedings* and the *Recommended Institutional Regulations on Academic Freedom and Tenure,* which include, among other safeguards, the opportunity to confront and cross-examine adverse witnesses.[77]

Post-tenure Review: An AAUP Response. Available at http://www.aaup.org/statements/Redbook/rbpostn.htm. Report approved by the American Association of University Professors.

frame for reviews, and corrective process vary according to the institution. The AAUP believes that the disadvantages associated with posttenure review outweigh the advantages, in terms of unacceptable costs in money and time, dampening of creativity and of collegial relationships, and threats to academic freedom. As presented in Box 4.1, the association has developed ten minimum standards to consider in a formal system of posttenure review.[28]

At many colleges and universities, posttenure review systems are designed to be constructive and developmental rather than punitive. The process may be standard procedure or triggered by a series of negative or poor performance reviews that identify deficiencies in teaching, research, service, interpersonal relations, other responsibilities, and/or overall contribution to the university. The chair and/or dean should meet with the faculty member to develop a corrective plan that identifies the deficiencies, develop in collaboration with the faculty member measures to overcome the noted deficiencies, establish expected outcomes, and identify a time frame for subsequent evaluations. Disciplinary actions may be initiated if the faculty member's subsequent evaluations do not show progress toward meeting the mutually developed goals. The educational institution should have policies and procedures to allow the faculty member to appeal and grieve an administrator's decision to initiate a posttenure review and any unsatisfactory outcomes.

DUE PROCESS

Due process is mandated when a nonrenewal decision infringes on the property or liberty interests of a faculty member. A property interest is the protection of interests a person has already acquired in specific benefits. It is derived from expressed employment contracts, state statutes and regulations, custom and practices, institutional policies, and oral promises. In contrast, a liberty interest is violated when one's actions damage or destroy a person's standing in the community or profession to the extent that it forecloses or impacts future opportunities. Tenured faculty members have a property interest in continued employment and the basis of or reason for their termination may implicate a liberty interest. To fulfill due process, the university must provide the faculty member with notice of the nonrenewal or termination, the basis thereof, and the opportunity to challenge the reasons and present rebuttal materials or evidence.

The concept of due process has been used to address the issue of whether a property interest requires the use of certain disciplinary procedures. In *Trimble v West Virginia Board of Regents,*[29] a tenured professor who organized and later became president of a teacher's labor organization was critical of the college president's implementation of computer software to write course syllabi. He did not attend several meetings related to the software, did not provide advance written notice of his absence as required by institutional policy, did not prepare a computer syllabus, and failed to appear at an office to draft the syllabus as directed by the college president. He was terminated for insubordination. The Court ruled,

- *Constitutional due process is denied when a tenured public higher education teacher, who has a previously unblemished record, is immediately terminated for an incident of insubordination that is minor in its consequences.*
- *Due process requires the educational institution to impose progressive disciplinary sanctions in an attempt to correct the teacher's insubordinate conduct before it results in termination.*[30]

The professor was reinstated with back pay, interest, and benefits. The Court noted, however, that the professor still had to adhere to mandates related to the computer syllabi.

The issue that arises in many cases is whether the faculty member was entitled to tenure-level status in the university system. This issue may arise because of certain provisions in the faculty handbook, state statute, institutional policies, or practices or customs. In *Board of Regents v Roth,*[31] a state statute provided that all state university teachers would be employed initially on probation and could only acquire tenure as a permanent employee after four years of continuous employment. After having acquired tenure, teachers were entitled to permanent employment during efficiency and good behavior with procedural protection against separation. Roth, hired as an assistant professor for 1 year to teach political science, characterized the administration as autocratic and authoritative. Although he was rated as an excellent teacher, the university did not renew his contract nor give him a reason for the nonrenewal. The Board of Regents rules stated that during the probationary period, no reason need be given for nonretention nor is the faculty member entitled to an appeal. Roth sued the university alleging that his nonretention was based on his criticism of the administrators, in violation of his First Amendment rights. Second, he alleged that failure to give him reasons for the nonrenewal violated his procedural due process rights.

Reversing the decisions of two lower courts, the Supreme Court ruled that Roth did not have a property interest in continued employment. His property interest only extended to the end of the contract period. The nonrenewal decision was not based on factors that would damage Roth's standing in the community nor affect future employment opportunities. "The fact that non retention in one job may make him less attractive to future employers does not raise to the foreclosure of opportunities mandated to establish deprivation of a liberty interest."[32]

In a similar decision decided the same year, *Perry v Sindermann,* the Supreme Court again addressed the due process rights of faculty. Sindermann,[33] like Roth, was a nontenured annual employee whose contract was not renewed after he criticized the college's administration. Sindermann had been employed as a teacher in the state college system for 10 years. During his last year of employment, he, as president of the teacher's association, publicly opposed and was critical of the board's position on changing the status of the college. The board did not renew his contract and issued a press release containing allegations of insubordination. Sindermann's lawsuit alleged infringement on his First Amendment protected speech right and violation of his Fourteenth Amendment's due process rights. The college argued that it had not adopted the tenure system. However, guidelines developed by the coordinating board for the college and university system provided that "the probationary period for a faculty member should not exceed seven years . . . subject to the provision that when, after a term of probationary services of more than three years in one or more institutions, a faculty member is employed by another institution . . . his new appointment is for a probationary period of not more than four years."[34] Sindermann had taught 4 years at another system junior college prior to the 4 years in his current position.

The absence of a written contract with an explicit tenure provision does not foreclose a property interest in continued employment. A teacher can establish the existence of a contract from works, actions, and other circumstances of employment. The rules and understanding fostered by state officials entitled Sindermann to a hearing granting him the opportunity to be informed of the reasons for the nonrenewal and to challenge the sufficiency thereof.

The AAUP supports faculty members' rights to be informed of the reasons for nonrenewal.[35] The information can be used to prevent future mistakes and to strengthen areas of weaknesses. However, one must also ponder the disadvantages associated with requesting information on reasons for nonrenewal. The faculty member may be under an obligation to share this information with future employers or this information could be provided to prospective institutions who inquire about the reasons for nonreappointment.

TERMINATION FOR CAUSE

A tenured faculty member can be terminated "for cause." The most common reasons are infractions involving moral turpitude, unethical conduct, insubordination, reduction in force/financial exigency, program reorganization or discontinuance, failure to maintain standards of sound scholarship and competent teaching, and neglect of professional duties. Policies and procedures to be implemented in for-cause terminations are outlined in faculty and university handbooks and manuals. When an institution is presented with dismissing a faculty member, the college should be prepared for the magnitude of its decision. The terminated faculty member will have supporters who oppose the administrator's decision. The problem is even more uncomfortable if the faculty member files internal grievances and appeals prior to initiating legal action. Nevertheless, administrators must implement the process in a manner that is not capricious, mean spirited, or arbitrary. Their actions should reflect an understanding of the faculty's rights, integrity, and dignity. The institution bears the burden of proving the need to take such action even though the nature of the required proof differs depending on which type of termination is involved.

Unethical Conduct

Unethical conduct is the failure to treat colleagues and students with respect and dignity and to be honest and fair in all university related dealings. In *San Filippo, Jr. v Bongiovanni*,[36] a highly respected tenured professor was dismissed for taking advantage of and exploiting visiting scholars from the People's Republic of China. Specifically, the professor was charged with:

- Forcing them to perform gardening and cleaning work
- Failing to provide health insurance after deducting monies from their salaries
- Using verbal language and threatening to send them back to China
- Allowing individuals working under his supervision to file false time reports
- Hiring postdoctoral fellows who did not have the appropriate credentials

Dr. San Filippo argued that the university's termination decision was based on ethical standards that were not a part of his conduct toward the visiting scholars and had no relationship to competent teaching and sound scholarship functions. Rejecting this argument, the Court held,

> • *[A]ll of Dr. San Filippo's charged actions sprang from his role as a faculty member at the University.*
> • *It is not unfair or unforeseeable for a tenured professor to be expected to behave decently towards students and coworkers, to comply with a superior's directive, and to be truthful and forthcoming in dealing with payroll, federal research funds or applications for academic positions.*
> • *Such behavior is required for the purpose of maintaining sound scholarship and competent teaching.*[37]

Misconduct and ethical violations can be the basis for disciplinary actions against faculty. Students should always be treated with respect and in a professional manner. Faculty should realize that they are in a position to exploit students for personal gain and should therefore seek guidance and clarification on using students for nonacademic activities.

Neglect of Professional Duties

The concept of neglect is defined as "to ignore or pay no attention to; disregard; to fail to care for or give proper attention to."[38] A neglect of professional duties is the failure of a faculty member to fulfill his assigned teaching, research, service, or other activities.

In *McConnell v Howard University*,[39] the Court addressed the issue of whether a tenured professor's refusal to continue teaching a class constituted neglect of professional duties to support dismissal. Dr. McConnell was teaching a demanding class so he advised the students to concentrate their efforts on class work. Two students were talking to each other and he asked them to refrain from the additional conversation. Words were exchanged and one of the students called him a condescending, patronizing racist. When the professor demanded an apology, the student refused. The professor taught the remainder of the class. At the end of class, when Dr. McConnell requested to talk, the student refused. She also failed to leave the class, so the professor called the Office of Security to have the student removed. On instructions from the dean, the student was removed from the class and escorted to the dean's office.

In response to the professor's request that appropriate action be taken, the student was told that her conduct was unacceptable and any further conduct of this kind would result in disciplinary action. At the next class the professor asked the student to apologize or leave. The student would do neither so the professor dismissed the entire class. The chairman of the Mathematics Department told the professor that the university could see these actions as neglect of his professional duties. The professor emphasized that he could not return to the class until the right atmosphere was reestablished. The professor asked the dean for disciplinary action to be taken against the student and for her to be removed from his class until the situation was resolved. The next class day the chairman of the department accompanied the professor to class where he again asked the student to either apologize or leave the class. In response to the student's refusal to leave the class, the professor refused to teach the class. He informed his students that he was awaiting the university's decision on the matter. The chairman of the department taught the class. The dean sent the professor a letter stating that slander was not an offense under the University System of Judiciaries and Code of Conduct and that no further action would be taken about the student. The professor met the chairman and the university's vice president for academic affairs who informed him that further action would be taken if he continued not to perform his teaching assignments. The professor said he wanted to teach but could not until the proper teaching atmosphere was restored. He did not return for the next class and was relieved of teaching that particular class but continued to teach his other classes.

The Grievance Committee found that the mitigating circumstances in this case were such that the proffesor's termination was not warranted and that a teacher can expect a university to protect the professor's authority in teacher/student relationships. Despite the Grievance Committee's findings and the support of the chairperson, the trustees' recommended that the professor be terminated. The professor filed a lawsuit alleging breach of contract. The Court of Appeals, ruling in favor of the professor, held that a valid issue existed as to whether the professor's failure to teach a class was actually neglect of professional responsibilities, which would warrant dismissal of a tenured professor. Dr. McConnell should be allowed to have a trial to determine if his reaction and actions were reasonable given the circumstances. In essence, one must look at the entire context and totality of the circumstances in issues involving neglect of professional responsibilities. The termination for cause of a tenured faculty member should be supported by a substantial amount of evidence and justice mandated that the professor be allowed to present evidence to counter the dismissal.

Incompetence

Faculty members are expected to be capable and well qualified to fulfill their assigned academic responsibilities. An incompetent teacher is one who continuously fails to fulfill his or her contractual obligations. Behaviors indicative of incompetence include inability to control student conduct in the classroom and improper grading of student projects. Incompetency may be the result of knowledge deficit, poor preparation, language barriers, and/or physical deficiencies. The behaviors identified in the case of *In Re Brantley*[40] are descriptive of incompetence. In the area of teaching, Brantley was not sufficiently acquainted with the subject matter he taught, his courses lacked content, he was unorganized, he was late for classes, he returned papers late, he reported his grades late to the registrar, and he was an easy grader.

When incompetence is combined with other improper or unprofessional behaviors, the faculty member may face severe academic sanctions. In *Agarwal v Regents of the University of Minnesota*,[41] a tenured professor was reprimanded for plagiarism of laboratory manuals. Eight of his current and former students filed a grievance against him alleging that he was incompetent as a teacher, displayed a lack of moral integrity in the plagiarism incident, and was unprofessional toward colleagues. The Court upheld the Judicial Committee of the faculty senate finding that Agarwal was "not competent as a teacher and that his level of competence was so low that it seriously impaired his usefulness to the University."[42]

When incompetence is an issue, the university can, for nontenure-track faculty, simply not renew their contract; whereas, for tenured faculty, administrators usually collaborate with faculty to develop remediation plans prior to undertaking an adverse employment action. Nevertheless, incompetency is a strong basis for implementing adverse employment actions.

Reduction in Force

Reduction in force (RIF) is a valid reason for terminating tenured professors. Institutions are not required to maintain tenure faculty members if severe financial conditions impede the operation of the university and certain programs. Standards devised for executing the reduction must be nondiscriminatory in nature and adhere to standards and contractual provisions. Courts will analyze the information presented to determine if a financial crisis actually exists or if the alleged reason is a pretext for some other motive such as reducing tenured faculty. The university has the burden of proving financial exigency.

In *Katz v Georgetown University*,[43] the operation of the medical center created a financial crisis for the university. Consequently, the university transferred control of the hospital and clinical practice to another corporation. Dr. Katz, a tenured professor at the medical center, was notified of termination of his tenure due to grave economic stringencies. He was offered a severance buy-out, nontenured employment with the new corporation, and installment payments of the salary difference. Dr. Katz filed a lawsuit after the university president rejected the grievance committee's decision that Dr. Katz was entitled to 1-year notice. Relying on the faculty handbook, the Court ruled that tenured faculty can be terminated for cause, which included grave economic stringency. No provision in the handbook required a 1-year notice to tenure faculty terminated for cause.

Administrators faced with a bona fide financial crisis must make good faith, reasonable attempts to avoid terminating tenure faculty. This includes reassignment to other departments or programs where possible and reasonable selection in the faculty positions to terminate. However, administrators are not obligated to retrain faculty members for new positions. For example, in *Hahn v University of District of Columbia*,[44] a professor with a dual appointment as a dean and tenured professor lost his position as dean during the merger of two colleges. Several years later, the university instituted a RIF due to a severe financial crisis and Dr. Hahn was terminated. The appellate court ruled that a determination must be made on whether Dr. Hahn's tenured position was "at-large" (general and not associated with a particular school or department) and if he was qualified to teach within another department in the college. Reduction-in-force situations are unfortunate and are valid reasons for downsizing and eliminating faculty positions. However, reasonable efforts must be undertaken to protect faculty positions whenever possible.

Program Discontinuance

Colleges and universities are sometimes faced with revising their academic curricula based on environmental changes and needs, poor student enrollment, and less than quality programs. In these situations, tenured faculty may be terminated and faculty may be denied tenure.

In *Roufaiel v Ithaca*,[45] the provost advised the dean that he could disregard the college's tenure rule and consider Roufaiel's application for tenure on its merits if enrollment figures were sufficient to justify another tenured professor. After determination by university officials that enrollment was insufficient, Roufaiel sued, seeking specific performance to grant her tenure or consider her pending application on its merits. Ruling for the college, the Court held that enrollment was a condition precedent to tenure. Enrollment figures were insufficient to justify a merit-only review.

Courts, like the AAUP, recognize the necessity of educational institutions to make decisions that promote and foster quality in academic programs. However, the institution has a good faith obligation to avoid termination if at all possible.

DISCRIMINATION

Title VII

Title VII of the Civil Rights Act of 1964[46] was designed to prevent or deter discriminatory acts against employees by public and private employers and their agents and to assure equality of employment opportunities. It provides a cause of action by individuals whose civil rights have been violated. The statute reads:

> "*It shall be an unlawful employment practice for an employer 1) to fail or refuse to hire or to discharge any individual with respect to his compensation, terms, conditions, or privileges of employment, because of such individual's race, color, religion, sex, or national origin; or 2) to limit, segregate, or classify his employees or applicants for employment in any way which would deprive or tend to deprive any individual of employment opportunities or otherwise adversely affect his status as an employee, because of such individual's race, color, religion, sex, or national origin.*[47]"

The Equal Education Opportunity Commission (EEOC) enforces the act. The commission has reasonable access to any evidence that relates to unlawful employment practices covered by the act that is relevant to the charge under investigation.[48] As applied to higher education institutions, Title VII prevents academic decisions that are discriminatory based on race, color, sex, religion, or national origin. A faculty member alleging a violation of Title VII must exhaust all institutional specific administrative remedies before filing a complaint with the EEOC. Similarly, if the state has an EEOC-related agency, the employee must initiate state proceedings prior to filing a federal action. The employer is the target and therefore supervisors or agents are not individually liable under Title VII. An EEOC complaint must be filed within 180 days of the adverse employment decision or action or 300 days if the complaint was initially filed with a state agency.

The case of *Brown v Trustees of Boston University*[49] highlights the protection against discrimination provided to faculty members in higher education institutions. In *Brown,* an assistant professor of English was denied tenure although she received unanimously favorable votes from her departmental colleagues and similar support at the administrative levels. Brown claimed that she had been discriminated against because of her sex and alleged that she had been held to a stricter standard than male peers in her department. In addition, she claimed that the president and dean had made derogatory remarks about her. Upholding her claim, the Court ruled that the university president's sexist remarks about the English Department established gender bias and awarded tenure and promotion to an associate professor's position as a remedy for discrimination on the basis of gender. The jury found that "but for" sex discrimination, Brown would have been granted tenure. The Court noted that the university's prerogative to grant autonomous tenure decisions must be subordinated to the goals of Title VII. The Court was required to fashion a remedy that provided comprehensive relief for victims of discriminatory employment decisions. It also rejected the university's claim that judicial imposition of tenure violated academic freedom maintaining that an institution's academic freedom did not include the freedom to discriminate against tenure candidates on the basis of sex or other impermissible grounds.

The application of the Civil Rights Act to religious institutions is fact-specific. The EEOC is prohibited from investigating cases where the practice or policy is a result of the educational institution's religious foundation, such as "teaching, spreading the faith, church governance, supervision of a religious order, or supervision or participation in religious ritual or worship."[50]

Theories of Discrimination

The two theories under which employees bring Title VII employment discrimination lawsuits are disparate impact and disparate treatment. Disparate impact occurs when a faculty member asserts that employment practices have either an intentional or unintentional negative, discriminatory effect on a protected group. Under the commonly used disparate treatment theory, the faculty or employee claims that an adverse employment decision, action, or environment was based on his or her race, color, sex, religion, or national origin. The typical allegations are that the faculty member was treated differently; held to a different, usually higher standard; or was the victim of bias and unfair treatment due to his or her sex, religion, race, color, or national origin.

Discrimination lawsuits are difficult, but not impossible to prove. The faculty member must establish a prima facie case of discrimination by showing that:

- He or she is a member of a protected class.
- He or she applied and was qualified for a job for which the employer was seeking applicants.

- Despite his or her qualifications he/she was rejected for the job; and
- After his or her rejection the position remained open and the employer continued to seek applications from persons of complainant's qualification.[51]

The prima facie case "raises an inference of discrimination only because [courts can] presume these acts, if otherwise unexplained, are more likely than not based on the consideration of impermissible factors."[52] The burden of proof then shifts to "the employer to articulate some legitimate, nondiscriminatory reason for the employer's rejection."[53] This presumption of discrimination must be refuted by the employer who must produce evidence that the applicant "was rejected, or someone else preferred, for a legitimate, nondiscriminatory reason."[54] A successful burden of production by the employer requires the employee to persuade the Court that the reasons offered are not true, unworthy of credence, and are pretext for discrimination. A case-by-case approach is used to determine if there is enough evidence for the plaintiff to establish intentional discrimination.

The remedies in discrimination cases that are available to employees are reinstatement, a new tenure and promotion review, back pay, compensatory damages (pain, suffering, mental anguish), attorney fees, and punitive damages in disparate treatment cases. A judicial grant of tenure will only be awarded in the most exceptional of circumstances.

In *Lewis v Loyola University of Chicago*,[55] the Court found that a professor who had been promised a recommendation for tenure would have been tenured because he met the objective criteria and the provost testified that it was uncommon for the dean's recommendation for tenure to be denied. Likewise in *Kunda v Muhlenberg College*,[56] the Court awarded a promotion and conditional tenure upon the completion of a master's degree as a remedy for disparate treatment discrimination. Kunda, like Lewis, met the qualifications for tenure, including positive recommendations and peer reviews.

Age Discrimination

The Age Discrimination in Employment Act (ADEA)[57] protects individuals 40 years and older from adverse employment decisions and actions based on age rather than qualifications and abilities. It makes unlawful the following acts of employers:[58]

1. Failing or refusing to hire or to discharge any individual with respect to his compensation, terms, conditions, or privileges of employment, because of such individual's age
2. Limiting, segregating, or classifying employees in any way which would deprive or tend to deprive any individual of employment, because of such individual's age
3. Reducing the wage rate of any employee in order to comply with this chapter

Like Title VII, the act applies to both public and private institutions, is enforced by the EEOC, and the employee has the burden of establishing a prima facie case of age discrimination. The employee must show that the employer's practice or policy had a discriminatory effect on persons protected under the ADEA. The burden then shifts to the employer to establish a business necessity for the practice.

The case of *Leftwich v Harris-Stowe College*[59] illustrates the application of ADEA in higher education environments. A legislative act transferred control of the college from a local board to a board of regents. The board of regents decided to hire a smaller faculty, which consisted of some faculty from the old college. Leftwich, a tenured professor, lost his position in the old college, but applied for the position in the new college. He was not hired, although he scored higher on his evaluation than his colleagues. Ruling in favor of Leftwich, the Court rejected the college's business necessity defenses of cost-saving measures and flexibility in hiring quality and innovative nontenured faculty based on the following analysis.

- *The plan was intended to reduce costs by eliminating some tenured faculty, who are higher paid than their non-tenured colleagues. A plan based on tenure status is suspect because of the "close relationship between tenure status and age." "The plan intent and effect of the defendants' practice was to eliminate older workers who had built up, through years of satisfactory service, higher salaries than their younger counterparts."* [60]
- *[The] assertion that younger nontenured faculty could have new ideas apparently assumes that older tenured faculty members would cause the college to stagnate. Such assumptions are precisely the kind of stereotypical thinking about older workers that the ADEA was designed to eliminate.* [61]

However, market-based practices such as hiring new faculty at salaries equal to or above tenured older faculty[62] and providing salary adjustment for faculty who present an offer of employment from another institution[63] have been upheld as "business necessity" against disparate impact claims.

As with other cases involving discrimination, the remedies available to victims must be consistent with their initial status. In the case of *Watlington v University of Puerto Rico,*[64] the faculty member alleged that the university failed to renew his full-time teaching contract and rejected his application for a tenure-track position because of age discrimination. The jury returned a decision in favor for the professor. However, the Court ruled favorably on renewing the professor's contract but rejected the jury's recommendation of the professor's appointment to a tenure-track position. The professor had not established a prima facie case of discrimination with regard to a tenure-track position. Further, an appointment to a tenure-track position would have placed the professor in a better position than he had at the time his full-time contract was not renewed. Finally, the Court held that the available remedies, liquidated damages and his subsequent earnings that exceeded the salary of his full-time contract, adequately addressed his economic status.[65]

For many colleges and universities, it is financially practical to replace older, tenured faculty who have higher salaries with less-experienced junior faculty at lower salaries. Federal and state law provides protection against age discrimination and ensures that adverse employment decisions are based on good cause.

Americans with Disabilities Act

The Rehabilitation Act of 1973[66] and the Americans with Disabilities Act (ADA) of 1990[67] prohibit employment discrimination against persons with disabilities in private and public entities. Its purpose is to eliminate unwanted discrimination against individuals with disabilities to guarantee those individuals equal opportunity. The ADA prohibits discrimination against a "qualified individual with a disability in job application procedures; the hiring, advancement, or discharge of employees; employee compensation; job training; and other terms, conditions and privileges of employment."[68] A qualified person with a disability is defined as an individual "who, with or without reasonable accommodation, can perform essential functions of the employment position that such individual holds or desires."[69] An employer must make reasonable accommodations for a qualified individual with a disability. To establish a prima facie or an ADA violation, the employer must allege that he or she has a physical impairment that substantially limits major life activity or is regarded as having such an impairment, that he or she experienced an adverse employment decision because of the disability, or that the employer failed to make reasonable modifications to accommodate the disability. The employer must then establish a legitimate, nondiscriminatory reason for the adverse employment decision. The employee has the burden of showing that the employer's reasons were pretext, not credible, or false. In *Meling v St. Francis College,*[70] a college refused to rehire an assistant professor of physical education following a car accident. She suffered a variety of injuries, including injuries to her shoulders and knees, which interfered with her ability to stand, sit, walk, and reach. After a year on medical leave, she attempted to return to work, but was informed by the dean that she could not have any limitations upon her return. The president of the university refused to accommodate the physician's mandated light-duty schedule or to discuss possible accommodations with Meling.

A prima facie case was established because Meling was a qualified person with a disability and because she had physical impairments that substantially limited her performance of one or more life activities, such as sitting, standing, walking, reaching, and lifting. She further established that the disability was the basis of the adverse employment decision. The Court rejected the university's argument that Meling was too physically limited to qualify as a proper supervisor in a physical education course even with accommodations. Ruling in favor of Meling, the Court awarded remedies to make her "whole" or fully compensate her for the unlawful employment discrimination, which included reinstatement and back pay. The Court, however, refused to grant her tenure. "The management of a college or university is primarily the responsibility of those equipped with the special skills and sensitivities necessary for so delicate a task."[71] Courts are ill-equipped to ascertain the future needs of educational institutions and therefore are reluctant to award tenure due to its long-lasting impact.

The ADA coverage also extends to recovering substance abusers, but excludes current drug abusers.[72] Educational institutions can establish and enforce a drug- and alcohol-free environment, with a zero-tolerance policy. The ADA does not mandate that employers accommodate an addicted employee. In *Griel v Franklin Medical Center,*[73] a nurse alleged wrongful discharge based on her status as a recovering drug addict in violation of the ADA. Griel informed the hospital that she was a recovering drug addict, enrolled in a 5-year impaired nurse program, and was terminated from her previous employment for diversion of narcotics. She fulfilled her employment responsibilities without incident until she injured her back while lifting a patient, which necessitated her taking a year off. Upon her return, she made a series of errors involving narcotics and was terminated. Griel attempted to show that the employer's articulated reasons for her termination were a pretext for discrimination because other nurses who made medication errors were not terminated. Ruling in favor of the hospital, the Court noted that the hospital was concerned when Griel, who apparently was in recovery from her drug addiction, began to make the type and number of mistakes in such a brief period of time. The ADA does not protect employees who violate policies and procedures of the organization. It is designed to protect against unlawful discrimination against individuals with disabilities who are otherwise qualified for the position. Individuals with disabilities cannot use the ADA as a shield against termination if their behavior or conduct would otherwise be a basis for termination.

Retaliatory Discharge

Faculty members allegedly terminated for cause usually bring lawsuits against the educational institution alleging the termination was in retaliation for some lawful act. To establish a Title VII violation under a theory of retaliation, the faculty member must prove:

- He or she engaged in a Title VII protected activity.
- He or she suffered an adverse employment decision.
- There was a causal nexus between the adverse action and the protected activity.

In *Albrechtsen v University of Wisconsin System*,[74] a professor alleged that he was denied a merit pay increase and two of his summer workshops were cancelled because of his protests against sex discrimination between 1987 and 1991. The file contained one letter dated 1997 in which he complained that the department was mistreating all faculty members, but did not mention the concepts of sex or gender. The university indicated that Dr. Albrechtsen refused to comply with the new department chairperson requests for his students' evaluations to determine merit and for his curriculum vitae to review his expertise to teach the workshops. Albrechtsen met the first element in that sex discrimination is a protected activity. A protected activity is defined as "any opposition to any practice rendered unlawful by Title VII, including making a charge, testifying, assisting, or participating in any investigation, proceeding, or hearing under Title VII."[75] Likewise he established the occurrence of an adverse employment action that interfered with his compensation and eliminated teaching assignments. However, he did not establish that but for the complaints, the same actions would not have been taken.

Ruling in favor of the university, the Court noted that the time gap between the alleged protected events and the adverse employment actions was too remote. "It would be bizarre for an academic department to wait most of a decade, promoting the faculty member repeatedly, [awarding him tenure] and allowing him to teach the summer workshops of his choice, only to retaliate" against him now.[76]

Family Medical and Leave Act

The Family Medical and Leave Act[77] was designed to balance the demands of the workplace with the needs of families. Employees can take leave for medical reasons; the birth of a child; or to care for a sick child, spouse, or parents who experience severe health problems. An employee who has worked at least 1,250 hours during the previous 12-month period is entitled to a statutory maximum period of 12 weeks of FMLA-mandated leave. An employer can require an employee to substitute vacation, personal, and or sick time for any portion of the leave period. The former runs concurrent with the 12-week FMLA leave.

An employer cannot interfere with, restrain, or deny the person's right to FMLA leave. Two types of lawsuits are brought against employers who unlawfully take adverse employment actions against employees: interference and retaliation. Interference occurs when an employer denies or places unreasonable restrictions and burdens on an employee who requests a leave. In contrast, to establish a claim of retaliation, the employee must show that:

1. He or she availed himself or herself of a protected right.
2. He or she suffered an adverse employment decision.
3. There was a causal relationship between the protected activity and the adverse employment decision.[78]

In *Raith v Johns Hopkins University,*[79] a research coordinator was terminated after she took medical leave to have surgery. Several negative comments were made to her including that, "People sometimes lose their jobs when they go out on disability." The university asserted financial difficulties as the basis for the termination. Rejecting this argument, the Court noted that two individuals involved in the termination decision had expressed hostility toward Raith and the clinic's costs increased because it hired another person at a much higher salary, extended the hours of another employee, and hired an outside technician. Therefore, the Court denied the university's request for a dismissal, instead indicating that there were several issues for a jury to resolve.

PROFESSIONAL DIMENSION

Faculty members applying for appointments at an institution should have knowledge and a clear understanding of established policies and procedures regarding the expectations of their responsibilities and duties of the position; policies and procedures regarding tenure and promotion including the time frame; and the emphasis placed on the areas of scholarship, teaching, and service by the institution. A faculty member should carefully consider an academic offer in relation to his or her philosophy, the potential for professional growth and development, and the feel of collegiality. All promises should be put in writing before the offer is accepted. The decision to accept a position should be made after careful and deliberate consideration. Once in an academic position, faculty should remain focused on achieving promotion and tenure. The university has a responsibility to create an environment that facilitates faculty members' abilities to fulfill their academic roles. Faculty have a responsibility to seek experiences and collaborate with others to fulfill the requirements needed to ensure success.

ETHICAL DIMENSION

Faculty members are aware of right and wrong and the dimensions of professional behavior. University dismissal policies may not cover every possible unethical behavior. Courts are not willing to rule that the failure of higher education institutions to specify certain behaviors as unethical create unconstitutionally vague regulations, which cannot be enforced. The academic environment is highly regarded by outsiders. To maintain this status, the actions of faculty within this environment must be professional and above reproach. Mistreatment of colleagues and students cannot be tolerated.

- Faculty should have contracts reviewed by an attorney or someone familiar with academic norms and traditions.
- Faculty should understand the institution's norms and history of granting tenure.
- It is important to request a detailed midtenure review that outlines the strengths and weaknesses toward tenure.
- Due process mandates that contract and tenured faculty are informed of the reasons under-lying adverse employment decisions and given a hearing to refute the allegations.
- Tenured faculty can be terminated for cause.
- A faculty member must file a complaint within the time frame mandated by EEOC, counting from the date of the adverse employment decision and not the date of termination because appeals or grievances do not stop or toll this time period.

Implications for Educators

- Understand the importance and significance of the interview process.
- Reduce all negotiations to writing because oral promises are difficult to prove and may not be considered in the face of a written contract.
- Accept a nontenure-track position if an earned doctorate has not been obtained in the specialty or related area, unless the tenure guidelines do not require a doctorate. Preparation for tenure starts at the time of the appointment or promotion to a tenure-track position. Attempts to complete a doctorate may deter from the focus of meeting the criteria for tenure.
- Obtain a copy of the tenure and promotion policy and review the policies and procedures with the department chair and the dean.
- Carefully consider any reductions in and credit toward tenure. Investigate whether the institution will consider scholarship and teaching performance from other institutions and determine the weight given these materials.
- Review and follow the guidelines, policies, and procedures for promotion and tenure outlined in the faculty handbook or other written documents. Oral promises do not supercede written criteria.
- Request extensive reviews and suggestions on strengths and weaknesses in the progression toward tenure and promotion.
- Serve on the appointment, promotion, and tenure committee, if available.
- Talk with other faculty members who have gone through the process. Review their tenure portfolio or dossier.
- Meet with the department chair and dean to discuss and review progress toward tenure and promotion. At the midtenure review, ask for a written mock evaluation based on the tenure dossier.
- Follow the internal grievance process.

Strategies to Avoid Legal Problems

RESPONSE TO CRITICAL THINKING QUESTIONS

1. **What mistakes, if any, did Kevin make during the interview and negotiations process?**

   The interview process is a time for the faculty and administrators to evaluate the candidate and for the candidate to evaluate the department and its missions, operations, and personnel. Kevin should have inquired about the gender mixture within the school, the number of tenured faculty, the denial rate for tenure, the reasons for denying tenure, faculty attrition, typical teaching loads, his expected teaching assignments and responsibilities, and the school's philosophy on student evaluations. The policies and procedures governing faculty members are outlined in the faculty handbook. Kevin should have reviewed these prior to the interview and used these as the basis for specific questions related to workload expectations, evaluations, progression, and tenure. A prospective faculty should closely investigate the ethics of the organization that is superficially outlined in the mission and philosophy statements. Direct and focused questions by the interviewer or potential employee will elicit additional information upon which to evaluate the institution. Kevin ignored the red flags that were raised during his interview with the dean of social work about the intensiveness of the tenure process. Instead of relying upon his own investigation and the truth confronting him in written format, Kevin accepted an oral promise.

2. **What is the likelihood of Kevin prevailing on a breach of contract claim against the dean?**

   Kevin based his breach of contract claim on what was said to him rather than the terms as outlined in the faculty handbook. Only the chancellor has the authority to grant tenure. His signed contract specifically incorporated the faculty handbook whose terms were binding on all faculty. Kevin cannot use oral promises to contradict expressed or written rules and regulations. Given Kevin's knowledge of the process, which was explicitly explained to him by the dean of social work, it was unreasonable for him to rely on oral promises.

3. **What is the likelihood of Kevin prevailing on a sex discrimination claim?**

   There is no doubt that Title VII applies to higher education institutions. Courts, however, note that tenure decisions are distinct from other employment issues and exercise great caution to avoid infringing into areas concerning the competence of faculty members. To prevail on a discrimination claim, Kevin must first establish a prima facie case of discrimination by showing that: (1) he belonged to a protected class; (2) he was qualified for tenure; (3) he was denied tenure; and (4) the denial of tenure gives rise to an inference of discrimination. If Kevin established the above, the burden of production then shifts to the university to articulate a legitimate, nondiscriminatory reason for the tenure denial decision. Kevin then has the ultimate burden of persuading the fact finder that the reasons provided are false, not credible, and a pretext for discrimination. As a male member in a predominately female profession, Kevin can establish that he is a member of a protected class and he was denied tenure. The comments made by some faculty members that he overheard are additional inferences of discrimination. However, whether Kevin was qualified for tenure will present a more challenging hurdle. The handbook clearly identified the weight given to teaching performance in the tenure evaluation process. Kevin's teaching evaluations were consistently average with comments that were critical of his teaching style. Unfortunately, there is no evidence that the dean or P&T Committee tried to provide assistance to Kevin in this area, which is readily correctable. The standards established for tenure eligibility at the university were not vague, nor disputed. There is no evidence that Kevin was treated differently because he was a male.

4. **What remedies, if any, does Kevin have under the Family Medical and Leave Act?**

As a full-time faculty member who has been employed for 12 months and has 1,250 hours of service during the previous 12-month period, Kevin should be able to take leave because he is an eligible employee under the FMLA. Likewise, the university met the definition of an eligible employer under FMLA because it had more than 50 employees in 20 or more work weeks and was engaged in commerce or any industry effecting commerce. Kevin will most likely bring a retaliation claim against the university. He probably cannot substantiate an interference claim, which will require him to establish that the university burdened or denied his medical leave application. Kevin will probably assert that his denial of tenure was in retaliation against him for his serious health problem that necessitated medical leave. To establish a prima facie case of retaliatory discrimination, Kevin must show that: (1) he engaged in a protected activity, (2) he suffered an adverse employment decision, and (3) the two were causally related. The first two elements are not difficult to establish, because he applied for medical leave under FMLA (a protected action) and he was denied tenure. The dean's comments to him were insensitive and provided evidence that she was not pleased with his request for medical leave. However, as with the discrimination issue, Kevin's greatest challenge is establishing that his tenure denial was based on his application for medical leave. The university's evidence is that Kevin simply did not meet the qualifications for tenure as specified in the faculty handbook and any other issues are peripheral. Because tenure is a multistep process, it is highly unlikely that the recommendation of the dean will determine the final outcome.

ANNOTATED BIBLIOGRAPHY

Nardi v Stevens Institute of Technology, 60 FSupp 2d 31, 41 (EDNY 1988).

Nardi initially joined Stevens in 1965 as a visiting professor in the Physics Department and later as a research professor. The dean, provost, and president told Nardi he could stay at Stevens as long as he had research grant support. Although he acknowledged the statement, he contends that these statements did not create a binding contract that Nardi could only be terminated if he failed to obtain research funding. Held for the institute: "No academic institution would ever accept such a limited definition of cause. It would mean that they could not discharge a professor for unprofessional conduct such as falsification of research data or sexual assault. If the parties had intended that the contract include such a definition of cause, they should have clearly and unambiguously state it, but did not."

Nicholas v Pennsylvania State University, 227 F3d 133 (2000).

Nicholas, initially hired as associate professor of PSU's human performance laboratory, received tenure in 1973. He supplemented his income with various external jobs. Nicholas disputed the university's claim that he worked full time as an emergency room physician and thus was unable to work regular hours at the laboratory. In 1993, the university hired a new director for the laboratory. Upon his arrival, the director requested Nicholas to provide information on his CV, research plans, and work schedule at the laboratory. Nicholas did not provide the information. After several warnings, Nicholas was informed that he would be terminated if he failed to provide the information. He was terminated for insubordination after he refused to comply. Nicholas also complained to the medical board about the director's method of allowing nonmedical personnel to perform muscle biopsies without medical supervision. The university subsequently agreed with Nicholas. This was the basis of his claim of a vendetta against him by the director. Held for Nicholas: The university breached its contract with Nicholas who was awarded nominal damages of $1,000 because he made more money after his termination than he did at the university. The Court reduced the damages to $1 and awarded 1-year severance pay. He was not entitled to the specific performance of reinstatement.

A truck driver instructor was hired on a 1-year contract. During this period, she received several letters regarding perceived deficiencies, probationary status, and reassignment of duties. She resigned after 3 months and brought a lawsuit for breach of contract under a theory of constructive discharge. Under state law, the handbook did not create a contract and thus could not be the basis of a property interest.

Yates v Board of Regent of Lamar University System, 654 FSupp 979(ED Tex 1987).

Yates argued the existence of a property interest based on custom and prevailing practices at the university. Held for Yates: Evidence indicated an understanding on the part of the university that nonprobationary employees could only be dismissed for cause.

LaForge v State University System, 997 P2d 130 (Nev 2000).

A nontenured university professor was given 369 days notice of his nonrenewal. The code required 365 days notice. He sued alleging that the university should have followed the procedures outlined in the by-laws. Held for the university: No language in either the code, by-laws, or state statutes required anything other than notice.

Moosa v State Personnel Bd., 126 Cal Rptr2d 321 (Cal App 3 Dist 2002).

A tenured professor known for demanding rigorous work of students had high student withdrawal rates and low grades. He believed students lacked adequate preparation for university-level work. The dean believed the professor was the problem and initiated a review. The committee consisting of tenured faculty found Dr. Moosa to be a resourceful and knowledgeable faculty member and agreed with him as to the root cause of the problem. No suggestions were made for improvement. Dr. Moosa was demoted after he failed to comply with the dean's directive to develop an improvement plan. Held for the Professor: Under the collective bargaining agreement, the dean lacked the authority to direct Dr. Moosa to develop an improvement plan. The provision allowed for a discussion of the Professor's strengths and weaknesses and suggestions for improvement.

Morgan v American University, 534 A2d 323 (DC App 1987).

A faculty member's contract was rescinded after he failed to disclose on his activity form that he worked full time at another institution. He brought an action alleging the university did not grant him the for-cause termination procedures stated in the handbook. Held for the university: A rescission of a contract is different from termination.

Kakaes v George Washington University, 790 A2d 581 (DC 2002).

A university failed to provide a nontenured faculty member notice of its denial of tenure decision according to the time frame established in the faculty handbook. A provision in the handbook read, "Any such faculty member who is not so notified shall acquire tenure at the end of the term." Remedy: The Court agreed that the university had contractually obligated itself to grant tenure, but noted that the handbook did not specify a remedy or relief available for the breach. Therefore, the Court found the monetary remedy appropriate.

Sackman v Alfred University, 717 NYS2d 461 (Supp 2000).

The university required proven teaching performance as the prime criteria for tenure, followed by scholarly activity, student advising, professional activity, and participation in campus activities. The handbook required the chairperson, through classroom visitations and other means to remain current on the teacher's performance. The chairperson made one classroom visit over a 6-year period. Dr. Sackman was denied tenure because his overall tenure portfolio showed a weakness in teaching skills. He sued, alleging that the university did not follow its own rules as established in the handbook. Held: One visit was insufficient to evaluate the professor's teaching performance. However, failure of a university to follow its own rules regarding tenure review does not establish a breach of contract. The professor was offered and accepted a tenure-track position, but was never guaranteed tenure. The handbook simply outlined the criteria and procedures.

Westheimer v New University, Available at: http://www.aaup.org/publications/Academe?02so/02spNB.htm

Joel Westheimer was the only nontenured professor who testified at a hearing held by the National

Labor Relations Board (NLRB) that graduate students at NYU should be able to unionize if they elected to do so based on the fact that teaching assistantships in his department were more like jobs than supervised learning experiences. The university disputed this contention and was strongly opposed to the graduate students ultimately successful union bid. Westheimer filed charges with the NLRB claiming that he was denied tenure in retaliation for his testimony on behalf of the graduate students. A regional office of the NLRB issued a formal complaint against NYU. Settlement reached: Prior to the case being heard by an administrative judge, a settlement was reached for the faculty. Westheimer received a financial sum of $15,000 and his record indicating that he was denied tenure was expunged. As consideration for the settlement, Westheimer agreed to withdraw his NLRB complaint and his tenure application.

Anderson v State University of New York at New Paltz, 169 F3dkk7 (2nd Cir 1999), remanded by 120 SCt 929 (US 2000).

Dr. Janice Anderson sued the administration, alleging a number of claims, including violation of the EPA. She claimed that since 1984, she had been paid less than male faculty of similar rank at her institution despite her equivalent or superior qualifications, record, and workload. The university sought to dismiss the suit, contending that it was immune from the Equal Pay Act (EPA) claim under the Eleventh Amendment. The district court rejected the university's argument and the university appealed. The AAUP joined a friend-of-the-court brief that was authored by the National Employment Lawyers Association (NELA). A federal district decision has not been issued in this case.

Smith v Virginia Commonwealth University, 856 FSupp 1088 (ED Va 1994), rev'd 62 F3d 659 (4th Cir 1995).

Following a statistical study that demonstrated a disparity of $1,300 between the salaries of men and women professors that could not be explained by permissible factors, Virginia Commonwealth University established a special fund for female faculty to apply for increases. A group of male faculty members whose regular increases remained undisturbed challenged as discriminatory this one-time pay adjustment made to 170 female faculty members. The lower court found that the university's program did not unnecessarily trammel the rights of male faculty members. AAUP filed a friend-of-the court brief to the Fourth Circuit, arguing that a one-time salary adjustment program to correct a statistically identified imbalance favoring male faculty members was consistent with Title VII and the judicial standards for such affirmative action programs. A three-judge appellant court sent the case back to the lower court for trial, unwilling to accept the adequacy of the university's statistical study without further evidence. Later, the full Fourth Circuit granted en banc review, and it ruled that a trial was necessary, although several different rationales were offered for the outcome.

DeSanto v Rowan University, 2002 WL 31011231 (DNJ 2002).

DeSanto, a temporary replacement faculty member, alleged discrimination and violation of due process after being denied a tenure-track position and sought as a remedy to be awarded a tenured position at the university. Held for the university: The faculty member was not entitled to tenure and could not introduce evidence that he was entitled to tenure or possessed a constitutional property interest in tenure.

Thornton v Kaplan, 937 FSupp 1441 (D Col 1996).

Professor alleged discrimination in violation of Title VII when colleagues denied the faculty member application for tenure. Held: Split decision for the faculty member and the university. The jury awarded the professor monetary damages but the Court declined to reinstate the professor with tenure.

Linn v Andover-Theological School, 638 FSupp 1114 (D Mass 1968).

Linn was fired at the age of 62, after 31 years of service to the institution. Linn sued, claiming this his employment was terminated in violation of the ADEA and a breach of his employment contract with the institution. The executive committee of Andover-Theological School ordered the president to reduce the budget of the institution to at least $50,000 and appointed a four-member faculty advisory committee to make recommendations to the implementation of its order. The faculty committee recommended Professor Linn be terminated from the institution. The Executive Committee accepted the decision and Professor Linn received notification from the president giving him 1-year's notice of his discharge. His discharge was approved by the Executive Committee and supported by the full faculty. The institution claimed that the professor was discharged due to a bona fide financial exigency and discontinuance of his position. The university failed to present adequate evidence of cause for terminating Linn and had not followed its own policies and procedures in determining financial exigency. The court ruled that the institution breached its contract with Professor Linn by violating the terms of his contractual academic tenure rights. The established criteria had not been followed when dismissing the faculty member.

NOTES

1 *McEnroy v St. Meinrad School of Theology,* 529 US 1068 (2000).
2 *Trimble v Washington State University,* 993 P2d 259 (Wash 2000).
3 *Lewis v Loyola University of Chicago,* 500 NE2d 47 (Ill App 1 Dist. 1986).
4 *McJamerson v Grambling State University,* 769 So2d 168 (La App 2 Cir 2000).
5 *Shebar v Sanyo Business System Corp.,* 544 A2d 377 (1988).
6 *Shebar.*
7 *Orem v Ivy Tech State College,* 711 NE2d 864 (Ind App 1999).
8 *Orem* at 871.
9 *Orem.*
10 *Brown v Bhuiyan,* 10 P3d 888, 891 (Okla 2000).
11 *Dixon v. Regents of Univ. of CA,* 5Cal.Rptr 3d 564 (2003)
12 *Kakaes v George Washington University,* 790 A2d 581, 584 (DC 2002).
13 *Kakaes.*
14 *Sackman v Alfred University,* 717 NYS2d 461 (Supp 2000).
15 AAUP, 1940 Statement of Principles on Academic Freedom and Tenure. Available at http://www.aaup.org/statements/Redbook/1940stat.htm.
16 AAUP, 1940 Statement of Principles on Academic Freedom and Tenure.
17 *Craine v Trinity College,* 791 A2d 518, 526 (Conn 2002).
18 *Craine* at 527.
19 *Craine* at 528.
20 R. O'Neill. Alternatives to Tenure. *Journal of College & University Law,* 27, no. 3 (2001), 573–602, 575.
21 *Craine.*
22 *Craine.*
23 *Craine.*
24 *Craine* at 533.
25 *Craine* at 534.
26 *Craine* at 543.
27 AAUP, 1940 Statement of Principles on Academic Freedom and Tenure.
28 AAUP, Post-Tenure Review: An AAUP Response. Available at: http://www.aaup.org/statements/Redbook/rbpostn.htm.
29 *Trimble v West Virginia Board of Regents,* 549 SE2d 294 (W Va 2001).
30 *Trimble* at 304.
31 *Board of Regents v Roth,* 408 US 564 (1972).
32 *Roth* at 568
33 *Perry v Sinderman,* 408 US 593 (1972).
34 *Sinderman* at 601.
35 AAUP, Statement on Procedural Standards in the Renewal or Nonrenewal of Faculty Appointments. Available at: http://www.aaup.org/statements/Redbook/Rbrenew.htm
36 *San Filippo, Jr. v Bongiovanni,* 961 F2d 1125 (3d Cir 1992).
37 The American Heritage Dictionary *San Filippo.*
38 W. Morris, (Ed). The American Heritage Dictionary of the English Language. Boston Houghton Mifflin Co., Publishers, 1979.
39 *McConnell v Howard University,* 818 F2d 58 (DC Cir 1987).
40 *In Re Brantley,* 518 NE2d 602 (1987).
41 *Agarwal v Regents of the University of Minnesota,* 788 F2d 504 (8th Cir 1986).
42 *Agarwal* at 506
43 *Katz v Georgetown University,* 246 F3d 685 (2001).
44 *Hahn v University of District of Columbia,* 789 A2d 1252 (DC 2002).
45 *Roufaiel v Ithaca,* 721 NYS2d 124 (AD 3 Dept 2001).
46 42 USC Section 2000e et seq.
47 42 USC Section 2000e-2(a).
48 AAUP, Court Cases Involving Tenure As Remedy For Discrimination. Available at: http://www.aaup.org/Legal/info%20outlines/legtendis.htm
49 *Brown v Trustees of Boston University,* 496 US 939 (1990).
50 *EEOC v Catholic University,* 65 FEP Cases 320 (1994).
51 *McDonnell Douglas Corp. v Green,* 411 US 792, 802 (1973).
52 *Furnco Construction Co. v Waters,* 438 US 567, 577 (1978).
53 *Furnco.*
54 *Furnco.*
55 *Lewis v Loyola University of Chicago,* 872 F2d 424 (7th Cir 1989).

56 *Kunda v Muhlenberg College,* 621 F2d 532 (3d Cir 1980).

57 29 USC Section 621 et seq.

58 Section 623.

59 *Leftwich v Harris-Stowe College,* 702 F2d 686 (8th Cir 1983).

60 *Leftwich* at 691.

61 *Leftwich* at 692.

62 *MacPherson v University of Montevallo,* 922 F2d 766 (11th Cir 1991).

63 *Davidson v Board of Governors of State Colleges and Universities,* 920 F2d 441 (7th Cir 1990).

64 *Watlington v University of Puerto Rico,* 751 FSupp 318 D PR (1990).

65 *Watlington.*

66 29 USC Section 794.

67 42 USC 12101 et. seq.

68 Section 12101(a).

69 Section 12111(8).

70 *Meling v St. Francis College,* 3 FSupp 2d 267 (EDNY 1998).

71 *Meling,* quoting *New York Institute of Technology v State Division of Human Rights,* 353 NE2d 598 (1976).

72 42 USC 12101 et. seq.

73 *Griel v Franklin Medical Center,* 234 F3d 731 (2000).

74 *Albrechtsen v University of Wisconsin System,* 309 F3d 433 (2002).

75 *Albrechtsen* at 438.

76 *Albrechtsen* at 439.

77 29 USC Section 2601 et. seq.

78 *Earl v Mervyns, Inc.,* 207 F3d 1361, 1367.

79 *Raith v Johns Hopkins University,* 171 F. Supp. 2d 515

5

Faculty Relations in Academic Environments

INTRODUCTION

The academic community is founded on principles of professionalism, respect, trust, autonomy, and good will. Administrators, faculty, and staff have a responsibility to maintain an academic environment where scholars strive and students succeed. Administrators and staff ensure efficient operations. These goals are threatened when faculty and administrators fail to hold themselves in high esteem by engaging in behaviors that are detrimental to the educational institution, colleagues, students, and themselves. This chapter discusses the basis of faculty relations in educational environments and addresses issues faculty may encounter in their relationships with administrators, colleagues, and students.

Dr. Constance Langstone is a tenured professor at Mountain Green University in the College of Health Sciences. She teaches courses in theory, finance, and leadership and administration to students within the college. Her fiancée works in the Department of Public Safety. She has established therapeutic professional relationships with the majority of her colleagues, having served on numerous committees with them, coauthored publications, mentored new faculty, and written numerous grant proposals. Her ties with the community are varied. She works 5 days a month at Greentowns HMO as a consultant administrator and is active in numerous civic leagues and charitable organizations. During her 8-year tenure at the university, Constance has received 22 awards and recognitions for her community and professional service. The faculty expects her to succeed the chair when he retires next year.

Two years earlier, Constance was assigned to mentor Dr. Tom Soffy, a new tenure-track assistant professor of nursing. However, after one semester he requested the dean to assign him another mentor, stating that Constance was obnoxious, overbearing, and outdated in her teaching content and methods. He voiced these concerns in a faculty meeting and requested a review of Constance's teaching materials. He also accused her of publishing students' papers/projects without giving them the appropriate credit. Constance responded by denying the allegations and with an accusation that Tom had problems working with women and was closed-minded. The chair, Dr. Wanton, warned them to keep their personal differences out of the work environment and to discuss issues with him prior to broadcasting them to faculty.

To meet the last-minute needs of the college, Constance agreed to teach a doctoral-level course in health care finance. She noticed a name on the roster that made her feel uncomfortable. During the first class, she indeed verified that her previous boyfriend was enrolled in the class. Their volatile relationship ended 8 years earlier when she left town to escape his stalking and emotional abuse. They had no contact since then and she was unaware he was in the same town. After class, Charlie came up to her, apologized for their past relationship, and offered to use his position as executive director at the Memorial HMO to collaborate on future projects. He currently worked with Tom, who had kept him apprised of Constance's activities. She suggested he take another course; however, he assured her that their past would not impact his academic performance. Constance did not discuss this situation with Dr. Wanton. She was aware that university policy prohibited romantic or sexual relationships between faculty and students.

Shortly thereafter Constance and Charlie began a romantic relationship. She reasoned that Charlie, at age 36, was not the typical naïve young adult and that they had a previous relationship. About three months after they resumed their relation, Tom saw them together at an entertainment/dance club. He announced this during a faculty meeting, stating that Constance was violating university policy and demanded an investigation. Dr. Wanton refused to discuss the issue and told them to meet him after the faculty meeting. Constance truthfully explained that she went to the club with a female friend who became ill and left early. Charlie was there with several of his friends and asked her to dance. They shared one dance and she left. Dr. Wanton did not ask nor did Constance volunteer additional information about their relationship. Two hours later, Charlie called and informed Constance that he told the sexual harassment investigator from the Office of Human Resources that they were not involved in an intimate relationship. Constance and Charlie agreed to table their relationship until the course ended.

Tom came to her class during a break to talk with Charlie about receiving an endorsement from his organization to support a grant proposal. During the conversation, he commented loudly, in front of other students, that he heard of Charlie and Constance's affair. Charlie denied the allegations and walked away. In response to one of the student's request to comment on her relationship with Charlie, Constance replied, "Sam, you need to focus your attention on successfully completing the requirements for the course. After all, you have failed the first two quizzes." An upset Sam left the classroom.

CRITICAL THINKING QUESTIONS
1. How should Constance handle the sexual harassment issue?
2. What actions, if any, can or should be taken against Tom? Against Charlie?
3. Does Sam have a cause of action against Constance for a FERPA violation?

• • •

FACULTY-TO-FACULTY RELATIONSHIPS

Faculty-to-faculty relationships should be based on respect, collegiality, and shared goals to advance the quality of the education process. Faculty members must cooperate, compromise, and collaborate and be collegial in the design of the curricula, teaching of classes, advising of students, securing external funding, promoting faculty development, building relationships within the university, and promoting the professional and financial growth of the academic unit. The American Association of University Professors (AAUP's) position is that

> " As a colleague, the professor has obligations that derive from common membership in the community of scholars; respects and defends the free inquiry of associates, in the exchange of criticism and ideas, shows due respect for the opinion of others, acknowledges academic debts and strives to be objective in professional judgment of colleagues and accepts a share of faculty responsibilities in the governance of the institution." [1]

Numerous factors affect the personal and professional relationship among faculty in departments, colleges, and universities. Respect, collegiality, collaboration, support, and trustworthiness are factors that facilitate a movement toward positive accomplishments. For example, respect, defined as a willingness to show consideration for another and a courteous yielding to the opinion, wishes, or judgment of another, promotes an environment that fosters the free exchange of ideas.[2] Likewise, support for colleagues is manifested in the provision of any type of aid to keep them in the best academic position possible. It may take the form of encouragement to keep one's spirit lifted, collaboration on projects to facilitate professional growth, or simply listening as one ponders a decision or voices frustration.

Conversely, hostility, vindictiveness, dishonesty, competition, and isolation produce stagnation, tension, and sometimes destruction within academic arenas. The following story reported in the *Chronicle of Higher Education* depicts the negative impact of poor faculty-to-faculty relationships.

> " *Interdepartmental fighting between professors in the economics department at the University of Cincinnati has reduced the faculty to just 11 and led to the closure of its doctorate program. The division over an emphasis on research or an emphasis on improving teaching has continued.* " [3]

Collegiality

Perhaps the most important factor in the foundation of faculty-to-faculty relationships is collegiality, defined as "the capacity to relate well and constructively to the comparatively small bank of scholars on whom the ultimate fate of the university rests."[4] From the perspective of a university president, collegiality is "the ability to work with your department to make sure that the University's going to move ahead, that your best interests-your interests are in the best of the University."[5]

Courts have upheld the lack of collegiality as the basis for the nonrenewal of faculty contracts or denial of tenure. In *University of Baltimore v Iz*,[6] a faculty member denied tenure brought a breach of contract claim against the university alleging that she was evaluated on the unwritten criterion, collegiality. The dean noted that Dr. Iz was reluctant to accept peer evaluation. Likewise, the chair described Dr. Iz as "inflexible, defensive, and unwilling to take constructive advice." Ruling in favor of the university, the Court noted that collegiality is an inherent concept in both teaching and service.

- *With respect to teaching, collegiality is certainly an important factor pertaining to "excellence in instruction, as indicated by an examination of all relevant sources of information, including input from students, peers, and administrators."[7]*
- *With respect to service—particularly, internal service—collegiality is fairly included within the criterion that includes "contributions to the university through faculty or administrative committee service, acceptance and fulfillment of special assignments from faculty organizations or the administration."[8]*

Courts have consistently upheld the expectation of collegiality in faculty relationships with students, colleagues, and administrators. Although these cases involved faculty who had deficits in other areas, such as teaching or research, their poor professional conduct and negative attitudes were viewed by the courts as adverse to the promotion of collegiality. Very few people want to work in an environment filled with dissent, tension, hostility, and drama. The academic community is no exception and in essence, noncollegiality definitely cannot be tolerated in a community of scholars. In the pursuit of the truth and dissemination of knowledge, a faculty member cannot work in isolation. The very nature of the progression and promotion process is dependent on positive, productive, and promising relationships. Faculty members are expected to be an integral part of their academic community. They must participate in committee assignments, discussions that promote the fulfillment of the department and university goals and objectives, and accept constructive feedback that promotes their personal and professional development. They cannot succeed in isolation.

The concern for some is that the use of collegiality, as an unwritten factor for promotion and tenure decisions, can promote unfairness and unwarranted surprises in the evaluation process. Faculty members should be informed that their behaviors and attitudes are considered noncollegial, be provided specific examples of the behaviors, and be given suggestions for improvement. These faculty may not have insight into their behaviors and how it negatively impacts others. Some senior faculty may perceive the outspoken advocacy for change by junior faculty as disruptive and unnecessary. Disagreements and conflicts with colleagues when appropriately channeled can be the impetus for change and growth. It disrupts the status quo and forces an evaluation of different perspectives, which in itself is an educational process. However, differences in opinions must be handled in an appropriate manner. It should not be revealed to students nor publicly displayed to the detriment of the department. One's personal grievances with colleagues, whether based on personality conflicts or perceived wrongdoings must be handled in a professional, yet effective manner. At worst, you may have to agree to disagree; at best, a collegial dialogue will result in a mutual understanding and acceptance of each other's perspective and beliefs.

FACULTY-TO-STUDENT RELATIONSHIPS

The AAUP recognizes that educators have special responsibilities and obligations to their students. Professors should:[9]

- Demonstrate respect for students as individuals and adhere to their proper roles as intellectual guides and counselors
- Make every evaluation of students reflect each student's true merit
- Respect the confidential nature of the relationship between professor and student
- Avoid any exploitation, harassment, or discriminatory treatment of students
- Acknowledge significant academic or scholarly assistance from them

The Court's statement in the following case exemplifies the professional nature of the faculty-student relationship. In *Korf v Ball State University*,[10] the Court rejected the professor's claim that the AAUP's statement did not apply to consensual sexual relationships with students and upheld the committee's finding that he had exploited students for his private gain. It reasoned that the professor's behavior must be judged within the context of the faculty-student relationship and not that of an ordinary person on the street. Educators have an important role in society and should not demean their status by engaging in behavior that is unbecoming and suspect.

Theoretical Foundations

Law in higher education was at one time almost nonexistent. The prevailing thought was that ill will, evil motives, and harmful intent were not associated with a community of scholars; therefore, intrusion by external forces, such as lawyers and judges, was unnecessary.[11] "Interference by such 'outsiders' would destroy the understanding and mutual trust that must prevail in academia."[12] Faculty members were held in high esteem as the producers and disseminators of knowledge. Attendance at higher education institutions was seen as a privilege and not a right. Therefore, courts accorded deference to faculty and administrators in their relationships with students. The following section describes the trends in theoretical perspectives that have governed faculty-student relationships.

In Loco Parentis Theory

The doctrine of in loco parentis reinforced the judicial hands-off practice that encompassed the world of academia. The case of *Gott v Berea College*[13] illustrates the extent of control faculty had over their students. The faculty revised its rule to add a clause that prohibited students from entering noncollege-owned houses and places of amusement. Gott's restaurant, which was dependent on students' patronage, was negatively affected by the rule. He sued seeking an injunction against the enforcement of the policy. Ruling in favor of the college, the Court acknowledged the overwhelming authority of college officials over students under the doctrine of in loco parentis. Although *Gott* involved a boarding school, similar policies and judicial deference existed in the public sector. Many students left high school and went directly to college, where they became "adults." Thus, higher education institutions were viewed as an extension of parental shelters. College officials had almost unchallenged authority to direct, guide, control, and discipline college students.

As illustrated in the case of *Dixon v Alabama*,[14] the face of academia began to change in the 1960s with the civil rights movements, enrollment of postwar veterans, and student protests against societal values and government.[15] Concurrently, the strength of the in loco parentis doctrine faded. In *Dixon*,[16] the university used its policy that allowed for the expulsion of any student at any time who becomes unpleasant and difficult to expel nine students who participated in a civil rights demonstration and insisted on service at a "whites only" lunch counter. Ruling in favor of the students, the Court noted that the students' constitutional right to due process (notice and a hearing) outweighed academic policies and regulations. The college did not have unlimited authority to expel students and to act in an arbitrary manner.

Negligence Theory

With the demise of the in loco parentis doctrine, courts were confronted with the issue of defining the basis of the relationship between higher education institutions and students. Students have sued colleges and universities based on a theory of negligence derived from tort liability. The argument was that a special relationship existed between the college and the student. Based on the nature of the relationship, the institution had a legal obligation or duty to exercise reasonable care to prevent injury or harm to the student. The University breached its duty to conform to certain standards of conduct, such as exercising reasonable care, which was a direct and proximate cause of an injury, loss, or harm suffered by a student. In tort law, damages are based on monetary value of the harm or injury. Tort liability is usually not appropriate as the basis for the faculty-student relationship in higher education institutions. It presupposes that faculty owe students a duty based on a special relationship, similar to that of the nurse-patient relationship. Duty is the first element that must be established in cases alleging negligence or malpractice. The educator-student relationship is not based on a special relationship that gives rise to a duty, Therefore, many courts do not recognize a cause of action for educational malpractice.

Contract Theory

The current, although not perfect, theory is that the relationship between a college and student is contractual in nature. The weakness in this theory is that usually parties to a contract share an equal or almost equal bargaining power. This is not the case with students, who must accept existing admission standards, program of study, and policies and regulations regarding progression and graduation. In essence, students have little bargaining power in their contractual relationship with education institutions. Uniform admission, progression, and graduation standards must exist to protect faculty from claims of arbitrary and capricious decisions. Faculty establish uniform criteria that apply to students in their respective disciplines. Attempts to negotiate course content and grading policies with a class of students invites disaster. Students simply cannot pick and choose what and how they want to learn and the basis upon which to assign grades. Diversity in students needs, learning styles, and work habits would create difficulty in reaching student consensus regarding learning assignments. Further, in making decisions regarding curricula for programs of study, faculty must consider and incorporate criteria established by professional organizations and accrediting bodies. Students are often not aware of these educational mandates.

Many courts accept the contract theory because it provides a basis upon which to determine if college officials have acted in a capricious and arbitrary manner. The Court in *Bilut v Northwest University* discussed the contractual basis of the faculty-student relationship.

> *The foundation of the relationship between educational institutions, their students, and faculty is the understanding that the students will abide by and adhere to the disciplinary regulations and academic standards established by the faculty and the university; and that upon the satisfactory completion of their studies, they will be awarded a degree in their chosen discipline.*[17]

This includes an inherent concept of good faith and fair dealing. In *Sharick v Southeastern University,* the jury found that the university's decision to dismiss Sharick from the program after he was given a failing grade in the final course required for graduation "was arbitrary, capricious and/or lacking any discernable rational basis."[18] Finding that the university had breached its contract with Sharick, the Court ruled that Sharick was entitled to recover more than just his tuition payments. Because he was deprived of his degree, he could pursue monetary damages in the form of loss earning capacity or the money he would lose by not obtaining his degree. If he was able to obtain his degree at another institution, he would be entitled to the costs of acquiring the degree, plus the present value of his income during the time period for obtaining the degree. The Court's message was that education officials cannot waste the student's time and then arbitrarily withhold his or her degree.

Basis of the Contract

The language in the course catalog, student handbook, and course syllabus is frequently analyzed to determine the basis of the university's contract with the student. The student handbook usually provides information for students on admission, academic progression, registration, deadlines, tuition and costs, progression, and graduation. The specific discipline's handbook will contain pertinent information on the requirements for obtaining the specific degree. In many upper-level degree programs, students must apply for specific admission into the program and will be evaluated based on the program's published criteria. For example, a typical nursing program may require students to complete prerequisites before applying to the nursing program. The selection process may incorporate grade point average, interview, and/or student goals. Once enrolled, the course syllabus provides the terms of the agreement.

Courts look to syllabi to determine whether the faculty exercised good faith and fair dealing. With some exceptions, faculty members enjoy academic freedom in the development of the course syllabus, although they must contain core information. Essential or core areas include:

- The professor's academic credentials
- The course number, title, and description
- Placement within the curriculum
- Objectives
- Attendance policy
- Course content and class schedule
- Reading assignments
- Course projects and examinations
- Grading policies and scale
- Evaluation methods
- Due dates for assignments
- Required and recommended textbooks
- A statement of the honor pledge

Handling Conflicts

There are times, however, as with any community of individuals, that conflicts will arise between students and faculty members. The student may feel that the professor is singling him or her out for negative treatment. Procedures should be in place to allow students to challenge any perceived negative treatment, curricula, or interaction issues. If left unresolved or the outcome is not satisfactory to the student, litigation may result. Faculty's position is strengthened if established procedures were followed. Flynn, a nursing student, experienced several conflicts with Professor Ambrose. In October 1994, the professor rejected Flynn's request for an extension on a paper, although Flynn alleged that other students were given extensions. A second request made in November due to personal illness and involvement in custody litigation was also rejected. Flynn indicated that she was called lazy and told by Professor Ambrose that she did not like her. She appealed and the director of the nursing program required Professor Ambrose to accept the late paper. Flynn received a grade of "F" on the paper.

In December 1994, the director informed Flynn that she was in danger of failing Professor Ambrose's class. Flynn relayed to the director and the assistant dean that the professor was treating her unfairly. Ultimately, Flynn received a "D" in the course and complained to the assistant dean that she should have received a grade of "C." Flynn was informed that she could continue in the program with the "D" grade and that greater than 50% of students received a "D" in Professor Ambrose's course.

In summer 1995, Flynn alleged that Professor Ambrose refused to give her a recommendation for an externship because she would embarrass the nursing program. Flynn then obtained a job at a nursing home that was approved by the assistant dean as an externship. However, Professor Ambrose, who supervised the externship, informed Flynn that she would fail the externship if any of her clinical journals were late. Flynn expressed concern to the assistant dean that Professor Ambrose would fail her even if she mailed her journals on time. Based on the recommendation of the assistant dean, Flynn withdrew from the externship.

She received a grade of "F" in another nursing course for failure to complete the coursework after being granted an extension. She blamed her difficulties on the stress of having to take another course with Professor Ambrose the next semester.

In the spring semester, Flynn registered for a required nursing course taught only by Professor Ambrose. Minutes before the first examination, Dr. Ambrose approached Flynn and indicated that she had an important letter to give her after the examination regarding her status as a student at the university. Flynn alleges that she was unable to concentrate and received an "F" on the exam. The letter was related to a trivial matter. Due to Flynn's performance on the exam, Professor Ambrose advised her that she would not successfully complete her work and advised her to withdraw from the program. She thereafter met individually with the dean, assistant dean, and director of the nursing program, repeated Professor's Ambrose comments, expressed her concern that Professor Ambrose would fail her, and requested to withdraw from the class.

The next spring, Flynn needed three courses to complete the nursing program, one of which was taught by Professor Ambrose. The dean refused to change her class assignment. Flynn alleges that during the class, she was humiliated and intimidated by Professor Ambrose. For example, the professor refused to answer what she labeled a "dumb question" asked by Flynn. On another occasion, the professor told the class that only one group failed—referring to Flynn's group—because they were lazy and careless. Meetings with the nursing administrators failed to resolve the student-professor conflicts; consequently, Flynn withdrew from the nursing program.

The Court rejected Flynn's claims of breach of contract and intentional infliction of emotional distress (IIED). Flynn could not provide evidence that the School of Nursing promised to assign her to courses not taught by Professor Ambrose or promised to provide her with a mechanism to address conflicts and grievances with professors, which would be necessary to substantiate a cause of breach of contract. Likewise, the Court ruled that in cases involving IIED, state law required a showing of outrageous conduct. Noting that "Ambrose may be the professor every LaSalle nursing student hopes they can avoid as an instructor," demeaning comments and humiliation do not rise to the level necessary to establish IIED.[19] Nevertheless, students should not be subjected to intentional abusive behavior by faculty. If the above student allegations were true, administrators breached their duty to provide an academic atmosphere conducive to student learning. The university has a responsibility to protect students from vindictive, unprofessional faculty members.

Likewise, the university must support its faculty from the misconduct of students. Faculty should not have to tolerate threats, negative comments, sexual innuendos, or other types of abuse from students. In many instances, the cases can be addressed under the disciplinary code; however, the university must be willing to enforce the code.

The case of *McConnell v Howard University*[20] illustrates the results of conflicts between faculty and administrators in handling a student's misconduct. A student called Dr. McConnell a "condescending, patronizing racist" in front of the entire class. The university would not discipline or make her apologize to the professor. The dean only advised the student that her conduct was unacceptable and future incidents would result in disciplinary procedures. However, the professor was disciplined after he refused to teach the class. He felt that he could not establish the proper teaching atmosphere until the student apologized or was removed from the class. The grievance committee found that the university procedures for handling this type of student incidents were inadequate, noting that "A teacher has the right to expect the University to protect the professional authority in teacher-student relationship."[21] The Court ruled that Dr. McConnell could assert his theory that the university had a duty to take and implement measures to protect his professional authority in the classroom.

- *Among a community of scholars, one who is assigned to teach must have some semblance of control over the classroom.*
- *If control is lost, learning invariably will be obstructed and the teacher will be unable to fulfill a professional responsibility.*[22]

Collegiality, cooperation, and collaboration are the basis for faculty-student relationship. Students provide input on curricula and instructions methods, either directly through service on committees or communications with faculty or indirectly through written evaluations. Ultimately, however, faculty are in charge of the students' learning environment.

FAMILY EDUCATIONAL RIGHTS AND PRIVACY ACT OF 1974 (FERPA)[23]

FERPA was enacted to allow students access to their education record and to protect their privacy rights by limiting who can receive their information without their consent.[24] The extent of coverage enacted by Congress for the protection of academic records is broad. FERPA extends to public or private educational agencies that receive federal funding and are authorized to direct and control or to provide instruction or services from the kindergarten to postsecondary education level. Educational institutions are required to protect students' educational records and personally identifiable information (PII) contained within these records or risk losing their federal funding.[25]

Education Records

Education records are defined as "those records, files, documents, and other materials which (i) contain information directly related to a student; and (ii) are maintained by an educational agency or institution or by a person acting for such agency or institution."[26] Educational institutions can withhold certain personal information on students and their families from numerous state and federal governmental agencies unless they obtain the proper release. Written consent of adult students or parents of minor children must be provided before this information can be released or disclosed. PII includes any information that could be used to identify a student such as his or her name, address, social security number, student number, or personal characteristics. Information on students' parents or relatives that can be used to trace the student is also subject to nondisclosure.[27] An educational agency or institution may disclose personally identifiable information of a student without consent to other school officials, including teachers within the institution who have a legitimate educational need or interest.

Many institutions have student directories that may contain personally identifiable information, such as the student's name, address, telephone number, e-mail address, date and place of birth, a photograph, dates of attendance, enrollment status, honors and awards received, degrees, most recent educational institution attended, and participation in activities and sports.[28] Although this information may be considered harmless and not an invasion of privacy, institutions must have an opt-out provision or "no release" form, which allows students to refuse the release of directory information.

A major issue under FERPA is what constitutes "education records." FERPA provides a basis to deny grade forms that contain the telephone number, class attendance record, and final grade of students;[29] to prohibit the posting of students' grades using their social security numbers;[30] to grant students access to letters of recommendations;[31] to allow peer grading;[32] and to correct assigned grades.

In *Lewin v Cooke,*[33] the Court elaborated on what constitutes education records and emphasized students' limitations to educational materials. Lewin's unsatisfactory performance on a pharmacology exam led to his subsequent dismissal from the medical school. Relying on the provision of FERPA that gives students the right to challenge inaccurate, misleading, or inappropriate data in their records,[34] Lewin asked the Court to correct two of his answers, which he contended were incorrectly graded. Refusing to decide the correctness of examination questions, the Court noted that FERPA "only permits actions to correct ministerial or technical inaccuracies in education records." He also alleged FERPA violations because the medical school failed to provide him with:

1. Access to his pharmacology examination within 45 days
2. The answer key to the pharmacology examination
3. Access to the unabridged tape recording of the hearing and deliberations of the student progress committee that voted to expel him

The first issue was not addressed by the Court due to legalities—the issue either was or should have been litigated or tried in the first lawsuit against the medical school. The second issue was denied because a master grade sheet was not viewed as an education record because it did not contain any of his personally identifiable information nor personal information on his education performance. FERPA only allows students' access to their education record. Finally, the Court ruled that although he was entitled to the tape as an education record, the Department of Education (DOE) had already instructed the medical school to give Lewin a copy of the tape. Therefore, he had already received the proper remedy allowed under FERPA for the violation, which was to correct the wrong by providing him access to the tape.

Access to Records

Case law supports the premise that educational institutions must balance the rights of the public to access records of governmental affairs with the privacy rights of its students. In *Osborn v Board of Regents of University of Wisconsin,*[35] Osborn requested public records of students who attended the university as well as records of matriculating and nonmatriculating students from several of the university's campuses, the law school, and the medical school in order to analyze and compare data on admission policies and practices. The university complied with some of the requests but refused to provide information on Scholastic

Aptitude Test (SAT) and American College Testing Assessment (ACT) scores, grade point averages, class rank by race and sex ethnicity, and socioeconomic background based on the following reasons:

- such personally identifiable information is prohibited from disclosure under FERPA,
- the public interest in disclosure is outweighed by the public interest in nondisclosure,
- the information sought . . . is only maintained in individual student education records and extracting the information requested would amount to creating a new record, which, . . . is not required under the open records law.[36]
- it had no duty to redact, extract, or create new records to comply with his request,
- the time and costs required to redact information exceeded that required by the open records law, because state statutory language required the custodian of record to delete any information that is not subject to disclosure, and
- the information requested implicated the personal privacy and reputation interests of individual students and applicants for admissions.[37]

Conversely, Osborn argued that:

- FERPA only prohibits disclosure of the entire education record and of personally identifiable information.
- The data from student records allow "the public to research and conduct studies to gauge the effectiveness and appropriateness of the University's admission practices and policies."[38]

Ruling in favor of Osborn, the Court acknowledged that, under FERPA, the university could not release PII without written consent of students, unless it was considered directory information. However, the information requested by Osborn was not considered PII because it "is not sufficient, by itself, to trace the identity of an applicant."[39] In addition, the Court found:

- *The public interest in nondisclosure (protecting privacy and reputation) was not outweighed by the public interest to disclosure, and*
- *The time/cost obstacle does not override disclosure, because the cost of compliance can be shifted to the requesting party.*[40]

Faculty may receive request for student information from health care recruiters who are interested in discussing employment opportunities with students. To avoid potential FERPA violations, faculty should not release student information without consulting with the appropriate administrator. Likewise, faculty who need access to student information for research purposes should follow institution policies and procedures to ensure compliance with FERPA mandates.

Disciplinary Records

FERPA also addresses the issue of when and under what circumstances outsiders can have access to students' disciplinary records. These records are considered education records that are protected from access under FERPA. However, as discussed later, exceptions were created for victims of violent crimes, for students under age 21 who violated policies related to alcohol and controlled substance, and for emergency situations. Congress, by allowing these exceptions, attempted to balance the privacy rights of the accused/perpetrator with the rights of the victim and general population. They determined that the latter groups' rights outweigh the perpetrator's right to privacy. Therefore, an "alleged victim of any crime of violence . . . , or a nonforcible sex offense" (such as statutory rape or incest), is entitled to "the final results of any disciplinary proceeding conducted by such institution against the alleged perpetrator of such crime or offense with respect to such crime or offense."[41] Educational institutions can disclose the final results of any disciplinary proceeding conducted by such institution against a student perpetrator of any crime of violence if after a disciplinary proceeding, the student is found to have committed a violation of the institution's rules or policies with respect to such crime or offense.[42] Disclosure of the final results is limited to the student's name, violation committed, and the institution-imposed sanction.[43] Other information such as information on the student-victim or student-witness cannot be disclosed without his or her written permission.[44] A crime of violence includes arson, assault and battery, burglary, manslaughter, murder, destruction or vandalism of property, kidnapping, abduction, robbery, and forcible sex offenses, such as rape.

Students' educational records can contain information on any disciplinary action taken against them for conduct that posed a significant risk to their safety or well-being or that of any other student or member of the academic community.[45] In cases involving alcohol or controlled substances, FERPA allows educational institutions to notify the parent or legal guardian of a child/student under 21 years of age if after a hearing the student is founded to have committed the disciplinary violation.[46] Similarly, information can be disclosed to appropriate parties in connection with an emergency "if the knowledge of such information is necessary to protect the health or safety of the student or other persons."[47]

As the following case illustrates, FERPA allows, but not does mandate, a notification requirement. In *Jain v State*,[48] the father of an 18-year-old student who committed suicide after a previous known attempt initiated a lawsuit against the university for failure to exercise care and caution to protect his son and for failure to notify the parents of an emergency situation as allowed under and mandated by FERPA. The university had an unwritten policy that its officials would notify parents of a student's self-destructive behavior. The appeals court refused to address Jain's claim that the university misapplied the provision of FERPA to his son's detriment because the issue was not raised in the lower court. However, it noted its serious doubts "about the merits of plaintiff's argument. His claim rests, after all, not on a violation of the Act, but on an alleged failure to take advantage of a discretionary exception to its requirements."[49] FERPA allows parents to be contacted in emergency situations but does not mandate that faculty or administrators have to contact parents.

Compliance

The violation of FERPA provisions is a source of concern for faculty and administrators in their attempts to maintain student privacy, because of the ambiguous and confusing language and the emergence of new issues created by FERPA.[50] These concerns should be viewed in the context that the goal of FERPA is voluntary compliance with its provisions. When in doubt, the Family Policy Compliance Office (FPCO) will provide advisory opinions to assist education officials to address and resolve issues. Individuals cannot pursue a private cause of action against education institutions for FERPA violations. They can, however, contact FPCO who investigates complaints and makes recommendations to correct violations and to ensure compliance. In cases involving a pattern of FERPA violations, the

Department of Education is empowered to initiate actions to withhold or terminate federal funding from the education institution.[51]

SEXUAL HARASSMENT

Sexual harassment is a recognized form of sex discrimination prohibited by Title VII of the Civil Rights Act of 1964 and Title IX of the Education Amendments of 1972. Title VII makes it unlawful for an employer "to fail or refuse to hire or to discharge any individual, or otherwise discriminate against any individual with respect to his compensation, terms, conditions, or privileges or employment, because of such individual's race, color, religion, sex, or national origin."[52] Title IX of the Education Amendments of 1972[53] similarly prohibits discrimination based on sex and applies to educational institutions receiving federal funds. It reads, "No person in the United States shall, on the basis of sex, be excluded from participation in, be denied the benefits of, or be subjected to discrimination under any educational program or activity receiving federal financial assistance."[54] It applies to educational institutions receiving federal funds and covers students and employees. Religious institutions, military training schools, and traditionally unisex educational institutions are exempt. Both Title VII and Title IX prohibit sexual harassment, which includes unwelcome sexual advances, requests for sexual favors, and verbal or physical conduct of a sexual nature. Box 5.1 provides examples of verbal, nonverbal, and physical sexual harassment. Table 5.1 provides guidance on conduct and actions that are appropriate and inappropriate in relations with others to avoid allegations of sexual harassment.

Theories of Sexual Harassment

An employee who is the victim of sexual harassment can bring a lawsuit under the theories of quid pro quo or hostile environment.

Quid Pro Quo
Quid pro quo is based on actions by a supervisor who conditions employment on the employee's submission to unwelcome sexual demands, rewards an employee for unwelcome sexual submission, or punishes an employee or subordinate who refuses to comply with the unwelcome sexual demands. To establish a prima facie case of quid pro quo sexual harassment, the employee must show that:[55]

1. He or she belongs to a protected group.
2. He or she was subjected to unwelcome sexual harassment.
3. The harassment complained of was based on sex.
4. His or her reaction to the unwelcome behavior affected tangible aspects of his or her compensation, or terms, conditions or privileges of employment.

In essence, lawsuits under a theory of quid pro quo must involve carried-out threats.

Hostile Environment
A hostile work environment is created when the employee is subjected to offensive, abusive, and intimidating working conditions or the unwelcome sexual behavior interferes with the employee's work performance and environment. In addition to vicarious liability

Examples of Verbal Sexual Harassment:[68]
- Use of vulgar, sexually explicit language.
- Making sexual comments about a person's physical characteristics.
- Making sexual comments or innuendoes either directed toward the person or in general.
- Telling off-color, sexually based jokes or anecdotes.
- Asking explicity questions about one's sex life, fantasy, preferences.
- Making comments that are either explicitly or implicitly sexual in nature about a person's clothing, body shape, or look.
- Asking a person for dates, repetitively, when that person has turned you down.
- Using sexually derogatory terms to refer to women as girls, chicks, foxes, babes, honey, darling, bitch.
- Whistling, making kissing sounds or vulgar smacking sounds.
- Rumor-mongering about a person's sex life.
- Supposedly light comments that indicate sexual interest in the other party, "You know I need you, baby!"

Examples of Nonverbal Sexual Harassment:
- The giving of unsolicited or inappropriate personal gifts (lingerie, sex books, or any fit inappropriate in nature).
- Writing personal, sexually suggestive notes; sending unwelcomed cards.
- Keeping nude or suggestive photos, calendars, ads, cartoons posted anywhere in the workplace.
- Staring at someone repetitively or in a suggestive manner; similarly, giving them the once-over, the "up and down."
- Following a person around the hospital or facility.
- Blocking a person's path; moving unnecessarily and repetitively too close to them in hospital [or other] milieu.
- Licking lips, throwing kisses, making inappropriate facial expressions.
- Through hand or body movements, making sexual gestures or representations of sexual acts.

Examples of Physical Sexual Harassment:
- Touching a person's clothing, hair, or body.
- Standing inappropriately close to a person and then brushing them.
- Hugging or engaging in other physical touching, such as kissing, when no such activity has been invited.
- Rubbing against another person in a sexual manner.
- Giving an uninvited massage to a person's neck or shoulders.
- Pushing someone's hair out of their face accompanied with stares.[69]

Reprinted with the permission of Elizabeth J. du Fresne.

Sexual Harassment Dos and Don'ts

Table 5.1

DO	DON'T
Know the sexual harassment policy of all institutions with whom you work.	Assume H.R. policies are irrelevant to you as a professional.
Remember sexual harassment depends on the perception of the person to whom the words or actions are directed.	Believe that because you didn't mean to be offensive that solves everything.
Respect all who work with you regardless of their race, creed, color, national origin, gender, age, disabilities, pregnancy, or marital status.	Joke, kid, tell stories, ask questions or in any way verbally or otherwise denigrate or hold in ridicule anothers' race, color, creed, national origin, gender, age, disabilities, pregnancy or marital status.
Always behave and speak as would be appropriate if our spouse, spiritual advisor, and/or child were present.	Use vulgar, profane, or sexually explicit anguage or gestures in the work place.
Treat males and females in the workplace without abuse, intimidation, hostility, humiliation, or scorn.	Treat one gender differently and with hostility.
If someone says you personally have done or said something offensive, your response should be a sincere: "I'm sorry," spoken in a normal tone.	When someone says you have personally done or said something offensive, immediately argue with them and try to convince them they are wrong and you are right—that the behavior is not offensive. Raise your voice; make aggressive gestures (shaking person or your finger in their face).
Assist anyone who complains of sexual harassment in reporting.	Threaten, bully, or try to convince anyone who complains of sexual harassment to drop the complaint or charge.
Encourage staff to report sexual harassment and to resolve issues quickly.	Encourage cover-up and/or problem solving by persons not trained to resolve human resource issues.
Know that your personal actions and words are covered by law.	Assume you are the exception— "This doesn't apply to me because I am Italian" [or another race, national origin, etc.].
Keep your relationships professional at work.	Assume anyone is "one of the family" and accepts dirty jokes, vulgar language, and physical horseplay.

Sexual Harassment Dos and Don'ts (continued)

Table 5.1

DO	DON'T
Know that appropriate touching in the workplace is a polite handshake.	Hug, kiss, pat, touch, or ask to be hugged, kissed, patted, touched in the workplace.
Tell your superiors of any romantic or physical relationships you currently have with those who report to you.	Assume that if you are dating, or are romantically or physically involved with someone at work that it is your personal business.

Reprinted with the permission of Elizabeth J. du Fresne.

for its supervisors, an employer can be liable for the actions of coworkers if the employer knew or should have known of the behavior and failed to take appropriate action. To establish a hostile work environment claim, the employee must establish:[56]

1. That he or she belongs to a protected group
2. That the employee has been subjected to sexual harassment
3. That the harassment was based on the sex of the employee
4. That the harassment was sufficiently severe or pervasive to alter the terms and conditions of employment and create a discriminatory abusive working environment, and
5. A basis for holding the employer liable, under the doctrine of vicarious liability

The behavior involved in a hostile work environment claim must extend beyond regular horseplay, socialization, compliments about appearances, and flirtations. It must "approach tangible injury, including psychological injury" and is analyzed on a case-by-case basis for frequency, severity, whether the conduct is physically threatening or humiliating, and whether it unreasonably interferes with the employee's work performance.[57] In addition to the employee's subjective interpretation, he or she must establish that a reasonable person would interpret the work environment as hostile.

Vicarious Liability

Under the doctrine of vicarious liability, an employer is responsible for the civil wrongs of his or her employees acting within the scope of their employment. An employer can be vicariously liable for the actions of his or her managerial personnel when the sexual harassment has an adverse impact on employment or the educational progression of students. In essence, the educational institution and its administrators can be held liable for the misbehavior of its faculty. Because the Supreme Court has acknowledged that sexual harassment by a supervisor is outside the scope of employment,[58] the following conditions must be present to trigger vicarious liability:

 • *An employer is subject to vicarious liability to a victimized employee for an actionable hostile environment created by a supervisor with immediate (or successively higher) authority over the employee.*

> • *When no tangible employment action is taken, a defending employer may raise an affirmative defense to liability [that] . . . comprises two necessary elements: (a) that the employer exercised reasonable care to prevent and correct promptly any sexually harassing behavior, and (b) that the plaintiff employee unreasonably failed to take advantage of any preventive or corrective opportunities provided by the employer to avoid harm otherwise.*[59]

The employer must prove its affirmative defenses by a preponderance of the evidence. In essence, an employer can escape liability for the acts or conduct of its employees by showing that it had an enforceable antisexual harassment policy, it used reasonable measures to disseminate the policy to its employees, and the employee did not use reasonable care or follow the policy to trigger the safeguards in place to prevent or correct the harassment. Failure to establish these factors will result in liability for the institution.

The case of *Kraft v Yeshiva University*[60] illustrates the application of the hostile work environment theory and the doctrine of vicarious liability. Kraft, a doctoral student, had a 2-year consensual relationship with the program director, Gibelman. During this time, he had a successful academic program of study and successfully defended his dissertation proposal. After Kraft terminated his relationship with Gibelman, she demanded he withdraw his dissertation proposal. His attempts to get approval for new topics were unsuccessful. Gibelman participated in the evaluation of his new proposal topic and in the meeting in which his request for an extension was denied. Kraft was ultimately dismissed from the program. At all times, Dean Gelman was aware of the relationship, the negative attitude Gibelman adopted after the breakup, and of her postrelationship retaliations against Kraft.

Kraft sued Yeshiva University under the doctrine of vicarious liability for the actions of Gibelman and Gelman. The university was liable under the doctrine of vicarious liability because Dean Gelman was aware of the retaliatory incidents and adopted an attitude of "deliberate indifference." He had the authority to, but failed to, intervene and implement measures to protect the student from a hostile educational environment. The university could not establish any actions taken to correct the misbehavior and improper conduct of its faculty member.

Similarly, the case of *Gyda v Temple University*[61] illustrates how a student successfully established sexual harassment against a faculty member and a retaliation charge against the university. It also supports the premise that faculty should refrain from sexual relations with students. Gyda was admitted in 1992 to the doctoral program in biochemistry. He was involved in litigation against another university for alleged discrimination based on his dismissal from the medical program. As part of the biochemistry curricula, Gyda was required to conduct laboratory research, for which he received a stipend. After two years of working with his faculty advisor, he requested and was granted another advisor, Dr. Hatton. Shortly thereafter, Dr. Hatton and Gyda engaged in a brief sexual relationship. He terminated the relationship and requested a purely professional relationship. Dr. Hatton testified that she was relieved when Gyda ended the relationship, because she was beginning to feel uncomfortable. However, she also acknowledged that she felt ambivalent and conflicted. No further sexual comments or activities occurred between them.

116

Nevertheless, the working relationship between Gyda and Dr. Hatton was filled with distress. Gyda indicated that he was criticized and subjected to harsh and unwarranted criticism as a result of his rejection of Dr. Hatton. Conversely, Dr. Hatton testified that Gyda would not fulfill his laboratory responsibilities and failed to maintain the required regular hours, either by not coming in or leaving early without permission. He disrupted other students in the laboratory through his use of profanity, sexual innuendo, sexually explicit language, and display of sexually explicit materials in his work area.[62] One student actually brought assault charges again Gyda, which resulted in a guilty finding by the university disciplinary committee. Angered by the charges and outcome, Gyda left the laboratory and did not return.

Shortly thereafter, Gyda reported his affair with Dr. Hatton to Dr. Suhadolnik, the graduate program director, and Dr. Marks, assistant dean for graduate studies. A faculty meeting scheduled for June 16 to address the issue was adjourned when Gyda was denied permission to audiotape the meeting. On July 1, Dr. Suhadolnik had a private meeting with Gyda and presented him with a memorandum that contained the information that was to be discussed in the faculty meeting. Gyda objected to the memorandum because it did not express his views or concerns, refused to communicate further with university officials, did not return to work in the laboratory, and officially withdrew from the university on August 2. On September 8, he filed formal charges of sexual harassment and retaliation through the university's Office of Affirmation Action (OAA) against Dr. Hatton, alleging that he did not report the matter earlier because he feared retaliation. Dr. Hatton was given a verbal and written reprimand for violation of university policy, but the OAA did not find that Gyda was the victim of a hostile work environment.

Gyda brought actions against the university, Dr. Hatton, and several administrators, alleging sexual harassment and retaliation under Title VII and Title IX. The university argued for summary judgment or dismissal without a trial, based on its assertion that because the relationship was consensual and no further advances or requests occurred after the breakup, Gyda did not establish unwelcome sexual harassment, because his relationship with Dr. Hatton was a consensual relationship. Rejecting this argument, the Court noted that Dr. Hatton violated the university's sexual harassment policy and acknowledged her ambivalent and conflicted feelings after the breakup. Thus, Gyda had established enough evidence to allow the case to proceed to trial. Similarly, the Court rejected the university's motion for summary judgment on the retaliation charge.

Gyda established that he engaged in protected activity/conduct when he reported the sexual harassment, that the university and/or its employees took adverse employment and educational actions against him after he reported the harassment, and there was a causal link between the negative work environment, his constructive discharge (forcing him to quit), and his reporting the harassment. To establish the causal link, Gyda showed that the protected activity and employment or educational action were related.

This case exemplifies the reason many institutions have adopted policies strongly discouraging faculty-student intimate relationships. Faculty and students are not on the same bargaining level, regardless of the students age, maturity level, and/or experience. Faculty are in positions of authority over students and therefore any nonacademic relationships with students is problematic. Because of the power differential, students can allege claims of sexual harassment, based on the assertion that they did not feel free to reject the relationship. In addition, violation of established policies and procedures can create a strong inference of wrongdoing by the faculty.

Policies on Sexual Harassment

The Kraft and Gyda cases illustrate the inherent conflicts that can emerge from faculty-student relationships and provide an understanding of why many institutions of higher education have instituted policies against such relationships. Policies range from strongly discouraging to an outright prohibition of such relationships. For example, faculty and staff at the University of Florida are strongly discouraged from engaging in amorous or sexual relationship with students because "such relationships, even when consensual, may be exploitative, and they imperil the integrity of the work or educational environment. They also may lead to charges of sexual harassment."[63] The university puts the burden on the faculty to resolve the conflict by removing themselves from the situation, notifying and seeking the advice of supervisors, and implementing steps to ensure an unbiased evaluation of the student or subordinate.[64]

Similarly, the sexual harassment policy at Old Dominion University strongly discourages romantic or sexual relationships between faculty and students because of the inherent power differences and the difficulty faculty will encounter in combating charges of sexual harassment stemming from the relationship. The policy indicates that charges of sexual harassment against a faculty or supervisor involved in a relationship with a student or subordinate "is presumed . . . because the power differential . . . may restrict the student or employer's freedom to choose to enter into the relationship. . . . The faculty member must be prepared to prove, by a preponderance of the evidence, that the individual claiming sexual harassment entered into the relationship freely and voluntarily."[65] This can prove to be difficult if the employee or student is the person bringing the charges.

Therefore, some educational institutions, like the University of Chapel Hill, North Carolina, outright prohibit amorous or sexual relationships between faculty and students.[66] The basis of the prohibition is twofold:

1. Voluntary consent by the student is impeded due to the power differential
2. The potential negative effect that such relationships have on students and the academic community

Others may perceive favoritism or that special benefits may result from amorous or sexual relationships with faculty or superiors.[67] Officials in higher educational institutions are correct in discouraging or prohibiting faculty-student relationships to avoid conflicts of interest, breaching the public trust, and unnecessary expensive litigation.

PROFESSIONAL DIMENSION

Academic environments are based on collegiality and respect between and among administrators, faculty, staff, and students. Students should not have to avoid certain professors because of their negative treatments or comments. Professors should treat students with respect and dignity in the academic environment. The university must foster and promote an environment of mutual respect of the faculty-student relationship. Written policies, procedures, and language in catalogs, handbooks, and syllabi form the basis of contractual relationships with students and is the starting point in litigation to determine if the academic unit breached its contract with the student.

ETHICAL DIMENSION

Educators should not diminish the trust and admiration that society affords them by engaging in unethical behaviors. The exploitation of students for personal gain, including sexual relationship, while not illegal, is unethical. This type of behavior should and cannot be tolerated in academic environments whose goal is to foster the intellectual, professional, and personal growth of its students. Intimate relationships between faculty and students should be avoided due to the known power differential and inherent conflicts. Likewise, administrators and faculty should have trust in and respect for the other to foster an environment conducive to teaching and scholarly production.

Implications for Educators

- The university must work closely with faculty to establish an environment conducive for students to learn and faculty to teach. A university can assign its faculty to teach the courses it needs them to teach.
- A university has no duty to accommodate faculty's desire to teach specific classes. It can offer whatever courses it wants to offer.
- Faculty have a responsibility to establish collegial relationships and promote harmony within the academic unit.
- Faculty should avoid potential conflicts of interest and/or seek advice from superiors regarding such situations.
- Faculty should follow established policies and procedures in addressing students' concerns and handling conflicts.
- The relationship between faculty and students is contractual in nature.
- Written language in educational materials can form the basis of a contract.
- FERPA protects students' education records that contain personal identifiable information.

Strategies to Avoid Legal Problems

- Know university policies regarding relationships in the work environment.
- Know university policies on sexual harassment, including its definitions, behaviors that constitute sexual harassment, and its consequences.
- Clearly differentiate between friendship, mentoring, and romantic relationships with students.
- Avoid sexual relationships with students, teaching assistants, and subordinates.
- Never use students' social security numbers to post grades, which include posting by the last six digits.
- Always protect students' education records. Refer requests for students' records to the appropriate university official.
- Avoid discussing a student's performance in locations where the conversation can be overheard by others.
- Give credit to students for their contribution to faculty members' scholarly endeavors.
- Always treat students and colleagues in a courteous and respectful manner.

RESPONSE TO CRITICAL THINKING QUESTIONS

1. How should Constance handle the sexual harassment issue?

Constance has violated the university's sexual harassment policy that prohibits romantic or sexual relationships between faculty and students who are not married to each other. The policy applies to all faculty regardless of their age, sex, or previous relationships with the other person. Members of the university community who violate university policy are subject to disciplinary actions, ranging from reprimand to termination. Constance finds herself in the vulnerable position of her employment status dependent on the decision of the faculty judiciary committee. Her actions were unprofessional and disrespectful of the faculty-student relationship. Regardless of their previous relationship, she was in a position to exercise power over Charlie and evaluate his academic performance. His executive position at the HMO does not negate the degree of Constance's academic control over him. Because the policy does not allow Constance to rebut sexual harassment and establish voluntary consent, Constance is in violation of the policy. Any disciplinary action could have an adverse impact on Constance's academic progression within the university. The issue, as viewed by the other faculty, is that Tom is trying to discredit Constance to elevate his consideration for the chair's position. She has many supporters due to her tenure, academic leadership, and unblemished reputation within the academic community.

However, at present, no one in a position of investigatory authority has asked Constance if she had a relationship with Charlie. The investigator from the Office of Human Resources closed her file after Charlie denied a relationship with Constance, who was never questioned. If questioned, Constance had an obligation to tell the truth. An ethical issue emerges as to Constance's obligation to come forward and tell the truth or remain silent and hope the issue will disappear. As always, ethical issues are subject to debate based on one's perspective of right and wrong, values, and beliefs.

2. What actions, if any, can or should be taken against Tom? Against Charlie?

Tom's actions are noncollegial. He has shown tremendous disrespect to Constance and to the faculty by failing to follow the chair's directive and by subjecting the faculty to unwarranted personnel issues. As junior faculty, Tom has no understanding of collegiality and mutual respect for the academic community. He is disruptive and disrespectful. His handling of the situation warrants some type of disciplinary actions and education on collegiality as the basis of relationships within the academic community. Courts have upheld the factor of collegiality as a basis for adverse employment actions, noting as valid consideration the impact one's continued employment will have on the overall functioning and atmosphere of the academic unit.

The relationship between a student and university is contractual in nature. The university agrees to provide the student with an education and a degree, where appropriate, if the student successfully completes the program of study and adheres to university rules and regulations. Charlie has violated the terms of his contract by breaching the student honor code. He provided false information to a university official investigating an allegation of sexual harassment. However, Charlie neither brought the complaint nor wished to be a party to any investigation. He is a professional adult involved in a consensual relationship.

3. **Does Sam have a cause of action against Constance for a FERPA violation?**

Under FERPA, Sam's test performance and grades are considered educational records, which cannot be released without his consent. However, Sam cannot pursue a private cause of action against Constance or the university based on an alleged FERPA violation, because this was not authorized by Congress in enacting FERPA. He can initiate a complaint within the university, according to policy and externally to the Family Policy Compliance Office. Because there is no pattern of violation, FPCO will take corrective action, usually in the form of advice and suggestions to ensure compliance with FERPA. The conduct does not arise to the level of disciplinary action by the Department of Education.

ANNOTATED BIBLIOGRAPHY

McGill v Regents of the University of California, 52 Cal Rptr2d 466 (1996).

McGill was an untenured professor in the Mathematics Department. He had deficits in teaching, scholarly work, and interactions with graduate students. His department chair found that McGill was deficit in collegiality. All but two of the 25 faculty members in his department voted to deny him tenure. He brought a lawsuit alleging breach of contract because he was evaluated on the unwritten criterion of collegiality. Held for the university: Collegiality is an appropriate factor in consideration for tenure.

Stein v Kent State University, 994 FSupp898 (ND Ohio1998).

Stein filed a number of complaints against her superiors and the university, alleging gender discrimination, plagiarism, and retaliation. The charges were not substantiated based on the evidence. She was advised to work on her collegiality. Stein's reappointment was not renewed. Her director indicated that Stein exhibited a continual pattern of negative behavior that undermined the functioning of the department. Stein sued, alleging that the use of collegiality was a pretext for gender discrimination. Held for the university: When not a subterfuge for discrimination, collegiality is a valid factor in tenure consideration decisions.

Alcorn v Vaksman, 877 SW2d 390 (Tex App—Houston [1st Dist] 1994).

A graduate student was dismissed from the doctoral program. Vaksman was outspoken and critical of university policies and political issues, expressing his views in newspaper articles, on talk shows, and at seminars and lectures. He had completed all but the dissertation (ABD) requirements. He was appointed a new faculty advisor after his original advisors resigned from the university. The Graduate Committee met to consider Vaksman's request to change his focus and voted to dismiss him from the program, citing concerns regarding his teaching abilities and lack of academic progress. Vaksman's faculty advisor was not consulted. He sued, alleging violations of his First Amendment right to free speech and violation of his Fourteenth Amendment right to due process. Held for the student: The evidence supports that the committee had intentionally harmed Vaksman because of personal disagreements, his personality, and his speech. His dismissal was outrageous and extreme and went well beyond the limits for learned professionals.

Romer v Board of Trustees of Hobart & William Smith Colleges, 842 FSupp 703 (WDNY 1994).

Romer had an extremely volatile relationship with another professor in the department. The university had evidence that the relationship had a negative impact on students. The dean expressed concern that the two faculty members could not keep their private differences contained and that the public nature of their volatile relationship had a negative impact on the academic community. Romer's tenure evaluation also showed deficiencies in other areas. He was denied tenure and sued, alleging the university had evaluated him on collegiality, a criterion not stated in the faculty handbook. Held for the university: The Court noted that language in the handbook that faculty and student relationships are an important part of teaching and that teaching requires mutual respect and consideration supported an evaluation of collegiality.

Nelson v Temple University, 920 FSupp 633 (ED Pa 1996).

A female employee-student at the Student Activities Office brought sexual harassment charges against her administrator. An investigation by the university substantiated the harassment and the administrator was suspended. He later retaliated against the student-employee by defaming her, attempting to organize students to impeach her, treating her organization differently, and filing a lawsuit against her. She filed and received right to sue letters from the state Human Relations Commission and the EEOC. She then filed sexual harassment and retaliation against the administrator in his individual capacity and against the university. Held for the administrator on only the Title IX individual capacity claim: There is no cause of action against an individual in his personal capacity under Title IX.

U.S. v Miami University, 294 F3d 797 (6th Cir 2002).

A student newspaper made a request under the state's Public Record Act for student disciplinary records to track crime trends on campus. The university complied with the request, but redacted information related to identity; sex; age; and date, time, and location of the incidents. The Ohio Supreme Court ruled that the editors were entitled to their requests for the full record, but imposed certain redactions, which included the above. The United States Supreme Court denied certiorari. Another newspaper requested the full records, including names, social security numbers, and student ID numbers, contending that the state's Supreme Court had ruled that disciplinary records were not education records, protected by FERPA. The university notified the Department of Education (DOE) that based on the Court's ruling and the request for records, it cannot comply with FERPA. The DOE responded that the state's ruling was incorrect and that FERPA prohibits the release of personally identifiable information contained in the student disciplinary records. The university informed DOE that it intended to comply with the request for information. DOE filed a lawsuit against the university, seeking an injunction prohibiting the university from releasing student disciplinary records that contained personally identifiable information, except as permitted under FERPA. The *Chronicle* filed a motion to intervene. The Court ruled that "student disciplinary records are education records because they directly relate to a student and are kept by that student's university."

Tarka v Franklin, 891 F2d 102 (5th Cir 1989).

An applicant who was denied admission to the graduate program brought a lawsuit after the school refused to grant him access to his letters of recommendation. The student who had audited several courses had never officially been admitted to the university. Held for the university: A student who audits courses does not have the same standing as officially admitted students. FERPA does not grant rejected applicants the rights to access their letters of recommendations.

NOTES

1 AAUP Statement on Professional Ethics. Available at: http://www.aaup.org/statement/index/htm.
2 W. Morris, *The American Heritage Dictionary of the English Language* (Boston: Houghton Mifflin Co., 1979).
3 R. Wilson, Bickering Decimates a Department: U. of Cincinnati's Economic Professors Fight over Teaching versus Research. *The Chronicle of Higher Education,* 49, no. 8 (Oct. 18, 2002), A12(2).
4 *Mayberry v Dees,* 633 F2d 502, 514 (4th Cir 1981), cert. denied, 459 US 830 (1982).
5 *University of Baltimore v Iz,* 716 A2d 1107 (Md App 1998).
6 *Iz.*
7 *Iz* at 1121.
8 *Iz* at 1122.
9 AAUP Statement on Professional Ethics.
10 *Korf v Ball State University,* 726 F2d 1222 (1984).
11 W. Kaplin, & B. Lee, *A Legal Guide for Student Affairs Professionals* (3rd ed.) (San Francisco: Jossey-Bass Publishers, 1997).
12 W. Kaplin, & B. Lee, *The Law of Higher Education* (San Francisco: Jossey-Bass Publishers, 1995).
13 *Gott v Berea College,* 161 SW 204 (1913).
14 *Dixon v Alabama,* 294 F2d 150 (5th Cir 1961).
15 Kaplin & Lee. *The Law of Higher Education.*
16 *Dixon.*
17 *Bilut v Northwest University,* 645 NE 2d 536, 542 (1994).
18 *Sharick v Southeastern University,* 780 So2d 136, 138 (Fla App 3 Dist 2000).
19 *Flynn v LaSalle University,* US Lexis 14077, (1988).
20 *McConnell v Howard University,* 818 F2d 58 (1987).
21 *McConnell* at 61.
22 *McConnell* at 66.
23 20 USC Section 1232g (2000), as amended.
24 Joint statement, 120 Cong. Rec. 39858, 39862 (1974).
25 Joint statement.
26 20 USC at Section 1232g(a)(4)(A).
27 20 USC at Section 1232(g).
28 20 USC at Section 1232 g (a)(5)(A).
29 *Rathie v Northeastern Wisconsin Technical Institute,* 419 NW 2d 296 (Ct App 1987).
30 *Krebs v Rutgers,* 797 FSupp 1246 (DNJ 1992).
31 *Tarka v. Franklin,* 891 F2d 102 (5th Cir 1989).
32 *Falvo v. Owasso Indep. School District,* 534 US 426 (2002).
33 28 Fed Appx 186 (4th Cir. 2002).
34 20 USC Section 1232G(A)(2).
35 *Osborn v Board of Regents of Univer,* 647 NW 2d 158 (Wis 2002).
36 *Osborn.*
37 *Osborn.*
38 *Osborn* at 173.
39 *Osborn* at 171.
40 *Osborn.*
41 20 USC Section 1232g (b)(6)(A).
42 20 USC at (b)(6)(B).
43 20 USC.
44 20 USC at (b)(6)(C).
45 20 USC at (h)(1).
46 20 USC at (i)(1)(A) & (B).
47 20 USC at (b)(1)(H).
48 *Jain v State,* 617 NW 2d 293 (Iowa 2000).
49 *Jain* at 298.
50 Kaplin & Lee, The Law of Higher Education.
51 USC Section 1232g(b)(2).
52 42 USC Section 2000E-2.
53 20 USC Section 1681 et. seq.
54 20 USC Section 1681 et. seq.
55 *Burlington Industries, Inc. v. Ellerth,* 524 US 742 (1998).
56 *Burlington Industries, Inc.*
57 *Harris v Forklift Sys., Inc.* 510 US 17, 21–23 (1993).

58 *Burlington Industries, Inc. v Ellerth,* 524 US 742 (1998).

59 *Burlington* at 765.

60 *Kraft v Yeshiva University,* 2001 US Dist Lexis 16152 (2001).

61 *Gyda v Temple University,* 2000 US Dist Lexis 7099 (ED Pa 2000).

62 *Gyda.*

63 University of Florida, Policy on Amorous or Sexual Relationships in the Work or Educational Environment. Available at: http://www.aa.ufl.edu/aa/affact/harass/amorous.htm.

64 University of Florida, Policy on Amorous or Sexual Relationships.

65 Old Dominion University, University Policies and Procedures. 6320—Sexual Harassment Policy. Available at: http://www.odu.edu.

66 The University of North Carolina at Chapel Hill, Guidelines for Handling Concerns Related to the Board of Governors' Policy Concerning Improper Relationships between Students and Employees. Available at: http://www.ais.unc.edu/hr/spaman/appendices/app-02F.htm.

67 University of North Carolina, Guidelines for Handling Concerns Related to the Board of Governor's Policy Concerning Improper Relationships between Students and Employees.

68 E. J. Du Fresne, Sexual Harrassment Issues in Health Care (Employment and Labor Practic Group) (Miami, Fla.: Steel Hector & Davis, LLP, 1998).

69 Du Fresne, Sexual Harrassment Issues in Health Care, 9–10.

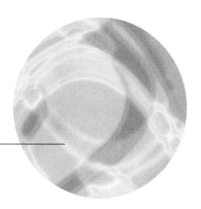

6

The Teaching Role of Faculty

RICHARDEAN BENJAMIN AND MABLE H. SMITH

INTRODUCTION

Teaching in the university setting has changed over the years. Ten years ago, the primary method of instructional delivery in the classroom was face-to-face lecture with occasional use of self-directed groups. Today, more often than not, university instruction occurs outside the classroom, and, in many instances, the instruction has a Web-based or online component. Technological advances in education have made it possible for students who live in remote locations to complete the requirements for a college degree without leaving their home town and in some instances without leaving their homes. With the increase in educational access and the different formats and medium to provide instruction, multiple issues surface not only in terms of the delivery format, but also related to student evaluation and grading. This chapter presents information on issues faculty encounter in fulfilling the teaching aspect of the faculty role.

Benny is a junior-level nursing student enrolled in the baccalaureate nursing program at Deansville University. He is taking a full course load including the first semester medical-surgical nursing course. His clinical group of six students is assigned to the Stepdown unit at the local community hospital. Each student is responsible for the care of two patients. The School of Nursing has employed Stephanie, certified as a clinical specialist in critical care, as an adjunct clinical faculty for three years. She is highly regarded by both students and faculty because of her clinical expertise and her ability to establish an effective student-faculty relationship. Students were aware that Stephanie had to check all medications before they were administered and observe all treatment provided to patients. This day Benny, an excellent student, was caring for a patient receiving a long list of medications and treatments. He was excited about the opportunity to work with this patient because this would be the first time he cared for a patient who required multiple treatments. He would administer intramuscular injections, change a Foley catheter, suction a tracheostomy, and monitor an arterial line. The patient's medications were scheduled for 10 A.M. It was now 10:15 A.M. and Stephanie was occupied with another student whose clinical performance had been marginal and required more direct supervision. The staff nurse instructed Benny to remain on schedule and administer the medication. In his excitement to do well, he administered the medications without Stephanie's knowledge or presence. However, he neglected to take the patient's blood pressure and pulse rate prior to administering the Digoxin. He immediately realized his mistake, decided to take the patient's blood pressure and record it as having been taken before the administration of the medication. The patient's blood pressure was 100/50 (normally 160/82), pulse rate was 50 (normally 84), and temperature was slightly elevated at 100.4F. He recorded the information in the medical records, but did not inform either Stephanie or the staff nurse. Later that morning, the patient experienced a significant drop in his blood pressure that resulted in his condition being downgraded from stable to serious.

CRITICAL THINKING QUESTIONS

1. How should Stephanie handle the situation with Benny?
2. What is the basis for allowing Benny to continue the clinical rotation?
3. What is the basis for failing Benny for the clinical rotation?

GENERAL TEACHING RESPONSIBILITIES OF FACULTY

Teaching a course includes several components from preparation and presentation of course materials to establishing and monitoring student performance. Faculty must be competent in their ability to develop and structure course content, organize delivery/presentation methods, identify evaluation methods, and assess learning outcomes. In addition, they must be knowledgeable of the subject matter and course content. The case of *Miller v Loyola University of New Orleans*[1] illustrates the disasters that can occur when faculty are unprepared to assume their assigned responsibilities. Professor Lepow, a tenured professor of tax law, was assigned to teach a course in professional and ethical issues, which was outside of her expertise. Miller, a student enrolled in the class, filed a complaint alleging numerous deficiencies in her teaching performance, including failing to timely order course materials, changing the time of the class without the prerequisite permission, requiring students' presentations on content that she was required to teach, failing to cover all the course content, and administering a final examination that contained numerous errors. In addition to validating the above complaints, an ad hoc committee also found that Professor Leprow's overall performance and responses to students' questions were below satisfactory and she had difficulty communicating with students. As evident from this case, this type and degree of ill-preparedness of faculty can have detrimental consequences for students, administrators, and the educational institution.

An important faculty role is assessing students' learning. This is accomplished using several evaluation methods, including, but not limited to, examinations, written work, projects, and presentations. Several questions arise related to evaluating student performance:

- How should faculty deal with student challenges to examination items/grades?
- What course of action should be taken when all members of a group do not contribute to the project?
- How should faculty handle incidents of cheating?

All of these issues are likely occurrences for faculty members. Faculty must ensure that students' rights are not violated while at the same time maintaining discipline and fairness in the classroom. This can be a challenging endeavor.

Course Syllabus

Course materials, such as the syllabus, are analyzed in legal cases to determine if the denial of an educational benefit to a student was arbitrary and capricious. The course syllabus, which includes the course description, course objectives, and evaluation measures, identifies what the faculty member will provide and what is expected of the student. It can be viewed as the contract between the faculty member and the student that spells out the terms of the agreement with respect to certain learning outcomes.

The Court in *Miller v Loyola University*[2] related the legal significance of the course description.

> - *Course descriptions are given to inform the student of what is generally covered in the course; they are not contractual provisions that bind the school to teach exactly what is written in the description.*
> - *There are many reasons why a particular course might not live up to its description. For instance, perhaps the students need extra instruction on a particular subject, which precludes every topic from being covered in a given semester. Current events may dictate that the course structure be changed to address more pertinent topics. Perhaps a teacher does not manage the course time optimally, and some subjects are not taught.*[3]

The course description is a cursory overview of the subject matter that will be taught during class sessions and does not provide a legal theory upon which to initiate a lawsuit.

Course Objectives

Behavioral or learning objectives provide a method for evaluating student performance and achievement. They provide a means for faculty to identify "behaviors that signify development within an educational program or relevancy to the needs of a particular group of learners."[4] Developing measurable learning objectives establishes the learning expectation between the student and the instructor. Learning objectives may be predetermined as in the case of a structured course or may be defined by the student in a situation when the student is enrolled in a course that involves independent work or one that is unstructured. Poorly stated learning objectives can obscure the measurement of student achievement, which directly impacts the student's performance and grade given on a particular assignment. Students must know the expected level of performance to successfully master the criteria.

The taxonomy of educational objectives is a system for ordering behaviors within the context of development.[5] It provides an excellent framework when developing behavioral objectives. Three domains are considered when developing behavioral objectives:

- Cognitive
- Psychomotor
- Affective

These three domains address the intellectual, emotion or value component, and performance aspects of students' learning. There are appropriate verbs for each level of the three taxonomies, ranging from simple to complex. Table 6.1 lists verbs that are used to create objectives. For example, in the *cognitive domain,* an objective that seeks to capture a simple concept in a course might require the student to "identify" or name the term; whereas, a more complex cognitive function would require the student to "evaluate" or "synthesize" the course content.[6] Beginning nursing students function at the lower cognitive level because they are learning and acquiring the basic foundation and general principles of nursing practice. A behavioral objective appropriate to this level, "The student will describe the signs and symptoms of diabetes," is descriptive of a lower level objective. Conversely, as students progress through the nursing curriculum, they are expected to build on previously learned knowledge and display higher levels of cognitive functioning. The behavioral objective "Develop a teaching plan for a patient with diabetes" requires higher level cognitive functioning because students must synthesize a variety of knowledge, such as signs and symptoms, complications, medications, diet, and exercise to develop the teaching plan.

Table 6.1 **Level of Cognitive Objectives and Action Verbs[47]**

KNOWLEDGE	COMPREHENSION	APPLICATION	ANALYSIS	SYNTHESIS	EVALUATE
Recall	Describe	Use	Examine	Formulate	Predict
Define	Discuss	Apply	Analyze	Arrange	Judge
List	Recognize	Demonstrate	Compare	Construct	Appraise
Name	Explain	Choose	Differentiate	Plan	Estimate
Relate	Identify	Illustrate	Discriminate	Organize	Defend

The *psychomotor domain* relates to the actual performance of selected skills. Clinical and laboratory experiences are used to evaluate the mastery of psychomotor skills. Students are expected to progress from guided learning to performance of skills with little to no guidance and cues. Faculty evaluate clinical growth as students progress through the nursing program.

The "3-R format" uses the classic film *Mrs. Reynolds Needs a Nurse* to evaluate student learning in the *affective domain* and has exercises that also incorporate the cognitive and psychomotor domains.[7] The film helps students learn the importance of caring and requires students to analyze the scenario in terms of the 3-Rs (their reaction to the scenario, their responsibilities to the patient, and the relevance and application to course content). *Mrs. Reynolds Needs a Nurse* is a film about an elderly white woman who was admitted to a busy neurological unit and placed in a bed in a hallway because all the rooms were full. As the story unfolds, Mrs. Reynolds gets labeled as a difficult patient by the nursing staff and nurses do not want to provide care for her. A nursing student, frustrated by the way the nurses are treating Mrs. Reynolds, initiates actions to address the many issues that emerge from this scenario. After viewing the film, students must respond to a series of questions derived from either visual or textual scenes. This evaluative format is designed for students to respond to the affective domain first, asking for their reactions. Second, they are asked the relevance in terms of a designated framework—course material. The third question requires students to respond in terms of their responsibility, which provides information about the psychomotor domain of learning.[8] Behavior objectives in each of the domains provide students with expected levels of performance and allow faculty to conduct a comprehensive evaluation of student performance to identify strengths and weaknesses.

The case of *Tobias v University of Texas*[9] illustrates the importance of identifying the student's expected level of performance. Tobias was required to complete a nursing process paper to fulfill a component of a clinical course. The paper required him to identify a patient problem, set goals, and plan interventions to resolve the patient's problems. In spite of the extra assistance provided to Tobias explaining and outlining the requirements, he did not analyze or synthesize the data to fulfill the requirements. Instead, he gave the professor "a stack of copied notes, charts, and medical records." After an independent evaluation by another instructor, Tobias was assigned a failing grade. He reenrolled but again failed the course under a different instructor due to his inability to synthesize patient information and develop "an articulable plan for himself or others to use."[10] Tobias was unable to function at the higher behavioral level of analysis and synthesis, instead remaining at the lower levels of identify and collect. The Court upheld his dismissal.

Assignments

The number and type of assignments must be considered based on factors such as the number of credit hours assigned to the course, the level of student, and the delivery format of the course. Criteria for successful completion of each assignment should be clearly outlined. Assignments are made to promote learning, provide measures of students' mastery of course material, and to foster critical thinking, decision making, and interdependent interactions. Individual and group assignments are used to achieve these outcomes. Some faculty are hesitant to assign group projects due to the inherent problems associated with measuring each student's level of participation and the related complaints from students that some group members did not participate or the quality of their participation was substandard. When students are assigned to work in groups, faculty should establish a system for evaluating the performance of each group member. This can range from a student self-report of his or her contribution to an evaluation by each group member of the other students' contributions. In online courses or those with a Web-based component, the use of discussion forums allows instructors to readily identify each student's contribution to the overall project.

The following story is an example of how a discussion forum can be used to determine the level of students' participation in group assignments. Students enrolled in the nursing leadership course were assigned to groups to complete a change project assignment and develop a group presentation that counted for 40% of each student's grade. A scenario, posted in the discussion forum, required students to identify the problem, develop strategies to correct the problem, and formulate an evaluation plan to measure outcomes. Students were instructed to use the online discussion forum to complete the assignment and to plan their group presentation. In the group, Sue's contributions consisted of a series of entries complimenting other students on their ideas or simply agreeing with the information provided by other students. After receiving 3 out of 10 possible points for participation, Sue challenged the grade, asserting that she had e-mailed her materials to the other students. Upholding the grade, the grade appeals committee noted that Sue did not adhere to the stated criteria for posting her comments, she was aware that the forum was the basis for the instructor to determine each student's level of participation, and she did not provide evidence from other students to support her degree of participation.

As illustrated in this scenario and summarized later, several principles provide the foundation for success in group assignments.

- Group projects, a popular approach to student learning, allow students to learn important lessons about shared responsibility, cooperation, and group dynamics, in addition to the content for a course.
- An inherent principle and expectation in all group projects is that each group member will equally participate to complete the project. An important aspect to emphasize with students is that group products are more than a sum of individual parts.
- Students who do not fulfill their group responsibility have not fulfilled the requirements to successfully pass the course and will not be unjustly enriched with a passing grade.
- The faculty member should investigate the participation of each group member.
- Each group member should complete a group participation form, which outlines his or her contribution to the group project.
- Students should sign the honor pledge with each assignment; therefore, if the student misrepresents or falsifies the degree of his or her participation, the faculty member has recourse to address the issue. In addition, failure to contribute to group projects and receiving full credit is a form of plagiarism, which is an honor code violation.

Whether the assignment is independent or group based, faculty should identify criteria for successful completion of assignments. Students are then evaluated and graded on the fulfillment of the established criteria.

Many valuable learning assignments may include repetitive content, designed to promote a different application of the material. For example, learning a theory in a theory course is different from using that theory as a theoretical framework for a project in a research course. Both courses require the student to learn the theory, but the application and overall outcome is different. The faculty member, as the content expert, needs to be clear about what students are expected to learn while at the same time documenting their level of mastery of this content. Successful completion of course assignments is the basis for the final course grade.

Modification of Assignments

The modification of an assignment from that on the initial course syllabus should not have a negative consequence, if students are properly notified and given the opportunity to complete the assignment. Faculty can revise assignments when confronted with factors such as curricula changes or unexpected changes in enrollment to create more effective learning experiences. Faculty have flexibility to alter the requirements of a course if it is done in a fair and unbiased manner, considering the student's status in his or her program of study. As presented in the *Bruner v Petersen*[11] case, "education must be flexible to accommodate changing circumstances."[12] Bruner, a student enrolled in an associate degree nursing program, had difficulty with the curriculum, having received 2 "Ds" and an "F" in previous nursing courses. After he received a grade of "no pass" in another nursing course, the chair required him to take a course outside the nursing curriculum, as a condition of reenrollment, to help him overcome his identified weakness. The faculty noted a lack of critical thinking skills, which hindered his ability to apply theoretical or didactic materials to clinical situations. They felt that Bruner would continue to have difficulty in the nursing curriculum and the identified course, Critical/Creative Thinking, would be beneficial in helping him in future nursing courses. Rejecting Bruner's breach of contract claim, the Court noted that the language in the student handbook specifically reserved the right of the chairperson and faculty to review and place conditions on reenrollment. In addition, the Court articulated the well-known judicial deference perspective, "The faculty is in the best position to determine how to help the student to succeed and must have the discretion necessary to maintain the integrity of the curriculum and the degree."[13]

Assignment of Grades

Grading is an area that can be the source of much unrest among students. Evaluating student performance is a very serious activity because their progression and graduation are dependent on a certain level of performance. Faculty must be objective in evaluating student performance and in assigning grades. The evaluation process is formulated during the development of the course. Clearly stated behavioral objectives, course requirements, and evaluation criteria facilitate this process. Evaluation components may include examinations, quizzes, written papers, and oral presentations. The goal of faculty is fair and accurate evaluations.

Students challenging grades have primarily been unsuccessful, unless the student can demonstrate some type of arbitrary and capricious behavior by the instructor. Courts defer to faculty to determine what to teach, how to teach, and how to evaluate students' performance. The practice of judicial deference, as discussed in Chapter 1, is based on the following principles:

- Courts are ill-equipped to evaluate academic performance and must guard against intruding into academic decision making.[14]
- Faculty have a wide range of discretion in decisions related to the academic performance of their students.[15]
- The same degree of deference is given to faculty judgment regarding students' performance in clinical courses as given to the theoretical components.
- A judicial decision will be upheld unless faculty acted arbitrarily, capriciously, or in bad faith in decisions concerning the progression and graduation of its students.[16]

TEACHING IN NONTRADITIONAL ENVIRONMENTS

Distance and online education programs have become part of mainstream education. Distance learning is defined as "any educational forum in which students and faculty are not in the same classroom at the same time."[17] Thus, distance and location are no longer access barriers to higher education. Colleges and universities have responded to requests from educational administrators, students, and business leaders to provide nontraditional access to higher education. Distance learners are individuals who, for a variety of reasons (e.g., costs, accessibility, scheduling), cannot or choose not to attend classes in traditional classrooms. Nontraditional learning environments create new issues.

The goal of distance education is to provide students in remote locations access to quality, affordable education through the use of technologies. Models range from settings where the professor simultaneously delivers the course content in a traditional classroom to students at distant or remote sites using a variety of technological means to completely Web-based and online instruction, where the computer is the communication piece between the student and professor. Successful distance learning programs combine effective teaching and learning strategies, computers, and audio-video technologies. Nontraditional education is a union between new ways of teaching and new ways of learning. The outcome is that students obtain higher education or specialized training from experts to attain undergraduate or advanced degrees or for continuing education. Courses offered using nontraditional methods must be "cognitively, pedagogically, and informationally aligned, reflecting in content and execution larger socioeconomic issues and using instructional technology to do more than simply access or transfer information."[18] Institutions, faculty, and students must continually adapt to changing technologies to make distance education a highly effective educational tool.

In nursing, many courses are offered via satellite through distance education or online as Web-based course. Distance education programs make it possible for registered nurses to complete a baccalaureate degree in nursing through a nontraditional education format.

Teaching Strategies

Faculty members have developed teaching strategies and learned technical competencies to effectively provide quality education to distance students. Faculty teaching nontraditional courses must be intrinsically motivated to develop learning experiences that promote critical thinking, decision making, professionalism, leadership skills, and group management skills.[19] They must use a variety of teaching-learning strategies, such as discussion forums, video streaming (the incorporation of video materials or verbal conversation into the slide or other graphic presentations), chat rooms, and PowerPoint presentations to accommodate the learning styles of diverse groups of students. Distance education can be an empowering experience for students, because it promotes "greater control over the acquisition of knowledge and skills" and greater direct involvement in the learning process.[20] Students who succeed in nontraditional learning environments are usually self-directed, accountable, focused, and intrinsically motivated.

Student Needs

Students value access to and interaction with professors. Important to students in all educational environments, especially in nontraditional programs, are the:[21]

- Instructor's recognition and response to their questions
- Instructor's professional behavior
- Instructor's encouragement of class participation
- Clarity with which class assignments are communicated
- Accessibility of the instructor outside of class
- Use of instructional techniques that facilitate an understanding of course material
- Timeliness with which written assignments are graded and returned

With today's technology, faculty-student interactions can occur via e-mail, telephone conferences, chat rooms, and instant messenger. Students have a tendency to expect an instant response to their e-mails and telephone calls. Faculty should clearly state when and how often they will check and respond to student e-mails and telephone calls. Every attempt should be made to address student concerns within 48 to 72 hours. Faculty should maintain regular office hours and be accessible to students at the designated times.

Behavioral Issues

Issues related to appropriate behavior, veracity, and honesty emerge with students in all educational environments. An educational institution and its respective units that have nontraditional learning environments should implement a policy addressing the expected standards for student conduct. Students enrolled in the university, whether on-campus, at remote sites, or online, are subject to all policies of the educational institution, including the honor code. For example, cheating in any course regardless of whether it is online or traditional should be promptly reported and addressed according to university policy. Some institutions have specific policies that outline acceptable and nonacceptable behaviors for all students. To "preserve academic integrity" and ensure that students have an environment conducive to effective learning, Old Dominion University identified examples of classroom behaviors that are considered disruptive and may be the basis for disciplinary action.[22] These include:

- Conversing during lecture
- Passing notes

- Eating
- Answering cell phones or pagers
- Arriving late
- Leaving early

Likewise, students must adhere to all university regulations and policies related to the honor code and are held accountable for their behavior. The presence of the site directors (individuals employed by the university to manage the distance sites) or proctors to disseminate exams and monitor the testing area are extremely useful in minimizing incidents of academic dishonesty. Faculty should include the honor code or pledge on the syllabus and require students to submit a signed copy with each assignment. Any form of academic dishonesty, including but not limited to cheating, buying term papers, and plagiarism, can be handled by the professor or referred to the honor council for investigation and disposition.

Professors should include expectations regarding student behavior on their syllabi and reemphasize the expected standard of conduct during the initial class. Students who impede the educational process by creating a disruptive educational environment are in violation of the honor code or student code of conduct. Students also have a responsibility to notify professors if other students are interfering with their ability to learn. A zero-tolerance policy for misbehavior and breaches of veracity can facilitate an educational environment conducive to learning. As students progress to the upper-level major courses, they are expected to conduct themselves in a professional manner in all academic related endeavors. Engaging in behavior that negatively impacts the learning environment is not professional behavior. Although prevention is better than reaction, the latter is better than no action.

Attendance Policies

In many nontraditional learning environments, the professor is unable to physically see the student during class. Therefore, faculty should carefully consider the formulation of their attendance policies. They should not mandate attendance policies that will not be enforced, nor do they forfeit the ability to enforce policies simply because the students are not directly visible. If attendance is mandatory, then the professor should have some mechanism to gauge students' attendance. Depending on student enrollment at distant sites, the professor may be unable to verbally call roll. However, students at distant or remote sites should use a sign-in and sign-out sheet that is sent to the instructor, who can then verify students' attendance during the entire class period. Another strategy is to randomly call students to answer questions. A record of attendance or participation is automatically created when students log into the computer; therefore, it is easier to identify attendance and participation in online courses or courses using computer-based assignments. A professor who does not have a consistent method to verify attendance or who does not exert much effort to determine class attendance should not have a grading policy based on attendance and/or participation.

RESPONSIBILITIES OF CLINICAL FACULTY

Generic nursing education programs provide the foundation for students to acquire the complex domain of applied knowledge and skills of decision making, clinical problem solving, critical thinking, and effective clinical reasoning.[23] The evaluation of clinical performance is an essential component in nursing education. Identifying the critical components and how one determines what constitutes acceptable practice versus unacceptable practice is the ultimate goal of the evaluation process. Determining clinical competency is not an issue unique to nursing; other practice disciplines such as teacher education and medicine share similar concerns. Clinical competence is described as the potential to perform, whereas "performance" represents the demonstrated ability to do something.[24] Another issue related to clinical competency is the appropriate time to evaluate student performance. Faculty must consider the level of the student and the length of time in the clinical practicum. The goals of clinical faculty in nursing include assisting students to acquire technical skills, develop professional responsibility and accountability, and progress from being dependent and narrowly focused to being interdependent and professionally collaborative.

Faculty Preparation

Clinical faculty must have adequate preparation to facilitate student learning and effectively assess their clinical competency.

Clinical teaching in nursing is complex for novice or junior faculty to learn.[25] Most tend to teach as they were taught. For example, they tend to be more focused on ensuring that patient-required treatments are implemented, medications are administered, and documentation is completed and less focused on student-related issues, concerns, and problems. They may miss "teachable moments" that capture the essence of the experience and provide an excellent teaching-learning opportunity for the student. Conversely, experts or experienced faculty with at least five years of supervising students in clinical settings have a broader view in that they tend to consider both the patient's and the student's learning. As novice clinical faculty become more experienced and develop expertise, they rely more on intuition and insight as a means of comprehending their clinical teaching practices and experiences with students.[26] These faculty recognize the needs of the patients and can skillfully match them with students to facilitate the best learning experiences. It is important that junior clinical faculty be provided with sound theoretical and structured support for making student-patient assignments, handling student issues, and developing positive relationships with clinical staff, rather than left to trial and error as the primary means of learning to teach students in the clinical area.

Because of the serious nature of the practice of nursing, safeguards in terms of who is allowed to teach students and methods used to assess clinical competence of students need to be in place to protect society. A tremendous responsibility falls on faculty members charged with teaching nursing students. As illustrated in *Morris v Francisco,*[27] if a student performs in an unsafe and careless manner, serious consequences such as patient injury, disability, or death may result. The patient, injured while under the care of a medical student, sued the faculty member who was responsible for supervising the care provided by the student. Upon learning that the clinical faculty member had allowed the student to make independent clinical decisions, the Court ruled in favor of the patient. Clinical faculty members can be held liable if they neglect to adequately supervise students. Teaching in clinical arenas is a serious endeavor.

Location

The location of clinical experiences should be planned based on the student's placement in the curriculum, clinical objectives, and desired outcome. More often than not, clinical experiences are being affected due to changes in the way health care is provided. Shortened hospital stays, shifts in focus from inpatient to outpatient or community-based care, and increased legal restrictions placed on educational programs in terms of student access to clients all have an affect on the clinical experience. Students may be assigned a patient the day before clinicals, complete all paperwork and readings in preparation for the clinical experience, only to find out on the day of the clinical experience that the patient has been discharged. Also, due to liability concerns, some health care institutions prevent students from performing certain actions, such as administering heparin or insulin, discontinuing wound drains, and taking telephone orders.

Clinical experiences outside the acute care facility create additional concerns. For example, sending students into a community for clinical experiences raises safety concerns from students and their families. Many urban neighborhoods are fraught with potential hazards and yet the residents of these communities are most in need of health care services.[28] What are the liabilities to the faculty and the university when these types of clinical experiences are course requirements? In cases where students sustain injuries while satisfying clinical requirements or during practice sessions in laboratory settings, courts will examine the foreseeable risks to determine the educators' level of responsibility. The courts have ruled that colleges have a special duty to students enrolled or involved in school activities that is greater than the duty it has to visitors to campus. Educational institutions have a duty to fully anticipate injuries that are foreseeable and instruct students on how to maintain safety.[29] Faculty must be diligent in evaluating students' learning situations to identify potential for their exposure to various dangers.

Student Preparation

Prior to the first clinical assignments, students must understand the clinical objectives, evaluation methods, clinical faculty policies and rules on patient care and treatment, and the rules and practices of the clinical organization. The course syllabus should clearly identify course requirements and the grading process. A clinical evaluation tool should identify the behavioral objectives that students are expected to master to successfully pass the clinical rotation. It is highly recommended that faculty establish what constitutes safe and unsafe clinical behaviors. Students are considered safe practitioners if they:[30]

- Demonstrate growth in clinical practice through application of knowledge and skills from previous and concurrent courses
- Demonstrate growth in clinical practice as they progress through courses and meet clinical expectations outlined in the clinical evaluation tool
- Are prepared for clinical practice in order to provide safe, competent care

Conversely, a student is considered unsafe when he or she causes, inflicts, or places patients in danger of physical harm or "creates an environment of anxiety or distress which puts the client or family at risk for emotional or psychological harm."[31]

Students should be required to attend a mandatory orientation at the clinical facility that covers topics such as emergency procedures, documentation, treatments and other practices that students cannot perform, staff-student relationship, and the philosophy of the institution. Issues such as when staff can supervise students, who reviews student's documentation, and the type and level of students' communication with staff and the medical team should be clearly addressed.

Student Evaluations

The student is entitled to know whether or not he or she is meeting the requirements of the clinical course; therefore, the course should incorporate formative and summative evaluation components. Formative evaluation, as an ongoing process, is done in such a way that students have the opportunity to make adjustments in their performance without detrimental consequences. If effective, the final grade, or summative evaluation, will not be a surprise for the student. Thus, the importance of clearly stated outcome criteria for which the student is evaluated is essential. Typically, a student is evaluated on an array of activities that are designed to capture a wide range of skills that are in the affective, psychomotor, and cognitive domains. These evaluations are based on direct observations, feedback from staff and/or preceptors, patient and family comments, written clinical coursework, and the student's ability to conceptualize the entire picture.

Although there are numerous ways to document students' performance in clinical, anecdotal notes are widely used and strongly recommended to document students' progress or lack thereof. Anecdotal notes contain information on students' clinical assignment, preparation, procedures performed, treatment administered, and strengths and weaknesses. These notes must be factual, objective, and nonjudgmental. They identify specific examples that reflect when the student is or is not meeting the course requirements. These examples are the basis for feedback to students to effect changes in their performance. Documentation attests to the diligence faculty exerted in helping students obtain positive learning experiences and allows others to review and evaluate the documentation to formulate an independent opinion in cases of student grade challenges.

An analysis and summary of anecdotal notes provide the basis for the summative evaluation. As illustrated in *Southwell v University of Incarnate Word*,[32] faculty members faced with a legal challenge to clinical grades can rely on the strength of their anecdotal notes and the principle of judicial deference to overcome student claims. In *Southwell*,[33] a nursing student was dismissed from the program the semester prior to her graduation. Southwell had successfully completed the didactic component of the nursing leadership/management course but was ordered off the unit by the clinical instructor during the practicum components because she had compromised a patient's safety. After negotiations between Southwell, her attorney, and the nursing program, she was allowed to complete the clinical component through an independent assessment. She again received a failing grade from another instructor because she failed to demonstrate competent and safe performance of required behaviors. Ruling in favor of the nursing program, the Court noted the evidence clearly reflected that Southwell did not successfully pass the course.

- *The determination of whether a student passed clinical is in the "professional discretion of the instructor who evaluated her and the nursing faculty as a whole. . . . Further, Southwell's grade is corroborated by [the instructor's] daily written evaluations."*[34]
- *The notes kept by both [clinical instructors] during Southwell's clinical evaluations were . . . consistent with the determination that Southwell failed the practicum. There were numerous mentions of unsafe and inefficient practices, as well as lack of certain basic clinical skills. Both instructors noted the need for close supervision of Southwell, particularly in reference to the administration of medication.*[35]

The determination of where and how long to keep anecdotal notes are determined by agency policy. A prevailing practice is to incorporate student data from the anecdotal notes into the final summative evaluation. Unless the evaluation is challenged, the notes can be maintained for a specific length of time and discarded. Summative evaluations are used to determine students' overall clinical performance throughout the entire nursing program.

Student-Faculty Conferences

Providing students feedback on their clinical performance is vital to their success in the nursing program and subsequently to their success in the profession. Clinical faculty should conduct and document formal and informal conferences with students to discuss their strengths, weaknesses, performance, and progress. Faculty and students formulate a plan to assist them to overcome their clinical weakness, maintain and build on strengths, and improve their overall performance.

The case of *Haynes v Hinsdale Hospital*[36] illustrates that faculty have a strong defense against student lawsuits when they have provided clear and precise documentation of student weaknesses and made suggestions for improvement. A phlebotomy student was failing the clinical component of a seven-week program. A memorandum from the program's instructors outlined numerous areas for improvement, including: repeating an exam and making at least a grade of 80, improving venipuncture skills, providing clear and concise instructions to facilitate better communication with patients, and listening actively to instructions provided by the instructors. Haynes retook the exam and scored 76.5% and received additional negative clinical performance evaluations. She challenged her dismissal from the program based on the instructor mischaracterizing a specific incident involving a patient. The Court noted that although the decision to dismiss Haynes was based on the totality of the circumstances, failure in any one area could provide the basis for dismissal. The school based its decision to expel Haynes on "all of the facts surrounding the conditions of her probation: she failed to achieve the necessary score on her make-up exam (this empirical fact alone would justify her expulsion); she failed to improve her phlebotomy skills; she failed to improve her communication skills or handling of the patients; and, she also failed to improve her ability to listen and take constructive criticism from her teachers."[37] As illustrated based on the case facts, the clinical instructor clearly identified the weaknesses and expectations required to pass the course. When students fail to fulfill a condition outlined by the clinical faculty, a valid reason for dismissal from the program is created.

STUDENTS WITH DISABILITIES

Educational institutions and its faculty must make reasonable accommodations for students with disabilities. Section 504 of the Rehabilitation Act[38] and the Americans with Disabilities Act (ADA)[39] were designed to minimize and hopefully eliminate unwarranted discrimination against persons with disabilities. However, pertinent to educators is the language that prohibits discrimination against and mandates that reasonable accommodations be made for "qualified students with learning disabilities."[40]

In *Southeastern Community College v Davis*,[41] the U.S. Supreme Court ruled that a student with a hearing impairment who was denied admission to the nursing program was not "qualified." Davis's hearing impairment prevented her from safely caring for patients and participating in the clinical program because she could not understand speech, even with the use of a hearing aid. In essence, the nursing program could not implement any accommodations that would overcome the deficiencies. The nature of nursing practice requires communication in providing care, responding to emergencies, and communicating with other health care professionals. In assessing qualifications, faculty and administrators can determine the mental disabilities that affect one's ability to function as a student and health care provider, to get along with other people, and to handle the stresses encountered in practice.[42] For example, in *Lekutis v University of Osteopathic Medicine*,[43] the Court upheld the dismissal of a student for serious problems in social functioning and mental instability. Lekutis displayed disruptive and unprofessional behaviors, including "dirty and unkempt appearance, a lack of tact, habit of walking with his hands clasped over his abdomen like a monk, inappropriate interactions, and repeatedly referred to a folded paper containing faculty's suggestions for improvement.[44] His emotional, mental, and physical behavior caused one hospital to abruptly terminate his clinical rotation privileges. Based on the behavior Lekutis demonstrated, faculty could not ensure that he did not pose a danger to himself or others. While educational institutions have an obligation to attempt to make accommodations for "otherwise qualified" students, they must ensure patient safety and adhere to standards mandated by clinical facilities.

Likewise, the case of *Hamilton v City College of City University*[45] reinforces the premise that reasonable accommodations do not mean diluting educational standards. A math professor twice allowed a student to use a calculator to accommodate his disability of dyslexia. However, the student's request was denied for the final examination, because the use of a calculator would interfere with the purpose and learning objective for that examination. Calculators were not allowed in class exams taken by the rest of the student's class members. The Court upheld the premise that "essential academic requirements of a course of study need not be altered nor is the College mandated to alter or effect substantial modifications of reasonable academic standards."[46] Reasonable accommodations can include, but are not limited to, allowing students:

- Extra time to take examinations
- To take exams in a separate room from other students
- Flexibility in turning in assignments
- To use mechanical devices such as calculators and computers

In reviewing allegations of discrimination on the basis of disability, courts will balance the rights of qualified students with the educational and professional requirements of the discipline. Faculty confronted with issues related to students with disabilities should consult the appropriate personnel. Many higher educational institutions have a department or office that provide faculty with a list of reasonable accommodations and guidance on issues encountered. In addition, faculty can contact the state or federal office of the Equal Employment Opportunity Commission (EEOC).

PROFESSIONAL DIMENSION

Nursing faculty must be competent in their specialty area. They must fulfill their role of helping students to transfer and apply theoretical knowledge to practice situations. They should continually evaluate the effectiveness of their current practice, while remaining open for more efficient methods of teaching and evaluating students. The faculty-student relationship is a significant factor in students' performance; therefore, faculty should continuously evaluate their objectivity in the relationship.

Educational technology has increased access for many students and has forced faculty to become creative in the development of learning strategies to effectively teach a more diversified student group. Development of course materials must incorporate this new technology to supplement the traditional lecture format to provide quality education to students. Students taking classes via nontraditional methods want to belong; therefore, faculty should incorporate activities that allow for connections with their peers to promote a sense of belonging, such as online group activities. Faculty in traditional programs must embrace technology to successfully prepare tomorrow's nurses.

ETHICAL DIMENSION

Many nursing courses also include a clinical component, which presents a challenge for some faculty members, because of what is viewed as a subjective aspect to the grading. Clinical faculty should be careful to not allow their biases and prejudices to enter into the evaluation process. They should assign grades based on the student's performance. Students must understand and incorporate the ethical principles of veracity, fidelity, confidentiality, and autonomy in their clinical practice. Today's clinical environment is filled with situations posing ethical dilemmas. Students must be educated in methods to address such dilemmas.

- Faculty can modify learning experiences and assignments to promote student comprehension and mastery of course content.
- Students should receive a course syllabus prior to or on the first day of class that contains course objectives, assignments, and evaluation methods and criteria.
- Course objectives should be consistent with learning outcomes.
- Course assignments are used to facilitate and measure student learning.
- The faculty-student relationship is a significant factor in students' performance.
- Faculty are not required to dilute educational standards or contravene the standards of clinical agencies to accommodate an "otherwise qualified" student.

Implications for Educators

Strategies to Avoid Legal Problems

- Adhere to the evaluation criteria outlined in the course syllabus, due to the contractual nature of the faculty-student relationship.
- Be flexible in giving students time to meet new requirements when circumstances or situations mandate a change in the grading process or course requirement and provide assistance in any way possible.
- Establish objective criteria upon which to evaluate students.
- Formulate professional judgments regarding students' competence in clinical practice. Support with specific examples from anecdotal notes.
- Protect patients from student-caused injury and maintain a safe learning environment. Base student grades and evaluations on their performance.
- Keep anecdotal notes on all clinical students that contain information on positive and negative performance.
- Make reasonable efforts to accommodate the needs of "otherwise qualified" students with disabilities.

RESPONSE TO CRITICAL THINKING QUESTIONS

1. How should Stephanie handle the situation with Benny?

Stephanie should immediately counsel Benny regarding the numerous errors he made in the care of the patient and his poor decision making. She should take Benny to a private counseling area, away from the other students and staff, and provide him with a verbal list of his errors. This immediate feedback highlights the magnitude of the errors and puts him on notice of the seriousness of the problem. It will also help him understand his actions within the context of the situation, rather than trying to recall specific details at a later point. After the oral counseling, she should make anecdotal notes of the events. Stephanie should schedule an office conference with Benny to address the issues in detail, identify incorrect and correct actions, make suggestions for improvement, and outline the consequences of failure to make improvements. Given the severity of the situation, Benny should receive a written warning or reprimand.

2. What is the basis for allowing Benny to continue the clinical rotation?

This is Benny's first clinical rotation. One issue that arises in clinical evaluation is, "At what point should a student fail the clinical rotation?" Should one incident be the basis for failing a student? Benny is eager, excited, and intelligent. He may not realize that success in the didactic component of nursing practice does not ensure success in clinical practice. The modes and basis of learning are different. Benny is a young, immature, novice nursing student who displayed extremely poor decision making. This experience can prove to be a valuable learning experience for Benny and a "teachable moment" for the instructor. He learned the hard way the importance of adhering to clinical guidelines and instructions.

3. What is the basis for failing Benny for the clinical rotation?

First, contrary to Stephanie's directions, Benny did not wait for her to administer medications to the patient. Instead he took instructions from the staff nurse and administered medications without supervision. He failed to inform the staff nurse that he needed to wait for his instructor or in the alternative, he could observe her administer the medication. The lack of this type of reasoning and decision making is reflective of the novice nursing student. In addition, and perhaps more troubling, is the lack of veracity in handling a problem. Benny realized after he administered the medication that he should have taken the patient's vital signs. Rather than admit his mistake, he engaged in deliberate deception to cover up the problem. Such behavior violates the ethical standard of veracity and raises serious concerns about his basic values. A student who will cover up errors is a walking time bomb to the profession. From a legal perspective, Benny's action put a patient's health and well-being in jeopardy, which could subject him, Stephanie, the educational institution, and the clinical facility to liability.

ANNOTATED BIBLIOGRAPHY

Wilson v Illinois Benedictine College, 445 NE2d 901 (1983).

Wilson was required to retake two economic courses after receiving grades of "D." His advisor, whom he met with every semester, never informed him that he needed to retake the courses. He did not specifically seek the advise of his advisor or review the bulletin to determine the consequences of the two "Ds." The bulletin read that only courses in which the student received a grade of "C" or better would apply toward graduation. Wilson was sent a notice the final semester before graduation that he had not completed all the courses needed for graduation. He initiated a lawsuit against the university alleging among other things, breach of contract. Held for the university: The language in the bulletin is clear and not ambiguous. Students are responsible for meeting the requirements of their major within the academic programs.

Nuttelman v Case Western Reserve University, 560 FSupp 1 (1981).

The requirements for admission to candidacy for the Ph.D. in nursing was successful completion of a three-part examination consisting of a clinical paper, a section on general knowledge, and a section on research methodology. Nuttelman passed the general knowledge section on the first sitting, the clinical paper on the second attempt, but twice failed the section on research methodology. She declined to take it a third time. She claimed the assistant dean failed to properly supervise the grading procedures and to ensure her anonymity during the grading process. Held for the university: The plaintiff did not prove ill will, bad motive, or arbitrary and capricious action. Educational institutions have wide latitude to determine their degree requiremnts.

Lilly v Smith, 790 SW2d 539 (Tenn App 1990).

A nursing student was dismissed from the program after receiving two "Ds" in accordance with the policy. The policy prevailed at all public community colleges and universities throughout the state. Therefore, Lilly could not enroll in any of the state nursing programs. She challenged the fairness of the policy. Held for the university: "While we may think the two 'D' policy is unfair or unwise, determining the wisdom of an academic policy is better left to the discretion of nursing faculty" (pg. 541). The nursing institutions seek to accept applicants who demonstrate professional potential and those who make two "Ds" do not hold this promise. Admission to a nursing program is not a civil right.

Lekutis v University of Osteopathic Meidicine, 524 NW2d 410 (Iowa 1994).

Lekutis was exceptionally intelligent, but below performance in the clinical components. A psychiatric evaluation revealed that "his affect was obviously inappropriate, often with bizarre facial expressions even during silence, which boarded on the austic at times." Testing results indicated "strong psychopathic tendencies and processes to impulsivity and acting out when angry and under stress." Lekutis rejected the psychiatrist's suggestion of medication and a medical leave of absence. Later, however, he requested a medical leave of absence due to a family illness. He had second thoughts based on his perception that he would not be readmitted. This led to a confrontation that resulted in Lekutis's admission to a psychiatric hospital. He was forced to take a 1-year medical leave of absence and his readmission was conditioned on a positive medical evaluation and proof of regular psychiatric care. He met the requirements and successfully completed the second year. However, he consistently failed the clinical components due to his mental condition and behavior. Held for the university: The record shows that Lekutis was deficit in his ability to deal with patients and staff.

NOTES

1 *Miller v Loyola University of New Orleans,* 829 So2d 1057 (La. App. 4 Cir. 2002).

2 *Miller.*

3 *Miller* at 1062.

4 D. E. Reilly, and M. H. Oermann. *Behavioral Objectives: Evaluation in Nursing* (New York: National League for Nursing, 1990).

5 B. S. Bloom, (Ed.), *Taxonomy of Educational Objectives. Handbook I: Cognitive Domain* (New York: Longman, 1956).

6 Reilly and Oermann, *Behavioral Objectives.*

7 J. J. Sadler, Mrs. Reynolds Still Needs a Nurse: Teaching Caring to Student Nurses. *Nurse Educator,* 26, no. 3 (2001), 111–113.

8 Sadler. Mrs. Reynolds Still Needs a Nurse: Teaching Caring to Student Nurses.

9 *Tobias v University of Texas,* 824 SW2d 201 (Tex App Forth Worth 1991).

10 *Tobias* at 205.

11 *Bruner v Petersen,* 944 P2d 43 (Alaska 1997).

12 *Bruner.*

13 *Bruner* at 48.

14 *Board of Curators of University of Mo. v Horowitz,* 435 US 78 (1978).

15 *Horowitz.*

16 *Regents of University of Michigan v Ewing,* 474 US 214 (1985).

17 H. Connors, *Distance Learning Technologies and Issues,19,* no. 3 (1998). National Council Publications. National Council of State Boards of Nursing available at: www.ncsbn.org/files/publications/issues/vol 193/distance 193.asp.

18 P. Privateer, Academic Technology and the Future of Higher Education. *The Journal of Higher Education,* 70, no. 1 (1999), 61–79.

19 Privateer, Academic Technology and the Future of Higher Education.

20 Connors, *Distance Learning Technologies.*

21 G. A. DeBourgh, Predictors of Student Satisfaction in Distance-Delivered Graduate Nursing Courses: What Matters Most? *Journal of Professional Nursing,* 19, no. 3 (2003), 149–163.

22 Office of Student Judicial Affairs. College Classroom Conduct. Old Dominion University, www.odu.edu.

23 DeBourgh, Predictors of Student Satisfaction in Distance-Delivered Graduate Nursing Courses; What matters most?

24 J. M. Scanlan, Learning Clinical Teaching: Is It Magic? *Nursing and Health Care Perspective,* 22, no. 5 (2001), 240–246.

25 J. M. Scanlan, Learning Clinical Teaching: Is It Magic? *Nursing and Health Care Perspective,* 22, no. 5 (2001), 240–246.

26 Scanlan, Learning Clinical Teaching: Is It Magic?

27 *Morris v Francisco,* 708 P2d 498 (1985).

28 R. Benjamin-Coleman, M. Smith, B. Alexy, and K. Palmer, A Decade of Distance Education: RN to BSN. *Nurse Educator,* 26, no. 1 (2001), 9–12.

29 K. A. Goudreau, and E.R. Chasens, Negligence in Nursing Education. *Nurse Educator,* 27, no. 1 (2002), 42–46.

30 J. Scanlan, W. Care, & S. Gessler, Dealing with the Unsafe Student in Clinical Practice. *Nurse Educator,* 26, no. 1 (2001), 23–27.

31 Scanlan et al., Dealing with the Unsafe Student in Clinical Practice.

32 *Southwell v University of Incarnate Word,* 974 SW2d 351 (Tex App—San Antonio 1998).

33 *Southwell.*

34 *Southwell* at 357.

35 *Southwell* at 357.

36 *Haynes v Hinsdale Hospital,* 872 FSupp 542 (1995).

37 *Haynes* at 545.

38 29 USC Section 794.

39 42 USC Section 12101 et. seq.

40 42 USC Section 12101 et. seq.

41 *Southeastern Community College v Davis,* 442 US 397 (1979).

42 *Doe v New York University,* 666 F2d 761 (2nd Cir 1981).

43 *Lekutis v. University of Osteopathic Medicine and Health Sciences,* 524 NW2d 410 (Iowa 1994).

44 *Lekutis.*

45 *Hamilton v City College of City University,* 173 FSupp2d 181 (SDNY 2001).

46 *Hamilton* at 184.

47 B. S. Bloom, M. D. Englehart, E. J. Furst, W. H. Hill, and D. R. Karthwohl, *Taxonomy of Educational Objectives: The Classification of Educational Goals.* (White Plains, NY: Longman, 1956).

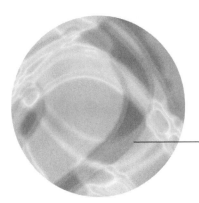

The Scholarship Role of Faculty

7

INTRODUCTION

The key to survival in academia for tenure-track faculty is productive and successful scholarship. In many institutions, scholarship includes, but is not limited to, research, publications, presentations at professional meetings, and securing external funding. Evaluation of excellence in scholarship in academia is a complex, multifaceted endeavor. The fundamental nature of scholarship is clearly articulated in the academic human resource policies of Michigan State University:

> *"The essence of scholarship is the thoughtful discovery, transmission, and application of knowledge, including creative activities, that is based in the ideas and methods of recognized disciplines, professions and interdisciplinary fields. What qualifies an activity as scholarship is that it be deeply informed by the most recent knowledge in the field, that the knowledge is skillfully interpreted and deployed, and that the activity is carried out with intelligent openness to new information, debate, and criticism."* [1]

Many institutions evaluate scholarship from a totality perspective, which incorporates both quantity and quality. This chapter explores the legal issues involved in the production and dissemination of knowledge, as it relates to research, publications, copyrights and patents.

Professor Larry Whate held a dual position as researcher at Cay Memorial Hospital and professor of nursing at Scenic College of Nursing. He taught nursing research, nursing theory, and leadership and management. Larry strongly believed in mentoring students and, thus, frequently engaged students in his research projects. At times, he would involve students in the drafting of his manuscripts to help them understand the fundamentals of publishing. On several occasions, he would assist students in publishing their research results and listing himself as second author. In his 8 years with the college, Larry had published over 50 articles, 40 as sole author and 10 with students. Scott Abbett, a first-year graduate student with a minor in statistics, was very interested in becoming a nurse-researcher. Larry recognized that Scott had extensive knowledge in research and believed that mentoring would assist him to meet his goal.

Larry was conducting a research study on the effects of Drug X on obesity in children. As always, he had assured his research participants that their information would remain confidential. Research data and findings did not show promise for the drug. However, the drug had a surprising side effect of reversing most of the symptoms suffered by children with attention deficit hyperactivity disorder (ADHD). Larry concluded the study and drafted a final report to submit to his funding sources, a private foundation and a governmental entity. Based on his study and the results, he also drafted two manuscripts. As was his usual practice, Larry did not submit the written material until the data and conclusions were validated by an independent statistician/researcher. Scott, who had assisted with the analysis of the research data, reviewed the draft manuscripts and added his comments. Without Larry's knowledge or consent, Scott drafted an independent manuscript using much of the same data, but written for a different journal and target audience. He reasoned that this was permissible because his manuscript was a derivative work.

Prior to the independent review, Larry received a subpoena from a Prudul drug company for all data, records, questionnaires, answers to questionnaires, and materials on his research methodology. Prudul was suing the maker of Drug X for patent infringement and needed Larry's research data to support their legal theory. Larry, through the university attorneys, filed a motion to quash or void the subpoena so he would not have to give them for his research data.

CRITICAL THINKING QUESTIONS

1. What copyright protection, if any, does Larry have in his manuscripts?
2. What is the probability of Scott being successful on a theory of derivative work?
3. What is the likelihood of the drug company gaining access to Larry's research materials?

• • •

DEFINING NURSING SCHOLARSHIP

The American Association of Colleges of Nursing (AACN) issued a position statement on defining scholarship for the nursing profession.[2] It defined the scholarship of nursing as activities that advance the research, teaching, and practice components of nursing through a process that is creative, significant to the profession, and subjected to replication, documentation, and peer review.[3] The four aspects of scholarship relevant to academic nursing are:[4]

1. *Discovery,* where new and unique knowledge that is germane to the profession is generated
2. *Teaching,* where knowledge is produced to support the transfer of information on the art and science of nursing to developing professionals and developing connections between the teacher's understanding and the students' learning
3. *Application,* where the emphasis is on the application of practice knowledge to solve society's problems and redefine community health problems
4. *Integration,* where new relationships among disciplines are created and knowledge is viewed in a larger more varied context

These standards can be used to guide faculty in their professional development and to evaluate their scholarship for the purposes of tenure and promotion. The form and supporting documentation as delineated by the AACN and summarized in Table 7.1[5] are specific in their focus on each area.

PUBLICATIONS

The art of writing can be a difficult and complex task that consumes a tremendous amount of time. However, as with any other task, the practice becomes easier the more one writes. Many faculty, especially junior faculty with little experience in writing, can expect a mandated revision of the manuscript before acceptance for publication. The comments provided by the reviewers provide constructive guidance for improvement to the writer. Responding to constructive feedback from the reviewers and enduring sometimes numerous rewrites is an intellectually growth-producing process.

Writing on topics of interests and in one's areas of knowledge may promote success in writing. The range of topics can include innovative teaching methods, case studies, critical analysis of problems with proposed solutions, and dissemination of research findings. Once a topic is identified, the prospective faculty-author should match the topic with appropriate journals. This involves perusing numerous journals for their mission, target audiences, and suggested topics. Once a target journal is identified, the faculty-author must incorporate the format and other publication requisites into the manuscript. After the manuscript is accepted for publication, it becomes the property of the journal.

Freedom in Publications

Writing for publication is just one aspect of scholarship. It is a component of scholarship that is a requirement to achieve tenure and promotion. The adage "Publish or perish" reflects the realism that faculty who do not have a record of publications have a limited

Table 7.1

Aspects of Nursing Scholarship

SCHOLARSHIP COMPONENT	FORM	SUPPORTING DOCUMENTATION
Discovery	Primary empirical research, historical research, theory development and testing, methodological studies, and philosophical inquiry and analysis.	Peer-reviewed publications, presentations, grant awards, mentoring junior faculty, recognition as a scholar and positive peer evaluations.
Teaching	Knowledge of the subject matter in the teaching-learning process, innovative teaching, development of evaluation methods, program development, learning outcome evaluation, and professional role modeling.	Presentations, design of outcome studies, published textbooks or other teaching aids, widespread recognition as a master teacher, application of technology to teaching and learning, learning theory development, case studies.
Practice/ Application	Development of clinical knowledge, professional development, application of technical or research skills, and service.	Policy papers, meta-analyses of practice problems, presentations, copyrights, patents, consultation reports, peer-reviewed publications, grant awards.
Integration	Conduction of reviews and analyses of policies, studies, literature, programs from an integrative perspective.	Interdisciplinary grant awards, publications, and presentations, policy papers, reports of interdisciplinary projects.

career in higher education environments. Faculty members are expected to engage in professional writing that results in published articles, monographs, and/or books.

Faculty enjoy a wide latitude in academic freedom in the selection of their publication interests. Case law is almost nonexistent on faculty's right to publish, the content contained therein, and where they can publish. As a general rule, administrators do not censure faculty's publications. Such an action would surely invoke lawsuits alleging violations of their rights under the First Amendment. The case of *Levin v Harleston*[6] is instructive in this area. Professor Levin published a series of articles in which he advocated that whites were superior to blacks. Many protested against his beliefs, which they found degrading and objectionable. Fearing a hostile academic environment and a disruption to the academic process, college administrators initiated a number of actions that had a negative impact on Professor Levin. The Court found the publications were protected expression and the university could not undertake measures designed to curb the professor's speech.

Box 7.1

Definitions of Selected Terms

Treatise	A systematic written "exposition or argument including a methodical discussion of the facts and principles involved and the conclusions reached."[59]
Derivative manuscript	A manuscript that is based on a previous work, but contains new materials.
Monograph	A scholarly book or pamphlet on a specific and limited topic.[60]
Refereed journal	Review of manuscripts by scholars and experts in the area on a particular topic, which incorporates a blind review process.
Blind Review	A review of a manuscript or other writings where the reviewer does not know the identity of the author.
Top-tier journals	Journal with high academic standards and reputation based on the required rigorous evaluation process and focus on valid and scholarly research methodologies.

Quality of Publications

Evaluation of published materials considers both the quantity and quality of the publications. A publication in a refereed, top-tier journal is weighed more heavily than a publication in a nonrefereed journal (Box 7.1). For example, in *Krystek v USM*,[7] the Court noted that a six-page article with minimal scholarly references and that was not peer reviewed did not meet the definition of scholarly work. A refereed journal requires a blind review of the submitted manuscript for review, analysis, and feedback from experts within the field. Once the reviews are compiled, the editor sends them to the author with a course of action, which may range from rejection of the manuscript, provisional acceptance with suggested changes to initial acceptance. The peer-review process elevates the status of journals due to the level of review the manuscript undergoes prior to its publication.

Because faculty are usually expected to publish in journals recognized as the top-tiered in their profession, the reputation of the publishing entity is a consideration in promotion and tenure decisions. In *Keddie v Pennsylvania State University*,[8] an ad hoc committee reviewing a candidate's tenure portfolio concluded that a published article and a manuscript accepted for publication was minimum or below minimum acceptable publishing standards. If the manuscript had been subjected to the blind, peer-review process, the professor would have had an excellent argument against the committee's conclusion.

Judicial Deference

As with other academic decisions, courts will not second-guess the professional judgment and decisions of educators and administrators in the area of quality of scholarly work.

In *Curtis v University of Houston*,[9] a professor sued after he was denied promotion from associate professor to full professor. Reasons for the denied promotion were that he:[10]

- Lacked the national visibility required to achieve the status of full professor
- Had not published a treatise in his field
- Had a long interruption from producing academic materials

Upholding the university's decision, the Court noted that the manual indicated that a professor should hold national recognition and be a respected expert in his field. Although one of the full professors in the department had not published a monograph, he had published two books, had edited two books, and had written over 30 articles (Box 7.1). In comparison, Curtis had no visibility in national and international conferences, had not contributed to any book chapters, and had only produced five articles.[11] Based on the totality of Curtis's scholarly production since his promotion to associate professor, the university was justified in the denial of his promotion to full professor.

RESEARCH

Like publications, faculty enjoy freedom in the pursuit of their research endeavors. The protection from unauthorized external intrusion into the research process is practiced under the auspices of academic freedom. Faculty members are free to conduct research and pursue the truth without fear that administrators, the government, or others will interfere with the planning, implementation, interpretation, and dissemination of the results. However, in legal challenges, this freedom is balanced against the administration of justice.

Legal Request for Faculty's Research Data

External parties have had mixed success invading the research realm of professors in higher education. Faculty cannot expect the courts to practice a judicial hands-off attitude when external parties request research information. As the following case illustrates, courts have not recognized the existence of a scholar's privilege in the academic research process. In the case of *In Re Grand Jury Proceedings, James Richard Scarce,* the Court refused to acknowledge the existence of a "scholar's privilege."[12] Scarce had written several publications, essays, and papers on the environmental movement and animal rights groups, including militant groups. After a break-in at an animal rights facility, the government subpoenaed Scarce to determine what he knew based on his associations with one of the suspects. The two were seen having breakfast after the incident. In addition, the suspect had house-sat for Scarce, who was out of town during the break-in. Scarce refused to answer the grand jury questions, citing a "scholar's privilege." In essence, he argued that the information was confidential in furtherance of his scholarly research. The Court noted that no court "has actually recognized a scholar's privilege to withhold from a federal grand jury confidentially obtained information which is relevant to grand jury inquiry and sought in good faith."[13] Scarce was charged with contempt of court when he failed to cooperate and comply with the subpoena.

Unpublished Data

In addressing requests for researcher data, the Court will balance the infringement on academic freedom against the requesting party's need for the information. While the Court acknowledges that compelled production of a researcher's confidential data may impede his or her data gathering ability, even confidential data may be revealed upon a showing of substantial need.[14] Nevertheless, a major factor in the courts' decisions is whether the information has been published or made available to other scholars or research sponsors. For example, in *The American Tobacco Company, R.J. Reynolds Tobacco Company, and Philip Morris, Inc. v Mount Sinai School of Medicine and The American Cancer Society*,[15] a court refused to force a professor to release his research data to several tobacco companies, who were being sued by relatives of individuals who had died of lung cancer. The companies wanted the professor's research data because it supported the plaintiffs' theory that the cancer was caused by a combination of cigarette smoking and exposure to asbestos.[16] A professor of medicine, who had nothing to do with the lawsuits, had conducted research and published several articles, which supported the conclusion that the combination increased the risk of cancer geometrically, which suggested a relationship between smoking and exposure to asbestos.[17] Research subjects had been assured that their personal data and other information would be kept confidential. The information sought was extensive to include raw data in its original form (which was being continuously updated for ongoing research), answers to questionnaires, responses to interviews, and documents that describe the research methodology. The School of Medicine and the American Cancer Society made a motion to quash or make void the subpoena because:[18]

1. The information requested contained confidential information that would take over a thousand hours to redact or remove the data that identified the study participants.
2. Removal of confidential information would unduly burden the researchers and interrupt their ongoing research.
3. Compliance with the subpoena requests would interfere with academic freedom, deny the doctors the opportunity of first publication of their research results, and discourage future scientific endeavors.

The New York Court agreed with the academic argument and quashed the subpoena. Courts will protect faculty's rights to pursue research and to protect their unpublished or ongoing data because the premature release of research data can have the potential for numerous negative consequences. The court in *Dow v Allen*[19] identified several of these consequences:

- *Public access to the research data would make the studies an unacceptable basis for scientific papers or other research;*
- *Peer review and publication of the studies [is] crucial to the researchers' credibility and careers and would be precluded by whole or partial public disclosure of the information;*
- *Loss of the opportunity to publish would severely decrease the researchers' professional opportunities in the future; and*
- *Inadvertent disclosure of the information would risk total destruction of months or years of research.*[20]

Given the emphasis on scholarship in the progression of faculty in higher education, courts are correct in preventing infringements that would impede completion, critical analysis, and publication of research findings.

Published Data

Published research data do not enjoy the same degree of protection from access by outsiders as do unpublished data. Once the research is completed and the findings published, researchers will encounter strong barriers in objecting to subpoenas for their research data. In the case of *The American Tobacco Company, R.J. Reynolds Tobacco Company, and Philip Morris, Inc. v Mount Sinai School of Medicine and The American Cancer Society*[21] discussed earlier, the Court rejected the tobacco companies' request for the unpublished data. The tobacco company then served upon the school subpoenas that requested primarily the raw data on computer tape that had served as the basis for the existing publications. Rejecting the medical school's argument of "research scholar's privilege," the Court noted that burden, academic freedom, and a premature release of findings were factors to consider, but did not determine the outcome of the case. The Court held that the time required to redact or remove confidential information could be performed by someone else and not the researchers and that the tobacco company had agreed to pay the associated costs. In response to the argument that the tobacco company could conduct their own studies, the Court noted that the professor, as the preeminent authority in the area, could anticipate that experts would rely on his findings. The knowledge derived from research data is published and shared with other scholars. Therefore, researchers should, upon request, produce the data that support their published research findings.[22]

The court ruled that:

- *Researchers accumulate basic data from an infinite number of sources. Sometimes it has been acquired by others and is used by the researcher. Sometimes it is acquired specifically for the research project. Sometimes and usually, both sources are used.*
- *The data are analyzed, compared and contrasted and from it all, the researcher draws conclusions using his analysis to document and support his report that in turn supports his conclusions. The value of the conclusions turns on the quality of the data and the methods used by the researcher in his analysis of that data as well as the skill and perception of the researcher.*
- *So if the conclusions or end product of a research effort is to be fairly tested, the underlying data must be available to others equally skilled and perceptive.*[23]

Critical examination and constructive criticism of published information is necessary to validate research results. The Court in this case allowed the release of raw data that had served as the basis of the published articles to allow interested reviewers to validate the published results and conclusions.

The Court in *Wright v Jeep Corporation*[24] reached the same conclusion regarding published research data and articulated numerous reasons for ruling against a professor's objection to a subpoena for research data after he had published his findings. The Court ruled that:

- *The administration of justice may require the parties to obtain data to help the court evaluate the validity of the conclusions.*
- *The First Amendment permits professors to write and speak without interference from government and external entities, but does not extend to the right to withdraw written and published materials.*
- *Compelled production of records and research data should not have any greater chilling affect for professors than the compelled testimony of a witness who sees or hears something. The possibility of being subpoenaed exists in many situations.*
- *A heavy burden is placed on any researcher who discovers information that becomes essential in litigation. However, the solution is to provide the information and compensate the researcher accordingly.*[25]

Researchers should be aware that their research may be criticized by their peers. Therefore, they should be prepared to respond to inquiries regarding the research process and the conclusions reached. Courts may not recognize the existence of a privilege in a researcher's data for use to determine the validity of the results and conclusions. In planning research and responding to request for research data, researchers should carefully consider methods to protect the privacy and identity of the research subjects or participants.

COPYRIGHT

Copyright applies to "original works of authorship fixed in any tangible medium of expression."[26] A work is considered "fixed in a tangible medium of expression when its embodiment in a copy or phonorecord . . . is sufficiently permanent or stable to permit it to be perceived, reproduced, or otherwise communicated for a period of more than transitory duration."[27] Thus, once a professor writes his or her lecture notes, they become copyrightable material. Copyright does not apply to "any idea, procedure, process, system, method of operation, concept, principle, or discovery."[28] For example, a professor has an idea for a publication and discusses this with another faculty member. The professor's idea is not protected by copyright. Under copyright law, the rights of an original work vest in the author of the work. Copyright protects the initial author or creator of work, who has the exclusive right to reproduce, transmit, or distribute it; to display or perform the work in public; and to create a derivative work from it.[29] Because, lecture notes belong to the professor, anyone who desires to use or reproduce them must seek the professor's consent.

Unauthorized Use of Lecture Notes

The practice by some Internet companies of hiring students to take detailed notes of a professor's lecture, copyright the notes, and then sell them for profit has raised the issue of the degree of protection afforded to professors in their notes. Internet companies defend their practice by arguing that the notes belong to the students, who may do as they please with the notes and posting a disclaimer that the notes represent students' versions of the lecture.[30] Universities are responding to this intrusion by adopting policies that prohibit students from engaging in note taking for commercial purposes[31] and initiating lawsuits against the companies that reproduce faculty lecture notes without the proper permission. To protect against the unauthorized commercialization of lecture notes, faculty should also include in their syllabus that their lecture notes are considered copyright and cannot be sold without their expressed permission. A sample prohibition policy that faculty can include in their syllabi reads:

> *Course materials (syllabus, lecture notes, etc) developed by Professor X for use in Class Y are copyright protected. Therefore use or reproduction of these materials require the express written permission of Professor X.*

This language applies to students and nonstudents who attend lectures or who have inadvertently accessed the course materials on the website. Because written lecture notes are copyrightable material, faculty members may assign or transfer their rights to the copyrighted work.

Reasonable Use of Copyright Materials

Unless the use of copyrighted materials falls within one the exceptions, faculty must seek permission to use copyrighted materials. The fair use and instructional exceptions contained in the Copyright Act are educator-friendly and allow for the fair use of copyrighted materials for teaching, research, and scholarship purposes. It is an attempt to balance the rights of the copyright owner with educators' interest in dissemination of knowledge. Copyright materials must be used in a reasonable manner, which is defined by four factors:

1. The purpose and character of the use
2. The nature of the copyrighted work
3. The amount and substantiality of the portion used
4. The effect of the use upon the potential market for or value of the copyrighted work[32]

Educators must consider the reasonableness of the amount used and market effect of the copyrighted material. For example, professors cannot copy entire books or a substantial portion for classroom use. A better practice is either to require students to purchase the book or recommend it as a supplemental textbook. The use of copyrighted materials, without permission, should not be used to make a profit. Faculty should use caution when putting copyright materials in course paks that will be purchased by students. The institution or copy shop must get permission from the copyright owner or licensing site.

Ownership of Faculty Work

Copyright of a faculty member's lecture notes, outlines, research, publications, and similar materials usually vest in the faculty who developed the materials. Courts have noted that if ownership of faculty members course materials were vested in the university, a professor who changes jobs would have to obtain the university's permission to use his own lecture notes, outlines, manuals, study guides, or other instructional materials at his new place of employment.[33] Therefore, as a general rule, universities do not assert ownership interests in these instructional and scholarly materials. Numerous courts follow the universal assumption and practice that "the right to copyright such writings belongs to the teacher rather than the college or university" because it "does not supervise its faculty in the preparation of academic books and articles, and is poorly equipped to exploit their writings, whether through publication or otherwise."[34]

Work Made for Hire Doctrine

Universities asserting an ownership interest in faculty-developed materials rely on the "work made for hire" doctrine, which is an exception to the rule that the rights in a work initially vest in the author. Under the work made for hire doctrine, the person for whom the work was prepared is considered the owner for copyright purposes, if it was "specifically ordered or commissioned for use . . . as an instructional text, as a test, as answer material for a test . . . if the parties expressly agree in a written instrument" of the work made for hire status.[35] Likewise, a work prepared for an employer by an employee that is within the scope of his or her employment is considered work made for hire.[36] Three factors are analyzed to determine scope of employment:

1. Whether the work is the kind that the employee was hired to perform
2. Whether it occurred within the authorized time and space limits
3. Whether the work was performed, in part, to serve the employer[37]

The Court in *Genzmer v Public Health Trust of Miami-Dade County*[38] applied these factors to determine the owner of a computer program developed by a medical doctor. Genzmer, who worked as a full-time Fellow in the pulmonary and critical care unit at Jackson Memorial Hospital, developed the software for a program to computerize the units consultation reports. His job description included patient care, ordering treatment, conducting research projects, and instructing house staff in his specialty area. Fellows were also expected to acquire skills to organize, administer, and direct a critical care unit.[39] The research requirement could be fulfilled through a variety of undertakings, including technological projects. Genzmer wrote the computer program on his own time, at home, using his personal computer. He discussed the program with his supervisor during the development stage. The test of the software was conducted at the hospital and revisions made based on the test. His supervisor provided input as to the final appearance of the reports generated by the software. Development of the program was included in Genzmer's evaluation and contributed to a more positive performance evaluation. Without objections from his supervisor, the hospital, or the Trust, Genzmer submitted and obtained copyright registration. Genzmer had programmed a bug into the program that made it inoperable after his employment ended. The department refused to comply with Genzmer's demands for payment and he initiated a lawsuit.

The Trust claimed ownership of the software, under the work made for hire doctrine. Applying the scope of employment test, the Court ruled for the Trust on the following facts:

- **Job Description.** *Genzmer was required to conduct a research project, which could involve computer programming. Organizing information would fulfill the requirement that he acquire skills in organizing a unit. His supervisor provided him with guidance and the program was a substantial factor in the improvement of his performance evaluation.*
- **Time and Space Limits.** *Genzmer was a salaried employee who was required to complete a research project. It is generally expected that he would work on the project away from the employment site. It is not a determining factor that the work occurred at a place different from the*

> *work environment and during nonbusiness hours. The significant factor is that the project was completed during the period of employment.*
> • **Motivation for the work.** *The software developed by Genzmer was tailored to the unit's needs. Prior to the software, the reports were done by hand. The program had a significant impact on the organization of information. It is sufficient that Genzmer was only partially motivated to meet the needs of the department.*[40]

Although Genzmer had received copyright protection, the Court ruled that he was not entitled to it. The outcome may have been different if the product was not related to employment responsibilities, was motivated by personal needs to achieve, and the supervisor had no input or did not approve of the project.[41]

As the following cases will illustrate, case law on the ownership of faculty-prepared material is inconsistent. For example, the Court in *Vanderhurst v Colorado Mountain College District*[42] interpreted the college's policy that a faculty member's duties included professional service activities such as course, program, and curriculum development to include as work made for hire an outline that the professor had created on his own time with his own materials. The Court reasoned, "[C]reation of the Outline was connected directly with the work for which he was employed to do and was fairly and reasonable incidental to his employment. Further, creation of the Outline may be regarded as one method of carrying out the objectives of his employment."[43] In contrast, the Court in *Weinstein v University of Illinois* reached a different conclusion.[44] Weinstein, an assistant professor of pharmacy, developed a proposal for a clinical program for pharmacists, which was funded by the university. He sought the assistance of Belsheim, the director of continuing education, and Hutchinson, the director of pharmacy practice, who assisted with the proposal and participated in the program. Belsheim and Weinstein did not agree on the drafts of the manuscript that were to be submitted for publication. Weinstein initiated a lawsuit alleging that the university violated his due process rights when Belsheim submitted the manuscript and did not list him as first author. The university argued that it owned the article under the work made for hire doctrine. Unlike the Court in Vanderhurst, discussed earlier, that focused on research and publications as terms and conditions of employment, the Court in Weinstein focused instead on freedom to publish and rejected the university's ownership argument. Acknowledging that faculty members do not obtain consent from the university to publish an article nor do they transfer to the university their ownership rights prior to submitting a manuscript for consideration for publication, the Court ruled in favor of the university. If the university did not own the manuscript, it could not deprive Weinstein of a constitutionally protected property interest.[45]

Faculty should clearly understand how their institution interprets the work for hire doctrine and applies policies regarding ownership of faculty-developed materials. Faculty-developed materials or work that is intended to be personal should not be commingled with the work environment. For example, the use of university resources, equipment, and supplies may subject a work to ownership by the university.

Jointly Authored Works

Jointly published or prepared manuscripts can create issues affecting transfer rights and other uses. A work is considered joint when it is "prepared by two or more authors with the intent that their contributions be merged into an inseparable or interdependent parts of a unitary whole."[46] The assistance provided by a graduate student, research assistant, secretary, or other colleague does not entitle the person to claim joint authorship.[47] Under copyright law, authors of joint works are considered coauthors and can publish either the original or a revision of the original article.[48]

Other issues arise as to the use of the original material in subsequent articles or professional undertakings. In *Weissman v Freeman*[49] two professors had worked together as researchers and coauthors on numerous publications in the area of nuclear medicine. Dr. Freeman put a copy of a manuscript prepared solely by Dr. Weissman in a packet for a lecture he was presenting. Although he complied with her request to remove the manuscript from the packet before it was distributed, Dr. Weissman filed a copyright infringement lawsuit against Dr. Freeman. Ruling in favor of Dr. Weissman, the Appellate Court noted that "joint authorship of prior existing works do not automatically make the two joint authors co-owners of the derivative work." Dr. Weissman had created a new copyrightable work at the time she solely created the new manuscript, because under copyright law, "where the work has been prepared in different versions, each version constitutes a separate work."[50] The fact that she had used material previously included in jointly authored articles was not the determining factor. Dr. Weissman had added new content, references, and pictures and had substantially rearranged materials from previous articles. Further, Dr. Freeman had not contributed to the new manuscript. Although the Weissman case discussed here involved a manuscript, the same issue can emerge related to jointly created online courses. Principles of joint ownership will govern situations where an online course was jointly created. As between the authors, they each have equal rights to the work as a whole. The institution's policy, however, will govern ownership of the course materials.

Ownership of Nontraditional Courses

Technological advances in education have created additional issues related to ownership of faculty prepared materials. The general practice of higher education institutions' deference to traditional instructional material is changing with the advent of distance education. The permanency of online courses and distance education has created a scenario where courses can be offered in subsequent semesters by someone other than the original professor.[51] Although the American Association of University Professors (AAUP) advocates that faculty members should remain the owner of materials prepared for academic instruction,[52] the policies of different universities are varied. Numerous issues have emerged related to copyright in online and distance education courses. Unfortunately, these issues do not have clear answers. Higher education institutions must balance the ownership rights of faculty with the tremendous costs involved in offering distance education and online courses. These costs include hardware, software, support personnel, and in some cases, the physical space. If ownership vested 100% in faculty members, they are free to take the end product to another institution or sell it, having invested only their time and intellectual knowledge. The educational institution is left with the expenses. If the university owned the course, they could "prohibit professors from teaching similar courses at other institutions, which would negatively impact the professor's career."[53] The major issues involved in faculty rights to online courses are based on several assertions:

- Traditionally, when a faculty leaves a university, so too does his or her expertise, class content, and teaching style.
- Online and distance education courses eradicate the above tradition.
- The faculty member developed the course and as such, whether online or face to face, the resulting product retains the "air" of the developing faculty.
- If the development of the online course is a part of the faculty's workload, then the work made for hire doctrine is more applicable.
- If the faculty member developed the online course on his or her time and without directives from university officials, he or she should retain ownership.

Policies addressing online courses should balance the university interests and expenses with the academic freedom and ownership rights of faculty. For example, the university can pay royalties or bonuses to faculty when their courses are financially profitable.[54]

PATENTS

A patent is the "exclusive right to make, use or sell an invention for a specified period (usually 17 years), granted by the federal government to the inventor if the device or process is novel, useful, and nonobvious."[55] The Patent and Trademark Office, within the Department of Commerce, processes applications for and issues patents. A patent prevents others from making or selling the patented invention. Higher education institutions are more likely to assert ownership in inventions because of the resultant profits. However, unless a specific agreement governs otherwise, patents are usually granted to the inventor. The policy governing patents will vary among colleges and universities, but the common practice is that the university owns the patent, or some portion thereof, and faculty-inventors are given a royalty for their inventions.

In situations where faculty members are required by university policy to assign their rights to the university, they should remain actively involved in or apprized of all negotiations. Faculty-inventors are more aware of the potential uses of their product and the market value. The university's obligation to faculty-inventors may be nonspecific and vague; therefore, faculty should clearly understand the patent policies. These principles are illustrated in *Kucharczyk v Regents of the University of California*.[56] Kucharczyk and Moseley, professors of radiology at University of California, San Francisco, invented a particular method for conducting perfusion magnetic resonance imaging technique (MRI), which was patented. University policy required employees to assign their inventions and patents to the university, and in turn the university would pay the inventors annually 50% of the net royalties and fees it receives. The professors' research was partially funded by a private company, Nycomed. Forms filed by the professors with the university's patent office and application to the U.S. Patent Office identified as coinventor a Nycomed researcher. The university entered into a license agreement with them that in exchange for exclusive rights to the patent, Nycomed would pay the university $25,000. Asserting that the patent was worth millions of dollars, the professors' initiated a lawsuit against Nycomed and the university.

The patent policy of the university was designed "to encourage and assist members of the faculty . . . in the use of the patent system with respect to their discoveries and inventions in a manner that is equitable to all parties involved."[57] Addressing the professors' assertion that the university had a contractual obligation to pursue negotiations vigorously, determine the true value of the invention, and obtain considerations in accordance with industry standards, the Court refused to interpret the patent policy to require these contractual responsibilities. Finding no evidence of bad faith on the part of the university, the Court noted that "the most that can be said is that the University was misled into signing away its rights to the patented method for substantially less than those rights were worth."[58] They allowed the professors to proceed against Nycomed on the charges of fraud, interference with contractual relations, and breach of the research funding agreement. The case was then settled out of court. As this case illustrates, faculty should remain involved in all negotiations regarding their inventions and should clearly communicate their expectations to academic administrators. The employing institutions should be fully and accurately appraised of all agreements and involved personnel.

PROFESSIONAL DIMENSION

The production and dissemination of knowledge is an essential aspect of the faculty role. Faculty enjoy autonomy in the selection and focus of their scholarship endeavors. Faculty are expected to show continual growth in fulfilling the scholarship role. As they develop and gain successes in this role, they gain internal confidence, are encouraged to continue their efforts, gain national and international recognition, and assume mentorship roles for junior faculty. The advent of technology and its widespread use in education has created challenges that many faculty embrace with enthusiasm, from the development of innovative teaching strategies to the dissemination of knowledge via nontraditional means. As higher education institutions continue to struggle with issues created by technology, faculty input is imperative in the development of policies and procedures governing ownership of course materials, patents, and other innovative inventions.

ETHICAL DIMENSION

The area of scholarship is fraught with numerous potential ethical dilemmas. Faculty should ensure that they are actively involved in the work in which they receive credit and should give credit to individuals who actively contribute. The practice of putting colleagues names on manuscripts that they did not contribute is an ethical violation, even under the best intentions. Likewise, faculty contributing to scholarly endeavors should have the knowledge base to make meaningful contributions.

Ethics would mandate that research results are accurately reported and never tailored to meet predicted outcomes. Because others rely on the outcome of research findings, data fabrication is a serious ethical breach. If multiple publications are anticipated from a single research study, each publication should address a different focus or question. This is possible if the researcher formulated and collected data to address multiple questions or hypotheses. Promises of anonymity promised to research participants must be upheld and their confidential information safeguarded.

Implications for Educators

- Publications in refereed journals, which employ a peer-review process, are considered quality and scholarly articles.
- Courts will allow external parties to access research data when the results have been published.
- Because policies regarding ownership of course materials vary from institution to institution, faculty should review their university policies and seek clarification when needed.
- Online course materials enjoy more indisputable copyright protection because they are readily fixed in a tangible medium.
- The advent of technologically based courses have blurred the line between faculty owned materials and materials that employers' own under the work-for-hire doctrine.
- Faculty should keep personal inventions away from the work environment to avoid employer's assertion of ownership.

Strategies to Avoid Legal Problems

- Review university policy to clearly understand the weight given to quality and quantity of scholarship.
- Consult with senior faculty and the department chair to identify top-tier journals.
- Contact legal counsel if external individuals request research or other sensitive information.
- Put a prohibition policy on syllabi acknowledging that faculty-developed lectures, outlines, manuals, and other materials is copyright protected.
- Review university policy on ownership of online and distance education materials.
- Bring the issue to the attention of the faculty senate or similar body if the policy governing ownership of online and distance education material is not satisfactory.
- Avoid commingling inventions. If inventions are intended to be private, then keep them away from the work environment.
- Clearly define each person's role in projects. If a project is to be jointly authored or conducted, have a clear written understanding of each person's expected contribution.
- Remain current on issues affecting faculty in the area of technology and alternate methods of instruction.

RESPONSE TO CRITICAL THINKING QUESTIONS

1. What copyright protection, if any, does Larry have in his manuscripts?

A work is subject to copyright protection from the moment it is written, because it is fixed in a tangible medium of expression. Larry's manuscripts are considered an original work of authorship. The fact that a work is unpublished does not diminish its copyright protection. The copyright owner possesses exclusive rights to prepare or authorize another person to prepare a derivative manuscript based on the copyrighted work. Similarly, a joint owner has equal and undivided rights in the work.

2. What is the probability of Scott being successful on a theory of derivative work?

If Scott is considered a coauthor of the original manuscripts, he is entitled to prepare derivative manuscripts. To prove joint authorship, Scott must show that he contributed to the manuscripts and at the time of their inception, both authors intended that their contributions would be merged into an independent and inseparable whole. Scott cannot prove joint ownership. There was no collaboration between Larry and Scott on the manuscripts and Larry did not intend for Scott to be a coauthor. Scott was given draft manuscripts to review as a learning activity. His comments on the manuscript did not elevate his status to that of coauthor. As such, Scott is not entitled to produce a derivative work. In addition, a derivative work must represent an original author of ownership. Scott's manuscript uses the same information from Larry's material to present it to a different author. If Scott attempts to publish the manuscript, Larry has a copyright infringement lawsuit and can get an injunction to prevent its publication.

3. What is the likelihood of the drug company gaining access to Larry's research materials?

Case law supports the premise that courts are more willing to protect research data when it is ongoing and incomplete. However, once the research is complete and the results published, courts have granted the subpoenaed information. Larry's research is at the in-between stage in that it is completed and manuscripts written. However, the results have not been verified. Applying the Court's analysis, the confidentiality of the information is not a major barrier to granting the request, because it can be removed. The cost of removal may be charged to the requesting party. Courts favor allowing data to be analyzed for analysis, validation, and criticism; however, they also respect researchers having control over their data for publication and other scholarly purposes. Larry has a strong argument that his research is not completed until the data are validated to ensure that conclusions drawn for the data are accurate. Because the data may be used in litigation and thus widely disseminated, he has a heightened interest in ensuring its validity. In addition, premature release of the information may impede publication opportunities and professional presentations. Once the material is published, however, Larry will encounter strong barriers in attempts to prevent the release of the data. If the study is ongoing, the release of data may be limited to that which support the published articles.

ANNOTATED BIBLIOGRAPHY

Wright v Jeep Corporation, 547 FSupp 871 (ED Mich 1982).

Dr. Snyder, a professor and research scientist with the Highway Safety Institute of the University of Michigan, published his research data that concluded that a particular Jeep experienced a disproportionately high roll-over rate when involved in an accidents. Jeep, the defendant in personal injury litigation, contended that the plaintiffs were likely to rely on the report and therefore subpoenaed all research and other data pertaining to the study. Professor Snyder objected to the subpoena on numerous grounds including an academic privilege not to testify, he was not a party to or expert in the lawsuits, his First Amendment rights as a researcher and writer protected him from forced testimony, and forced testimony would have a negative and chilling effect on researchers, scientists, and educators. Held for Jeep Corporation: The administration of justice requires the validity of the conclusions to be ascertained.

Dow v Allen, 672 F2d 1262 (7th Cir 1982).

Dow Chemical Company issued a subpoena to obtain research data, including raw data, notes, and working papers, from researchers at the University of Wisconsin who were conducting studies on the toxicity of certain herbicides. The study was funded by the Department of Health, Education and Welfare. Faced with threatened cancellation of certain of its herbicides by the Environmental Protection Agency, Dow wanted to evaluate the data prior to the hearings, although the research was incomplete. Held for the university: The Court ruled that the production of raw data prior to the study's completion was burdensome, interfered with the necessary peer review, and could preclude professional opportunities and future publications.

Deitchman v E.R. Squibbs & Sons, Inc., 740 F2d 556 (7th Cir 1984).

Dr. Herbst maintained an ongoing registry to monitor several aspects of genital tract carcinoma. He and his colleagues made an association between a female's exposure to DES in the womb and the early development of cervical and vagina cancer. They had hundreds of case files and published numerous articles from the data contained in the registry. Dr. Herbst made promises of confidentiality to his subjects. Squibb issued subpoenas, which would in effect require the production of all registry documents. Dr. Herbst objected to the subpoenas on the grounds that the registry would be destroyed if confidentiality was breached and disclosure would have a negative effect on the academic freedom. The Court balanced this with Squibb's argument that the data derived from the registry have become the basis upon which plaintiffs based their lawsuits and upon which their experts would rely. Remanded to the lower court: Rather than a blanket denial of an extensive and overly broad subpoena, the lower court must fashion a remedy that is reasonable and determine what information the requesting party can access.

Lawrence v Curators of the University of Missouri, 204 F3d 807 (8th Cir 2000).

Lawrence was denied tenure because of her weak research record and failure to publish in top-tier journals. She had one independently published article, which was from her dissertation topic. The other articles were coauthored. Four of the six outside reviewers expressed criticism of her publication record. Lawrence sued the university alleging that the denial was pretext for discrimination. Held for the university: The dismissal was upheld because there was no substantial showing of discrimination.

Lim v Trustees of Indiana University, 297 F3d 575 (7th Cir 2002).

A professor was denied tenure on the basis that she did not meet the university's tenure requirements. At the time of her hire, the department chairman made several deviations from standard policy to attract her. To achieve tenure, faculty members were expected to publish one to two articles a year and be first or senior author on at least half of those publications. At the time of her tenure application, Lim had five peer-reviewed articles, but was senior author on only one. Lim brought a lawsuit against the university alleging gender discrimination because other individuals with similar publication rates were tenured. Held for the university: The tenured individuals received tenure under a different chairperson. Lim did not meet the published standards and her deficits were clearly stated in her evaluations.

Hays v Sony Corporation of America, 847 F2d 412 (7th Cir 1988).

Two business teachers prepared a manual to instruct students on how to use the school's word processors. Shortly thereafter, the school district purchased new word processors and gave Sony the manual to modify for consistency with the newly purchased processors. The new manual was very similar to the old one and at times used verbatim language. The teachers filed for copyright protection and brought a copyright infringement lawsuit against Sony. Held for Sony: The dismissal of the teachers' lawsuit in the lower court was not appealed in a timely manner. However, the work made for hire doctrine may not be applicable in this case because high school teachers are not expected to publish and the work was done without directives, input, or supervision from their supervisors.

Seshadri v Kasraian, 130 F3d 798 (7th Cir 1997).

A professor and his graduate student submitted a coauthored paper to a journal. After a disagreement between the two, the professor wrote the journal and withdrew the manuscript alleging that the graduate student had provided erroneous content. He also requested that his name be removed from the authorship of the manuscript. The graduate student resubmitted the manuscript for consideration for publication solely in his name. He wrote the professor requesting approval to acknowledge his assistance in the preparation of the manuscript. The professor indicated that he had primarily written the article and indicated that he did not want his name associated with the manuscript. Each accused the other of academic misconduct. The student was cleared and the professor was suspended for a year and forbidden from advising graduate students. The professor sued, alleging among other things, copyright infringement. In response, the graduate student alleged that the professor had abandoned his interests in the manuscript. Held for the university: Rejecting the abandonment claim, the Court noted that the author of a joint work is joint owner who is entitled to copyright it and license it to a third party (the journal) and must only account to the coauthor for any profits.

NOTES

1 MSU Human Resources-Appointment, Reappointment, Tenure, and Promotion Recommendations. Available at: http://www.hr.msu.edu/Hrsite/Documents/Faculty/Handbooks/.

2 American Association of Colleges of Nursing. Position Statement On Defining Scholarship For The Discipline Of Nursing. (1999) Available at http://www.aacn.nche.edu/Publications/positions/scholar.htm.

3 American Association of Colleges of Nursing. Position Statement On Defining Scholarship For The Discipline Of Nursing.

4 AACH citing E. Boyer, Scholarship Reconsidered: Priorities for the Professoriate (Princeton, NJ: The Carnegie Foundation for the Advancement of Teaching, 1990).

5 American Association of Colleges of Nursing. Position Statement On Defining Scholarship For The Discipline Of Nursing.

6 *Levin v Harleston,* 770 FSupp. 895, aff'd 966 F2d 85 (2nd Cir 1992).

7 *Krystek v USM,* 164 F3d 251 (5th Cir 1999).

8 *Keddie v Pennsylvania State University,* 412 FSupp 1264 (Penn 1976).

9 *Curtis v University of Houston,* 940 FSupp 1070 (1996).

10 *Curtis* at 1073.

11 *Curtis* at 1077.

12 *In Re Grand Jury Proceedings, James Richard Scarce,* 5 F3d 397 (1993).

13 *Scarce* at 403.

14 *In re Grand Jury Subpoena Dated January 4, 1984,* 583 FSupp 991 (EDNY 1984).

15 *The American Tobacco Company, and Philip Morris, Inc v Mount Siniai School of Medicine and The American Cancer Society,* 880 F2d 1520 (1989).

16 *The American Tobacco Company.*

17 *The American Tobacco Company.*

18 *The American Tobacco Company.*

19 *Dow v Allen,* 672 F2d 1262 (7th Cir 1982).

20 *Dow* at 1273.

21 *The American Tobacco Company.*

22 *The American Tobacco Company.*

23 *The American Tobacco Company.*

24 *Wright v Jeep Corporation,* 547 FSupp 871, 874 (EDMich 1982).

25 *Wright* at 874–877.

26 17 USC Section 102(a).

27 17 USC at Section 101.

28 17 USC at Section102(b).

29 17 USC at Section106.

30 S. Seeley, Are Classroom Lecture Notes Protected by Copyright laws? The Case for Professors' Intellectual Property Rights. *Syracuse Law Journal,* 51, no. 1 (2001), 163–189.

31 Seeley, Classroom Lecture Notes Protected by Copyright laws?

32 17 USC Section 107.

33 *Williams v Weiss,* 237 Cal App 2d 726 (1969).

34 *Hays v Sony Corporation,* 847 F2d 412 (7th Cir 1988).

35 17 USC Section 101.

36 17 USC Section 101.

37 *Genzmer v Public Health Trust of Miami-Dade County,* 219 FSupp 2d 1275 (2002).

38 *Genzmer.*

39 *Genzmer.*

40 *Genzmer.*

41 *See Roeslin v District of Columbia,* 921 FSupp 793 (D.D.C. 1995).

42 *Vanderhurst v Colorado Mountain College,* 16 FSupp 2d 1297 (D Colo 1998).

43 *Vanderhurst* at 1306.

44 *Weinstein v University of Illinois,* 811 F2d 1091 (7th Cir 1987).

45 *Weinstein* at 1093.

46 17 USC Section 101.

47 *Seshadri v Kasraian,* 130 F3d 798 (7th Cir 1997).

48 *Seshadri* at 1094.

49 *Weissman v Freeman,* 868 F2d 1313 (2nd Cir 1989).

50 *Weissman* at 1315.

51 AAUP, Statement on Copyright. Available at: http://www.aaup.org/statements/Redbook/Spccopyr.htm.

52 AAUP, Statement on Copyright.
53 L. Leslie, Application of the Teacher Exception Doctrine to On-line Courses. *Journal of Legislation, 29,* no. 1 (2002), 109–124.
54 Leslie, Application of the Teacher Exception Doctrine to On-line Courses.
55 B. Garner, (Ed.) *Black's Law Dictionary* (7th ed.) (St. Paul, Minn.: West Group, 1999).
56 *Kucharczyk v Regents of the University of California,* 48 FSupp 2d 964 (ND Cal 1999).
57 *Kucharczyk* at 970.
58 *Kucharczyk* at 971.
59 *Webster's Ninth New Collegiate Dictionary* (Springfield, Mass.: Merriam-Webster Inc., Publishers, 1984), 1257.
60 W. Morris, (Ed.), *The American Heritage Dictionary of the English Language.* Boston: Houghton Mifflin Co., Publishers, 1979), 849.

The Service/Practice Role of Faculty

8

RICHARDEAN BENJAMIN AND MABLE H. SMITH

INTRODUCTION

During the first part of the 20th century, nursing students were instrumental in the provision of nursing services and care to patients in hospitals. Educators and hospitals collaborated on the diploma-based curricula for these nursing students, most of whom became employees of the hospitals where their original education took place. Nursing faculty were usually employees of the hospitals and their primary focus was educating students. The apprenticeship style of teaching-learning was the method of teaching the art and science of nursing to students. As nursing education moved into baccalaureate- and associate-degree-granting institutions and curricula included general education and liberal arts requirements, nursing students were assigned to a variety of health care agencies for clinical experiences.[1] Moving nursing programs into academic settings created a new set of priorities and problems for faculty. Faculty appointments, promotion, and tenure are made on the basis of teaching, clinical expertise, scholarship, and service. Teaching assignments in most nursing programs are based on a faculty member's clinical expertise, because faculty are preparing students to enter the world of health care practice. The advent of changes in health care environments, advances in technology, and varied patient care models mandate that faculty maintain their knowledge of health care environments and clinical competence. However, the means (faculty practice, as an academic component) to achieve the end may not be as valued and rewarded as teaching and scholarship activities.[2] This chapter explores the service component of the faculty role and its related issues.

andi James has been a faculty member at Monitor Merrimack University for over 10 years where she teaches medical surgical nursing. Sandi's teaching schedule includes a 3-credit lecture course and two 4.5-credit clinical courses. In addition to course obligations, the university requires that Sandi maintain office hours for a minimum of 4 hours per week. Because Sandi can satisfy her university obligations in 4 days, she elects to work at the local hospital 1 day during the week, plus some weekends if needed to supplement her income. Some other faculty members engage in similar practices. Recently, however, the university drafted a proposal that would require faculty members to report all outside employment for approval by the dean and to restrict the number of hours that faculty can engage in outside employment to 8 hours per week. All revenues generated from hours that exceed the 8-hour limit would be subject to surrender to the university. The thinking of Sandi and her colleagues is that they are meeting all their academic work obligations and should not be restricted from working on their own time. Furthermore, as a teacher, she does not have set hours, the salary paid by the university is far below what she could earn working two 12-hour shifts at the hospital, and she is legally required to remain current in her practice area. She cannot afford to give up the additional income, but will not work to give money to the university.

CRITICAL THINKING QUESTIONS

1. Does Sandi's practice activities constitute service within the definition of the service component of her academic requirements?
2. How should Sandi and her colleagues address the policy issue to administrators and/or the faculty senate?
3. Given the nature of nursing practice, should more emphasis be given to clinical practice than to other service areas when considering a faculty member for tenure and promotion?
4. Discuss the validity of Sandi's argument that she is legally required to practice to remain clinically competent?

ACADEMIC RESPONSIBILITIES: SERVICE COMPONENT

Professional service to academia is usually differentiated into three major categories and reflects activities that occur within the academic environment and those that are external to the college or university. The service component of academic responsibilities include service to the department, school, college, and university; service to the community; and service to the profession. Selected examples of service activities in each category are listed in Box 8.1.

Faculty practice is just one aspect of the overall category of service. However, given the time commitment involved in holding employment in health care environments, nursing faculty may erroneously equate time with significance.

Educational institutions should recognize that faculty practice is imperative in practice disciplines, such as nursing. Because faculty have the appropriate knowledge and skills in their clinical area of practice, they are able to supervise students in clinical environments. State boards of nursing and accrediting agencies mandate that students fulfill a specified number of clinical practice hours. Faculty, therefore have the dual roles of clinical and theory teacher.

Examples of Service Activities

SERVICE TO DEPARTMENT, SCHOOL, COLLEGE, AND UNIVERSITY

- Student advising
- Involvement with student organizations, such as Sigma Theta Tau, Student Nurses Association
- Service as a member or chair of committees and task forces
- Participation in special events, such as recruitment activity, marketing, and orientation

SERVICE TO THE COMMUNITY

- Speaking engagements
- Consulting
- Involvement in community forums and groups
- Teaching on health issues to community groups
- Volunteering or organizing blood drives, food banks, or health fairs

SERVICE TO THE PROFESSION

- Participation in and/or holding leadership positions in professional organizations
- Reviewing for publishing companies
- Organizing continuing education activities
- Maintaining clinical competency, professional practice
- Mentoring

Faculty who are supervising students and not current in their practice area create increased liability for themselves, the educational institution, the clinical facility, and students.

FACULTY PRACTICE

Nursing is a practice discipline and its faculty are faced with the dual role of educator and clinician. With the shift of nursing education from hospitals to universities, nurse academicians are challenged to maintain their clinical competence and credibility with nurses and students. The American Association of Colleges of Nursing (AACN) and National Organization of Nurse Practitioner Faculties (NONPF) have endorsed faculty practice as a means to cement the relationship between education and service. Although nursing faculty are charged with educating students in theoretical/didactic content and teaching clinical skills, the majority of faculty themselves do not practice.[3] Due to nursing shortages and financial constraints in health care environments, the profession is seeking ways to restore and strengthen the connection between nursing education and practice. In its vision for nursing education for this decade, the AACN called for teaching based "in the reality of clinical practice," acknowledging that this development is likely to result in "practice becoming as integral to the faculty role as teaching, research, and service."[4] Faculty practice is essential for nurse educators to gain collegial respect, improve communication with students, and increase realism in the classroom.[5]

Definition of Faculty Practice

The definitions of faculty practice are varied. Its definitions and characteristics range from joint appointments to "moonlighting" to health centers run by nursing faculties.[6] "Faculty practice includes all aspects of the delivery of nursing service through the roles of clinician, educator, researcher, consultant, and administrator."[7] It is also viewed as a formal arrangement between a clinical facility and an educational institution whereby a faculty member interacts for or on behalf of clients. In contrast to clinical supervision and moonlighting, faculty practice is normally conducted in a scholarly and professional environment with outcome goals of research and publications. However, the definition that is consistent with the focus of nursing education relates faculty practice to "the provision or facilitation of the delivery of nursing care through advanced behaviors or research, mentoring, leadership, collaboration, and direct patient care with outcomes of scholarship and student learning."[8] Incorporated in each of the above definitions is the premise that faculty practice is a professional endeavor.

The variety of faculty practice implementation methods contributes to its varied definitions. On the one hand, faculty practice involves a work agreement that allows the faculty member to provide services at various locations, such as a school of nursing or university medical center facility, as a component of faculty's teaching workload. Yet another description of faculty practice includes an arrangement where nursing faculty members maintain employment outside of the university setting during nonacademic hours. Some colleges and universities require faculty to document their practice on faculty activity forms, while others view it as part-time employment unrelated to academic responsibilities.

Problems Integrating Faculty Practice

The professional model of nursing education includes clinical competence for its educators. Nurses maintain their clinical competence through the practice of nursing. Yet practice or service has not been valued or rewarded in the university setting. Although colleges and universities publicly advocate the traditions of teaching, service, and research, it is research and publications that garner the rewards at tenure and promotion time.[9] Clinical practice, often categorized as service, rarely enters the equation for rewards in the academic setting. The profession is continuing to demand increasing faculty involvement in practice although the academic environment does not provide a means to evaluate and reward this component of the faculty member's role.[10]

Faculty practice is easier to implement for nontenured, part-time, and adjunct faculty who do not have research and publication mandates. Most nursing faculty appointments are based on a full-time position within the academic unit. Employment contracts extend for a 9- or 10-month period, thus leaving faculty members without a source of income during the off months. Others, especially certified nurse practitioners or clinical specialists, must maintain a consistent level of practice to meet licensing and certification requirements. Working in clinical practice only in the summer or off months may not be feasible when one expects to establish long-term working relationships with an employer. However, working evening and night shifts and on the weekends during the academic term can create physical and emotional hardships.

FACULTY PRACTICE MODELS

Faculty practice provides an excellent opportunity to ensure that faculty remain up-to-date academicians and competent clinicians and are an excellent way for schools of nursing to provide leadership to the nursing community.[11] Several models exist that provide a theoretical and practical basis for integrating education and practice:

- Unification model
- Collaboration model

- Integration model
- Dyad model
- Research joint appointment
- Reverse joint appointment
- Private practice model
- Community-based services model

Each model is briefly described below:

The Unification model implemented at Rush University in Chicago and at Rochester University (Strong Memorial Hospital) in Rochester is a matrix organizational model in which the dean of the school of nursing is also the director of nursing service. Departmental chairpersons are leaders in education and service. Both Rush and Strong have combined university and hospital administrations, which facilitated the development of the model.[12]

The Collaboration model was developed at Case Western Reserve University with funding from a Kellogg Foundation grant. The model allowed for collaboration with the school of nursing and university hospitals. Under the structure of the model, various positions within the school of nursing and nursing department have shared appointments, which require that a specific percentage of time is allocated between the hospital nursing department and the school of nursing. The shared appointments included shared costs.[13]

The Integration model involves nursing centers that allow faculty and students to participate in direct care of clients in facilities that are under the direction of the school of nursing. The nursing centers, also known as academic nursing centers, are an integral part of faculty workload assignments that allow for clinical research for staff and students, generate income, provide high-quality care to the community, and promote visibility of faculty providing learning opportunities for students and clinical practice of faculty.[14]

The Dyad model of collaboration involves sharing services without sharing of cost. At the University of Maryland, faculty members were paired with clinical nurse specialists in the hospital and joint projects in education, practice, and research were implemented. Outcomes of the dyad model included increased job satisfaction for the clinical nurse specialists.[15]

The research joint appointment collaboration emerged when departments of nursing established the position of director of nursing research as a joint appointment with a school of nursing. The purpose was to implement research findings in practice and improve clinical decision making of practicing nurses. In this arrangement the researcher is a faculty member at a university school of nursing with an interest in conducting a research program in a hospital. The researcher educates the hospital staff about the research process and dissemination of research findings within the practice setting. Costs are shared between the nursing department and the university school of nursing.[16]

The reverse joint appointment (RJA) is the result of the need to add strong clinical faculty to schools of nursing. Albert Einstein Medical Center and La Salle University School of Nursing sought to test another model of faculty practice where master's prepared clinicians and nurse practitioners (NPs) were appointed as faculty to the school of nursing. The practitioner-educator role was labeled the reverse joint appointee, from practice to education. The characteristic features of this role required that the school of nursing purchase 40% of the RJA's time from the practice setting for a 9-month period. This includes two days of clinical teaching per week and attendance at all faculty-related meetings. The intent is that the clinical appointees would influence and participate in curricular decisions with the full-time faculty in the school of nursing.[17]

The private practice model, also known as "moonlighting," is when a faculty member practices nursing independent of any formal arrangement between the university and the clinical setting. This type of practice does not have the major aims of research and scholarship and may not be classified as faculty practice.

The *community-based services model* is the result of the changing focus of health care and nursing moving from the hospital to the community. Nursing faculty have been active in developing community-based health promotion programs in a variety of settings. These settings include homeless shelters, worksites, apartment complexes, and student and school-based clinics. Faculty provide clinical services to clients. They also serve as preceptors for students and mentor staff in these facilities.

A major barrier to faculty practice is its physical and emotional impact. Individuals holding joint appointments have reported work overload, feelings of discomfort moving between two different cultures, and frustration from the demands of two different systems. Another barrier is that institutional policies do not support and reward dual practice. Models that integrate faculty practice are more faculty-friendly than those that have practice as an "additive" component.

COMPENSATION FOR PRACTICE

Faculty members who perform clinical practice are entitled to compensation. A number of universities recognize and have capitalized on the marketability of the services of their faculty.

> "*Universities today see themselves as the total consumer of faculty time, talents and revenue. As a result revenue earned outside the university may be restricted, encumbered, or closely monitored. Therefore it is essential that these same institutions develop a culture and methods that recognize and reward practice activities. All incentive plans and recognition efforts are likely to prove futile if faculty practice activities are not valued by the university as an important component of the faculty role.*" [18]

The action taken by the University of Pittsburgh is an example of how faculty practice can be successfully incorporated into academia. Faced with a growing number of faculty electing not to pursue tenure-track appointments because of the competing demands of service (clinical practice) and research, the university decided to establish research and clinical track pathways. The research track is a tenure-track appointment; whereas, the clinical pathway is not tenure-earning. Criteria for the clinical track were established and included 4 hours of clinical practice per week in the area of the faculty's teaching responsibility in an agency where students have their clinical rotations. Faculty members receive 20% of the earnings with the remaining amounts distributed internally within the school or college.[19]

Faculty practice can generate significant income. The University of Texas-Houston Health Science Center School of Nursing generated an income of $1,188,609 from several faculty practice activities during a 1-year fiscal period.[20] Compensating faculty who work in nurse-managed health centers can take many different forms, from direct allocation to the faculty member for a specific percentage of the revenue generated, bonus pay, reduction in teaching assignments to flex credits. A credit system allows the faculty member to accumulate points to support teaching assistants, travel, and capital equipment such as computer hardware or professional dues and other expenses.[21] The decision to include practice in the faculty role may stem from the need to secure additional revenue sources to support the mission of the school and better compensate the faculty. Institutions value practice as a means to maintain a current curricula, maintain clinical expertise, collaborate for scholarship and research, improve patient care, and capitalize on opportunities for external funding. Practice is an integral part of the educational process, because it allows clinical instructors to remain current on technological advances and new approaches to treatment and to integrate research and theory into clinical practice. In essence, nursing is an innovative and constantly changing practice profession.

UNIVERSITY POLICIES REGARDING OUTSIDE EMPLOYMENT

Faculty practice is necessary for a practice profession that is accountable to the public for quality of care, current clinical skills, and effective teaching. "To believe that one can teach what one cannot practice is logically inconsistent."[22] Policies related to faculty practice emphasize that full-time faculty members are expected to provide full-time service to the university. Universities encourage external activities if they do not interfere with the faculty member's responsibilities to the university or create conflicts of interest, as determined by the department's chair or dean. External employment must also contribute to or enhance the faculty's academic and professional growth. Therefore, it is not uncommon for universities to require faculty to report and get approval from their administrators. The university may also impose time limitations on outside practice, which may range from a certain percentage of the faculty time per week to a specified number of hours per month. Exceptions to the time limitations are usually made on a case-by-case basis.

Courts have upheld outside employment policies that require surrender of additional revenue or siphoning off when faculty exceed the allowed number of outside employment hours. In *Gross v University of Tennessee,*[23] the university policy required full-time medical faculty to sign a medical practice income agreement that allowed medical earning above a certain level to be siphoned off. The purpose was to promote a greater commitment to academic responsibilities by limiting the doctor's outside practice. Upholding the policy, the Court ruled that it is reasonable to believe that outside employment could interfere with academic responsibilities and the method used to siphon off income was reasonably related to achieving educational purposes.[24] The goal is to ensure that faculty devote their time and energies to academic endeavors.

Deans and department staff will be hesitant to grant permission if faculty practice occurs during regular business hours or requires the use of university equipment, supplies, or facilities. Faculty in schools of nursing seeking permission to engage in outside employment must consider their teaching, research, and service activities in relation to their proposed work hours. In essence, the faculty's primary responsibilities are to the university.

Faculty whose external activities violate university policy or interfere with the performance of their educational-related responsibilities can be terminated. In *Marks v New York University,*[25] the Court found that the university had not breached its contract with a professor who held full-time teaching positions at two different universities. NYU's policy limited outside employment for faculty to one day per week to ensure they maintain a sustained level of commitment to their academic responsibilities. Professor Marks violated the terms of her employment as outlined in the university's handbook.

PROFESSIONAL DIMENSION

Faculty practice is necessary to remain competent in one's clinical area of practice. It also provides the opportunity to bridge the gap between education and service to improve learning for students, while simultaneously maintaining faculty expertise. Clinical faculty who practice independently on the units or in the hospitals where they take students have an advantage because they are familiar with the facility's policies and procedures, the nursing staff, and the type of patients. These faculty can usually rely on their nurse colleague to facilitate students' learning experiences. External practice activities must be fulfilled within the parameters established by educational institutions' policies.

ETHICAL DIMENSION

Faculty may encounter difficulty trying to practice independently to maintain clinical competence and meet the university requirements for tenure. Ethics mandate that faculty who are not clinically competent in their practice area refrain from supervising students. Educational institutions must give faculty practice its appropriate relevance. Faculty who maintain competence through outside employment must structure their time so they fulfill their teaching and scholarship activities. They must be mindful that their external activities and reputation can reflect on the educational institution.

Implications for Educators

- The academic model normally has four criteria for promotion: research, scholarship, teaching, and service. Clinical practice, often categorized as service, rarely enters the equation for rewards in the academic setting.
- Faculty practice is a labor-intensive endeavor, which is not recognized in many higher education environments as a significant educational component.
- Attempts to integrate faculty practice with other academic responsibilities—teaching, practice, and research—are complex and demanding for tenure-track faculty.
- Faculty can select one of several models to use as a guide in structuring their practice activities.
- Faculty practice has been viewed as valuable to the education of nursing students.
- Tradition in higher education mandates against labeling faculty practice as scholarship, which is reserved for those activities that increase the national and international visibility of faculty members, such as publications, presentations, and grants.
- Faculty practice is a local activity conducted in a well-defined and limited space.

- Review university policy on outside employment.
- Complete all required paperwork for outside employment and obtain permission, if required.
- Avoid situations that may conflict with academic responsibilities.
- Explore a faculty practice model that would benefit the faculty group. Remember, models can be creatively developed to meet the faculty's needs.

Strategies to Avoid Legal Problems

RESPONSE TO CRITICAL THINKING QUESTIONS

1. Does Sandi's practice activities constitute service within the definition of the service component of her academic requirements?

Faculty practice is considered a component of academic service. Many colleges and universities recognize that service involves activities external to the university. The current academic climate calls for increased faculty accountability in clinical expertise. Faculty employed in institutions with a faculty practice model will probably have fewer conflicts than faculty who engage in moonlighting activities. Although undertaken primarily for monetary compensation, moonlighting results in knowledge of the health care environment, improvement of clinical skills, professional development, and improved relations with clinical staff. Courts have upheld revenue surrender policies when they are related to fulfilling the objective of ensuring faculty remain focused on their academic responsibilities.

2. How should Sandi and her colleagues address the policy issue to administrators and/or the faculty senate?

Many college and universities administrators do not have intricate knowledge of nursing practice and the requirements placed on faculty. The first approach is to educate them about the requirements imposed on nursing faculty by accrediting agencies and the profession. For example, the National League for Nursing's Accrediting Commission (NLNAC) and Commission on Collegiate Nursing Education (CCNE) have developed specific accreditation criteria related to faculty competency in the area of instructional responsibility. The dichotomy for nursing faculty is that the profession is continuing to demand increasing faculty involvement in practice, although the work environment does not provide a means to evaluate and reward this aspect of the service component of the faculty member's role. Just as artists need to create their own art, or musicians need to practice their craft, nursing instructors need to practice nursing.[26] Institutionally imposed time constraints must be flexible for faculty in practiced disciplines. Nurses and other health care professionals work according to previously defined shifts. Therefore, a faculty member working a 3 P.M. to 11 P.M. shift may technically have an overlap with "normal business hours" if defined as 9 A.M.-5 P.M. However, faculty members do not work "defined" hours. Unless faculty compensation is based on a predetermined model, faculty should oppose any income-surrender policies. A better practice for faculty who cannot adhere to the imposed time limit is to change the classification of the faculty from full time to part time, obtain approved release time, or seek some other similar activity.

3. **Given the nature of nursing practice, should more emphasis be given to clinical practice than to other service areas when considering a faculty member for tenure and promotion?**

Faculty who are responsible for teaching undergraduate- or masters-level students with a clinical focus (e.g., nurse practitioners, clinical nurse specialists, nurse anesthetists, midwives) must be clinically competent. They need to practice in their specialty area. However, any college or university that is striving for national recognition must have faculty with national and international visibility and engaged in quality scholarly endeavors. This means that its scholarship cannot be limited to faculty practice. Because nursing is a practice discipline, the dean and/or chair must determine the appropriate weight and relevance of faculty practice, in relation to the mission and goals of the educational institution.

4. **Discuss the validity of Sandi's argument that she is legally required to practice to remain clinically competent?**

Sandi has a valid argument in that clinical faculty who supervise students should be competent in their practice areas. The same dangers that hospitals encounter in floating nurses to units outside of their clinical expertise exist with having unprepared and incompetent faculty supervising students. The risk for liability is heightened. Clinical faculty are charged with facilitating learning in a safe environment, while minimizing potential litigious situations. This entails being able to foresee and predict potential problems. Seasoned clinical faculty have insight into the type of patients and resultant risks and complications. In essence, they are able to provide competent care to patients, while simultaneously protecting students from errors. Unseasoned or unprepared clinical faculty create risk of liability for students, to themselves, the clinical facility, and the employing institution.

NOTES

1 J. Felts and R. Toms, Linking Practice and Education. *Journal of Nursing Administration,* 30, no. 9 (2000), 405–407. Retrieved January 10, 2004, http://netserv.lib.odu.edu.

2 E. B. Rudy, N. A. Anderson, L. Dudjak, S. N. Kobert, and R. A. Miller, Faculty Practice: Creating a New Culture. *Journal of Professional Nursing,* 11, no. 2 (1995), 78–83.

3 S. E. Barger, K. E. Nugent, and W. C. Bridges, Nursing Faculty Practice: An Organizational Perspective. *Journal of Professional Nursing,* 8, no. 5 (1992), 263–270.

4 American Association of Colleges of Nursing. A Vision of Baccalaureate and Graduate Nursing Education: The Next Decade. (1997). Available at http://www.aacn.nche.edu/Publications/positions/vision.htm.

5 I. Mauksch, Faculty Practice: Professional Imperative. *Nurse Educator,* 5 (1980), 21–24.

6 L. M. Martin, Nursing Faculty Practice: Challenges for the Future. *Journal of Advanced Nursing,* 21, no. 4 (1995), 743–747. Retrieved November 4, 2003,

7 M. Potash & D. Taylor, Nursing Faculty Practice: Models and Methods (Washington, D.C.: National Organization of Nurse Practitioner Faculties, 1993).

8 M. Campbell, Multidisciplinary Faculty Practice and Community Partnership. *Holistic Nursing Practice,* 7, no. 4 (1993), 20–27.

9 C. M. Hutelmyer and G. F. Donnelly, Joint Appointments in Practice Positions. *Nursing Administration Quarterly,* 20, no. 4 (1996), 71–79. Retrieved November 5, 2003, http://web3.infotrac.galegroup.com/itw/infomark/351.

10 K. Herr, Faculty Practice as a Requirement for Promotion and Tenure: Receptivity, Risk, and Threats Perceived. *Journal of Nursing Education,* 28 (1989), 347–353.

11 McNeal & Mackey, (1995)

12 A. Blazeck, et al. Unification: Nursing Education and Nursing Practice. *Nursing and Health Care,* 3, no. 1 (1982), 18–24.

13 Blazeck et al., Unification: Nursing Education and Nursing Practice.

14 S. Barger and R. Crumpton, Public Health Nursing Partnership: Agencies and Academe. *Nurse Educator,* 16, no. 4 (1991), 16–19.

15 I. Ingber and K. Peddicord, The Dyad Model of Nursing Practice. *Nursing Connections,* 2, no. 1, 5–17.

16 Hutelmyer and Donnelly, Joint Appointments in Practice Positions.

17 Hutelmyer and Donnelly, Joint Appointments in Practice Positions.

18 S. K. Krafft, Faculty Practice: Why and How. *Nurse Educator,* 23, no. 4 (1998), 45–48. Retrieved November 4, 2003, http://netserv.lib.odu.edu.

19 E. B. Rudy, N. A. Anderson, L. Dudjak, S. N. Kobert, and R. A. Miller, Faculty Practice: Creating a New Culture. *Journal of Professional Nursing,* 11, no. 2 (1995), 78–83.

20 McNeil & Mackey

21 Krafft, Faculty Practice:Why and How.

22 R. Lassan, Nursing Faculty Practice: A Valid Sabbatical Request? *Nursing Forum,* 29, no. 2 (1994), 10–14.

23 *Gross v University of Tennessee,* 620 F2d 109 (6th Cir 1980).

24 *Gross* at 110.

25 *Marks v New York University,* 61 F Supp 2d 81 (SDNY 1999).

26 Martin, Nursing Faculty Practice: Challenges for the Future.

Ethical Framework of Higher Education

9

Ethical Considerations in Education Environments

INTRODUCTION

There is often a thin line between what is illegal and what is unethical. While the law may not prohibit the commission or omission of certain behaviors, educational institutions may nevertheless prohibit them because they are unethical. For example, it is not illegal for faculty to engage students in external business ventures. However, it can be unethical because students may feel that they must participate or suffer negative consequences. The apparent power difference between faculty and students is a strong underlying factor in many ethical violations. Ethical concerns are pervasive throughout academia, from selection of textbooks to publishing a research article. This chapter identifies several ethical principles and ethical issues as they relate to faculty in higher education environments.

Donna Boyerts, an assistant professor of nursing, is scheduled to have her third-year review next year. She has not fully developed a research agenda, but has published three articles and has average student evaluations in teaching. The department chairperson reduced her teaching load for the first year to allow for the development of her research agenda and publication of research results. Donna has a regular teaching load during her second year and is finding it extremely difficult to balance scholarship, research, and teaching. She often comes to class unprepared and compensates by stimulating class discussions on the topics, relying on the honor students to provide the substance of the topics. Several students have complained that the textbook did not adequately provide information on the assigned topics and the tests did not relate to the assigned readings. Donna was paid $2,500 to review and provide comments as to the relevance of the book for junior-level medical-surgical nursing students. After a cursory review, Donna gave the book excellent ratings and adopted it for her course. She continues, however, to select test questions from the test bank derived from the previous textbook. Based on the students' performance on the tests, Donna lowered the curve to ensure that students received good grades.

Several weeks into the semester, Lisa, a 23-year-old single mother, came to Donna's office in tears. She confided that she is involved in an unwanted sexual relationship with Dr. Drew, the department chairperson, and does not know how to "get out of it." Lisa attributed her poor academic performance and probationary status to "relationship stress." She came to Donna because she listened to students and seemed genuinely concerned about their academic progress. Aware that the chairperson's recommendations on progression, promotion, and tenure issues were highly regarded, Donna told Lisa to inform the chairperson that although he was a wonderful person, the relationship was over and that she had confided in her about the situation. Donna told Lisa that although the chairperson was her boss, her students were more important and that she would risk negative repercussions to protect them. Donna suspected that Lisa was not telling the truth; however, she could use this to her advantage. Donna reasoned that if she communicated to the chairperson her support of him, then he would in turn be supportive of her during the third-year review. Feeling empowered, Lisa indicated that she, in turn, would protect Donna if the chairperson attempted any vendetta toward her. However, she preferred to keep this incident a secret, because she had been involved in relationships with other professors and she did not want that to come out. Two weeks later, Donna made an appointment with the chairperson to discuss her overall performance and his recommendations for her third-year review.

CRITICAL THINKING QUESTIONS

1. Identify at least three ethical violations in this scenario and discuss how each violation should be handled.
2. In the absence of a policy prohibiting such relationships, should faculty members engage in intimate relationships with students?

Colleges and universities are not immune from cases involving breaches of ethical standards. Ethics involves one's conformity to standards of professional conduct and norms and considers the duties that professors owe to the academic community. If the higher education community is indeed a microcosm of society, the magnitude and array of these breaches should not be troublesome. However, breaches of ethics in academia cast a shadow on the academic community and can provide the basis for disciplinary actions against faculty members. Many colleges and universities follow the ethical duties and responsibilities stated in the American Association of University Professors (AAUP) Statement on Professional Ethics, which are summarized below:

- Professors should practice intellectual honesty. They must "accept the obligation to exercise critical self-discipline and judgment in using, extending, and transmitting knowledge"; and they must not allow subsidiary interests to "seriously hamper or compromise their freedom of inquiry."[1]
- Professors should be role models for the meaning of ethical standards. They should treat students with respect and "adhere to their proper roles as intellectual guides and counselors." They should strive to "foster honest academic conduct" and to ensure that students are evaluated honestly and according to established criteria. Professors should maintain the confidences of students and refrain from exploitation, harassment and discriminatory behaviors. This includes giving students the proper credit and recognition for their contributions to professional and scholarly work.[2]
- Professors should demonstrate collegiality for and toward their colleagues.
- Professors should continuously strive to maintain the performance of their academic responsibilities and to balance external undertakings and obligations.

The AAUP acknowledges that, unlike the law and medical professions, which have professional organizations/entities to enforce their ethical codes and standards, the academic profession bears the burden of maintaining professional integrity. It states,

> "*the individual institution of higher learning . . . should normally handle questions concerning propriety of conduct within its own framework by reference to a faculty group.*"[3]

The formation of ethics committees in higher education environments has been advocated to educate faculty on ethical issues and to investigate and dispose of the allegations either through dismissal of unfounded allegations or the proper handling of founded allegations.[4] Committee members should be "tenured faculty chosen for their record and reputation of integrity, sound and mature judgment, and commitment to the welfare of the institution."[5] These committees or designated members of the academic community are charged with self-policing and peer review to ensure adherence to professional integrity.

Equally important is the need for the institution to quickly investigate claims or perceptions of unethical conduct to avoid giving the impression of indifference to ethical violations. However, the process should be organized and carefully structured to protect the rights and reputation of those involved. Due to the sensitive nature of the issues and the potential negative consequences, all proceedings should be kept confidential.

ETHICAL THEORIES

Faculty members will encounter ethical dilemmas in the academic environment. Many dilemmas do not have a definite right or wrong and may be the subject of considerable debate. For example, as a faculty member, is it wrong to have students paint your house and build a deck? Is it wrong for a university to prohibit intimate faculty-student relationships? The manner in which one addresses these dilemmas is based on his or her values, beliefs, morals, and education. Ethical theories provide a basis for viewing one's actions or decisions. They consist of "fundamental beliefs about what is morally right or wrong and propose reasons for maintaining those beliefs."[6] They are also used as a basis for making decisions and resolving ethical conflicts. Although there are several ethical theories, the two theories most applicable to health care professionals and educators are deontology and utilitarianism.

Theory of Deontology

The theory of deontology focuses on one's duty or moral obligations to others, which is the basis for one's actions. This theory values individualism and espouses that every person is an end and not solely a means to another person's ends.[7] For example, inherent in faculty relationships with their students and colleagues are the duties and obligations to treat them with respect and dignity and to respect their status as "free, rational, responsible," and equal individuals.[8] The deontologist believes "that there is a particular rule that he or she must follow regardless of his or her desires or any foreseeable results."[9] To do otherwise is unacceptable, because righteous is defined as doing one's duty. The following scenario illustrates how the same situation could be interpreted in different ways. The school of nursing's policy is that students must pass each course with a grade of "C" or higher and students are terminated from the nursing program if they fail two courses. Michelle, the president of the Student Nurses Association, is very active at the national level and is considering running for president of the National Student Nurses Association. During her first semester in nursing school, she went through a divorce and a contested child custody care and failed medical-surgical clinicals due to poor attendance. She repeated the course and received a grade of "A" in that course and all subsequent nursing courses. Michelle enrolled in an online leadership course during the first semester of her senior year. Due to her busy schedule, which included being the student keynote speaker at "Legislative Day," which was held at the state's capital, fundraising to fund student-initiated activities, and attending faculty governance meeting as the student representative, Michelle overlooked a major assignment that was worth 35% of the final grade. The professor's policy is to only allow make-up work in cases of emergencies. The chairperson and two other professors have requested that Michelle be given an extra credit assignment to raise her grade or to allow her to complete the project with a one-grade drop. To resolve the conflict, the professor, using a deontology framework, would focus on his or her specific duties and responsibilities, which are guided by specific rules and principles related to student performance and the assignment of grades.

Theory of Utilitarianism

In contrast, an advocate of utilitarianism would consider that the act of assigning a failing grade is not in itself good or bad but must be viewed in relation to the outcome or consequences.[10] A person's actions are evaluated as right or wrong based on their consequences.[11] Is it in the best interest of the school, university, or community to fail a promising nursing student, future clinician in times of a nursing shortage, and future nursing leader? The theory of utilitarianism holds that the correct course of action is the one that creates the greatest good for the greatest number of people.[12] Good is usually viewed in terms of the greatest happiness for the greatest number of people. Although the concepts of "good" and "happiness" are relative terms without a common meaning, this theory causes one to consider the consequences of one's actions, in terms of all involved persons. The common good is weighed more heavily than the individual good. Therefore, in the situation earlier, the professor will evaluate the situation to determine the impact of altering grading policies on the school and university. She will also consider the consequences of failing and of passing Michelle. The goodness or rightness of an action is viewed from a totality perspective. The final decision will be based on what will create the greatest happiness for the greatest number of people.

ETHICAL PRINCIPLES

Consideration of ethical principles provides a strong foundation for decision making and interpersonal interactions. Ethical principles "help in thinking through difficult moral issues and in defending subsequent decisions."[13] They offer "a firm grounding for moral judgment that can be used to resolve ethical dilemmas and be given in justification of our actions."[14] They are used to determine one's role based on the nature of the relationship and to provide guidance in morality-based situations and/or dilemmas. When ethical principles are in conflict, faculty should carefully analyze the situation to determine the dominant principle, which is often decided based on one's morals and personal value system. Many times, ethical dilemmas do not provide answers; they create more questions. The incorporation of ethical principles in faculty roles and decision-making processes promote actions and conduct that respect the rights, integrity, and dignity of students and colleagues.

Principle of Autonomy

The principle of autonomy is based on the belief that an individual has the ability to reason, to engage in logical thought, and to decide on a course of action. Every competent adult has the power to make his or her own decisions and choices and to have those decisions or choices respected.[15] Autonomy is eroded when one infringes on the ability of another person to make free choices. For example, a professor was required to have 12 students enrolled before he could teach his summer elective course. Eleven students registered for the course. The professor asked his graduate assistant to register for the course, but he refused, indicating that he had planned to spend the summer with his family. After unsuccessfully trying to find another student to take the course, the professor again approached his graduate student and offered to allow him to take the course as an independent study. The student again refused because he did not want any academic-related obligations. Is the professor creating a situation where the student does not feel free to refuse? Should the professor continue to ask the student to enroll in the course? Because professors often recommend courses for students to take, is the professor in this case

Box 9.1

Ethical Violation of Autonomy

An ethical violation would occur if the faculty member continued to ask the student or if he used his authority to make the student register for the course. An ethical violation is present, if for example, if the student registered for the course after the professor made a comment such as, "You will not get the type of recommendation you need for the honor's graduate scholarship next year. Sometimes we have to scratch each other's backs." The professor's coercive behavior was unethical and breached the student's right to decide whether or not to take the course. In essence, the professor's own selfish interest impeded the student's right to free choice.

exercising his academic responsibilities under his advisement role? How much autonomy do students have in the faculty-student relationship? Box 9.1 discusses the ethical violation of autonomy in this situation.

Principle of Veracity

The principle of veracity relates to one's ability to tell the truth.[16] Information must be presented in an accurate, comprehensive, and objective manner to facilitate understanding and acceptance of the material presented. A Pulitzer Prize–winning tenured professor of history misrepresented his "military service during the Vietnam War," his participation in the civil rights movement, and his "role as an anti-war activist"[17] to his students for several years. Is this a violation of veracity? To what extent can professors alter actual facts to promote learning in the classroom? Is embellishing considered lying? How does a discussion of the professor's personal life impact the teaching-learning process? If the professor's accounts of his military service promoted student interest, should negative actions be taken against him? Box 9.2 discusses the ethical violation of veracity in this situation.

Box 9.2

Ethical Violation of Veracity

These fabrications violated his ethical duty to practice intellectual honesty and negatively affected his status in the academic community. One can only speculate as to how the misrepresentations affected his students. Elliot Gorn of Purdue Unversity stated, "To lie to our students about ourselves, regardless of motives, is to patronize them, to not trust them, to fail them utterly by putting our own needs—for approval, for popularity, for control over the classroom—over their rightful claim to honesty."[26] The professor was suspended for violating the ethics of his profession.[27] Students are captivated by professors' real-life stories, which can be very effective teaching strategies. For example, nursing faculty usually relate personal experiences with patients and their family to their students to emphasize key points and to bring a degree of realism to the content. These examples should be based on true versions of the professor's encounters. When the "truths" are changed to emphasize a particular point, the professor can effectively engage students in critical thinking exercises by requiring them to consider alternative perspectives.

Box 9.3

Ethical Violation of Fidelity

The professor violated the principle of fidelity because she made a promise that she did not intend to fulfill. She should have explained the nature and purpose of the assignment so students would have a clear understanding of its purpose and intended outcome. The use of students to fulfill or meet the faculty's outside consultation activities has ethical implications, which in this case was magnified by the professor's withholding of the truth. Sharing the actual outcome of the case would have been an added benefit and learning experience for the students. Professor Hinley also exploited the students for her personal gain, by making them do research that she was hired to do.

Principle of Fidelity

The principle of fidelity requires individuals to honor their promises and commitments to others.[18] For example, faculty should make every effort to adhere to outlined evaluation methods and to keep their promises. Professor Hinley was hired as a legal consultant for a unique medical malpractice case. Using a similar scenario, she divided her students into two trial groups, one representing the plaintiff and one for the defendant to prepare for a mock or practice trial. Each student in the "winning group" that developed the correct legal theory and strategy was promised five extra-credit points. Unknown to the students, there were no correct theories or strategies, because this was the first time the facts of this case would be litigated or tried in court. At best, students could only prepare persuasive arguments. Students were extremely diligent in their efforts, which required extensive analytical research and creativity in their arguments. After the mock trial, Professor Hinley explained that she was just testing a new teaching strategy and that students would not receive extra credit, but the project would count as a component of the participation grade. After numerous students voiced their displeasure, the professor increased the participation grade to count 10% toward the final course grade. Has the professor violated the principle of fidelity? Should students be told the purpose of assignments? Should professors use students to facilitate and assist in their consultation activities? How much of a difference would it make if students were told the reason behind the assignment since they would still have to complete the assignment? Did the professor correctly remedy the situation by increasing the participation grade? Box 9.3 discusses the ethical violation of fidelity in this situation.

Principle of Confidentiality

Faculty should respect and maintain the confidences of students or colleagues. Relationships with students and colleagues are encouraged to assist their intellectual and professional development. At times, confidences may be divulged that faculty should respect, but which may create a dilemma. For example, Jared confides in you that his clinical instructor, a highly regarded faculty member, made sexual innuendoes toward him. He requests guidance on how to handle the situation, but mandates that it be kept secret. University policy strictly forbids sexual harassment, which is a basis for termination. Faculty members

Ethical Violation of Confidentiality

Faculty have a responsibility to maintain student confidences unless someone is in danger of being hurt. For example, if a student confided that he or she planned to do harm to another person or student, the faculty may have a legal duty to report the student. However, absent the legal requirements associated with duty to a third party, faculty should strive to maintain student confidences. Jared should be encouraged to discuss the situation with the appropriate administrator who handles sexual harassment issues. The faculty member should also seek guidance in how to handle the dilemma of maintaining student confidences and upholding university policies.

must uphold and adhere to university policy. Do you inform Jared that the allegation must be reported? Do you tell Jared to rethink what happened and determine if he misinterpreted the situation? Would you discuss this with the professor? What if Jared had a vendetta against the professor and was going to various professors imparting the same information in an effort to discredit the professor? Should the professor be made aware of the accusation? Box 9.4 discusses the ethical violation of confidentiality in this situation.

Principle of Justice

The principle of justice requires equal and fair treatment of others.[19] As a general principle, faculty should adhere to the same policies and practices for each student and make available for all what is made available for one. For example, Professor Lockes allowed a student to write a paper for extra credit to increase her grade from a "C" to a "B" to keep her from losing an academic scholarship. Another student who had also gotten a "C" requested the same treatment because she needed to increase her GPA in order to get into graduate school. Several other students then made similar requests. Should the professor give all students the option of doing extra-credit? Can a professor make a benefit available to only one student? How much discretion does the professor have in exercising authority to make extra course assignments?

Has the professor violated an ethical principle if he does not allow all students to do extra-credit work? Box 9.5 discusses the ethical violation of justice in this situation.

Ethical Violation of Justice

If Professor Lockes denies their requests, he subjects himself to allegations of bias and unfairness and if he grants their requests, he has increased his workload. What may initially appear to be a helpful act may have widespread consequences if the overall impact is not considered. The principle of justice requires reflection on the overall impact. Professor Lockes should strive to treat all students fairly and provide uniform assignments and grading policies.

PROFESSIONAL DIMENSION

As professionals, faculty are viewed as possessing an extensive body of knowledge and holding competence in their specialty area. This is the basis of the trust, admiration, and respect given to them by students and the community. Education environments maintain a professional image through the behavior, attitude, and actions of their faculty. Thus, faculty should exemplify their knowledge in the classroom, in research, in professional presentations, and in service activities. This requires them to be prepared, have a syllabus and adhere to it, make revisions based on students' understanding and performance, and have time to provide assistance to students to help them grow and develop. They should refrain from crossing the line between personal and academic relationships.

ETHICAL DIMENSION

Many ethical issues do not involve the law. As a general rule, the law is not particularly suited to address ethical issues and problems. The law is a system of rules and processes that govern the actions and behavior of individuals in society.[20] A violation of the law usually results in criminal charges and/or monetary judgments. Therefore, when addressing an issue, one must first ask, does a law prohibit this action or behavior? If the answer is no, then one is most likely dealing with an ethical issue. For example, a faculty member alleged that the failure of administrators to enforce actions that promoted control over his classroom violated his First Amendment rights.[21] The dean and department head had berated the faculty in front of his students, interrupted his class, criticized his teaching, and changed his grade. The administrators' actions and behaviors did not infringe on the professor's freedom of speech and thus did not violate the law. However, they were clearly unprofessional and unethical. Ethics involve the norms, standards, and professional responsibilities members of a profession have toward others. Members of a profession are socialized into the role, either through formal education or by observing the behavior, conduct, and actions of senior members and by adhering to professional guidelines established by professional or licensing organizations. The basic guideline for behavior is to be honest, sincere and reasonable in one's dealings with others. To avoid ethical violations, faculty should treat students and colleagues with respect and dignity and be truthful in their dealings and interactions with others.

Implications for Educators

- Senior faculty should educate and assist junior faculty members to recognize and respond to issues involving ethical dilemmas.
- Ethical considerations for students entail treating them as responsible adults and avoid engaging them in personal service activities, financial/business ventures, and intimate/sexual relationships. All students should be respected and treated equally and fairly.
- Ethical considerations for the teaching role involve adequate preparation for teaching, from developing the syllabus to assigning the final grade.
- Ethical considerations for the research role involve protecting research participants, reporting fair and accurate results, and adhering to publishing guidelines.
- Ethical considerations for the service role involve balancing service activities to prevent interference with academic responsibilities.
- Ethical considerations for faculty involve treating colleagues in a collegial manner and assisting them to develop professionally in the academic environment.
- Ethical considerations for self involve being honest, professional, caring, and considerate in interactions and endeavors with others.

- Understand the faculty role and adhere to it.
- Read course materials prior to class and present current content.
- Design exams to test knowledge rather than to gain popularity.
- Assign grades based on students' performance on grading criteria outlined in the syllabi.
- Make extra credit options available to all students.
- Adopt textbooks based on their quality.
- Use university supplies, equipment, and staff for educational purposes.
- Maintain the confidences of students and colleagues.
- Attend lectures and workshops on ethical issues in higher education to remain updated on frequently encountered problems.
- Avoid engaging students in nonacademic activities.
- Refrain from intimate and sexual relationships with students.
- Ensure honesty in conducting and accuracy in reporting research findings.
- Uphold and enforce the institution's policies and procedures.
- Treat colleagues and students in a professional manner and with courtesy and respect.

Strategies to Avoid Legal Problems

RESPONSE TO CRITICAL THINKING QUESTIONS

1. Identify at least three ethical violations in this scenario and discuss how each violation should be handled.

- Donna has an obligation to promote honesty. She believes as false the allegations made against the chairperson; therefore, Donna should not lead the student to believe that she will assist her in promoting these charges. The effect of these allegations can have detrimental consequences on students, the chairperson, and the department. In addition, Donna may actually undermine her ability to develop positive relationships with her colleagues. The chairperson is entitled to respect and fairness. To protect the integrity of the academic environment and the student, Donna should guide the student to the office or committee who can conduct a proper investigation into the charges.

- The practice of accepting money from publishers to adopt their textbook is an ethical dilemma. If Donna had actually reviewed and selected the textbook because it was the best book available for the course, then it is not unprofessional conduct. However, to adopt a textbook motivated solely by financial gain is unethical behavior. Donna has engaged in the "commercialization of academic integrity"[22] by accepting payment for the adoption of the publisher's textbook. This practice created problems for Donna, because she did not review the textbook, reading assignments were inconsistent with the tests, and students did not get a quality education. Donna has an ethical duty to avoid selecting textbooks because of publisher incentives and to base her decision on what is considered the best textbook to provide students with quality content.

- Donna is not fulfilling her role as an intellectual counselor and guide to the students due to her inadequate preparation for class. Faculty members are charged with dissemination of knowledge. It is their responsibility to facilitate the development of the students' skills and knowledge of the subject matter. To accomplish this, the professor must be knowledgeable and his or her class presentations must be organized and informative. Donna should read the textbook and related materials to ensure she is adequately prepared for class. She can combine lectures or presentations with class discussion, but she should have enough knowledge of the topic to be an effective facilitator.

- Students are not being evaluated honestly and according to established criteria. The syllabus that Donna distributed should have outlined the assignments and grading policies. Inherent within these policies is the assumption that exams would be derived from class assignments and presentations or lectures. Although Donna changed textbooks, she continued to use the test bank developed for the old textbook. Therefore, students' grades were not based on class content. Curving the grades compensated for their poor performance, but does not address the frustration felt by students when they study course materials, only to have an exam that is unrelated to that material. Donna is also exploiting the honor students by, in essence, making them teach the class. When used correctly, class discussion is an excellent teaching strategy.

2. **In the absence of a policy prohibiting such relationships, should faculty members engage in intimate relationships with students?**

Faculty-student relationships that extend beyond the academic environments into business, service, financial, and intimacy can create numerous ethical issues. Faculty should carefully assess the potential impact that these relationships can have on students, colleagues, and the university. Problems often emerge because the power differential between student and faculty create the potential for, an inference of, or actual situations of exploitation, conflicts of interests, and erosion of academic integrity.[23] Little guidance is provided to faculty members by professional organizations in defining their relationship with students.[24] However, faculty should recognize that the "line between an appropriate professional faculty-student relationship and one that is exploitative or compromises faculty objectivity is not always clearly drawn, and as a relationship extends into more personal realms and increases in intensity, both potential benefits and risks increase."[25] The best course of action is to avoid any relationship that gives the appearance of unprofessionalism.

NOTES

1 AAUP, Statement on professional ethics, 1987. Available at: http://www.aaup.org/statements/Redbook/Rbethics.htm.

2 AAUP, Statement on professional ethics, 1987. Available at: http://www.aaup.org/statements/Redbook/Rbethics.htm.

3 AAUP, Statement on professional ethics, 1987. Available at: http://www.aaup.org/statements/Redbook/Rbethics.htm.

4 R. B. Sweeney, Ethics for Academics. *Management Accounting* (USA), 74, no. 8 (1993), 14–17.

5 Sweeney at 16. Ethics for Academics.

6 J. T. Catalano, *Ethical and Legal Aspects of Nursing* (2nd ed.) (Pennsylvania: Springhouse Corp., 1995).

7 E. L. Bandman, Tough Calls: Making Ethical Decisions in the Care of Older Adults. *Geriatrics,* 49, no. 12 (1994), 46–51.

8 K. A. Strike, and J. F. Soltis, The Ethics of Teaching (3rd ed.) (New York: Teachers College Press, 1998).

9 G. L. Husted, and J. H. Husted, Ethical Decisions Making in Nursing (St. Louis: Mosby-Year Book, Inc., 1991), 61.

10 Bandman, Tough Calls: Making Ethical Decisions in the Care of Older Adults.

11 Bandman, Tough Calls: Making Ethical Decisions in the Care of Older Adults.

12 S. Denig, and T. Quinn, Ethical Dilemmas for School Administrators. *High School Journal*, 84, no. 4 (2001), 43–54.

13 A. Limentani, The Rule of Ethical Principles in Health Care and the Implications for Ethical Codes. *Journal of Medical Ethics,* 25, no. 5 (1999), 394–398.

14 Limentani, The Role of Ethical Principles in Health Care and the Implications for Ethical Codes, 396.

15 E. Bandman, and B. Bandman, *Nursing Ethics Through the Life Span* (4th ed.) (Englewood diffs, N.J.: Prentice-Hall), 2002.

16 Bandman and Bandman, *Nursing Ethics Through the Life Span.*

17 W. W. Roworth, *Professional Ethics, Day by Day.* Academe, 2002. Available at: http://www.aaup.org/publications/Academe/02JF/02jfrow.htm.

18 Bandman and Bandman, *Nursing Ethics Through the Life Span.*

19 Bandman and Bandman, *Nursing Ethics Through the Life Span.*

20 G. Pozgar, *Legal Aspects of Health Care Administrators* (8th ed.) (Mass: Jones & Bartlett Publishers, 2003).

21 *Parate v. Isibor,* 868 F2d 821 (6th Cir. 1989).

22 T. Bartlett, Selling Out: A Textbook Example. *The Chronicle of Higher Education* (June 27, 2003), A8–A10.

23 P. A. Rupert, and D. L. Holmes, Dual Relationships in Higher Education. *Journal of Higher Education,* 68, no. 6 (1997), 660–679.

24 Rupert and Holmes, Dual Relationships in Higher Education.

25 Rupert and Holmes, Dual Relationships, in Higher Education, 662.

26 Roworth, Professional Ethics, Day by Day.

27 Roworth, Professional Ethics, Day by Day.

A

Abrogate. To annul, make void, or abolish.

Absolute Immunity. A complete and unlimited exemption from all civil liability.

Academic (judicial) Deference. The reluctance of courts to interfere with academic decisions of faculty and administrators.

Academic Freedom. The ability of faculty to speak freely and openly on academic, political, and societal issues without fear of negative consequences by administrators and external individuals.

Acceptance. An agreement to accept the terms of an offer in a contract.

Anecdotal Notes. Written comments and notes of a student's performance made by a faculty member in the course of certain academic experiences, such as clinical rotations.

Appellant. A party who, dissatisfied with the outcome or decision of the lower court, appeals to a higher court to reverse or modify the outcome or decision.

Appellee. A party who wins in the lower court and responds to appellant's appeal of the lower court's ruling by asking a higher court to uphold the decision.

Arbitrary and Capricious. Unpredictable and impulsive actions and decisions that are based on bias and prejudices rather than on established policies and procedures.

At-large Position. A position that is not associated with any predetermined entity and usually represents the general public or goal.

Autonomy. The right to self-determination and to make independent decisions.

B

Blind Review. A review of a manuscript or other writings where the reviewer does not know the identity of the author or contributor.

Bona Fide. An action that is sincere, genuine, and made in good faith.

Breach of Contract. The failure of one party to a contract to fulfill the terms and conditions outlined in the contract.

C

Collegial. Being friendly and mutually respectful of others.

Color of the Law. Presenting or representing that one has the authority of the position; appearance of valid power and authority.

Compensatory Relief. Payment of monetary or other type of damages to a person as compensation for any injury or wrong.

Confidentiality. Maintaining the words, expressions, and confidences or secrets of another.

Consideration. A mutually agreed upon benefit between parties to a contract in exchange for the performance of an act or refraining from certain acts.

Contract. A legally binding agreement between two or more competent parties (individuals) that outlines the terms and conditions of the agreement.

Contract of Adhesion. A contract that contains preestablished or standard terms that are usually non-negotiable and signed by an individual with substantially less or no bargaining power.

Contract Theory. A theory describing the relationship between a faculty and student as based on legal obligations and mutually accepted terms.

Copyright. The legal right granted to certain individuals, such as writers, composers, publishers, and the like, to exclusive rights and ownership of their works. Copyright protects works fixed in a tangible medium of expression.

Cyberspace. Related to electronic environments, including the Internet and World Wide Web.

D

De Novo. Means "a new trial." An appeals court will hear the case as if there had not been a previous trial.

Declaration. A formal announcement or statement.

Declaratory Judgment. A judgment that establishes the legal rights or obligations of the parties to resolve a dispute about a legal right but does not award any damages.

Declaratory Relief. A court order that declares the legal rights of the parties.

Defendant. The person who is being sued and must defend against the lawsuit.

Deference. Deferring or yielding to the belief, act, or judgment of another person or entity.

Deontology. The ethical theory that focuses on a person's obligation or duty to another person.

Derivative Manuscript. A manuscript that is based on a previous work but contains new materials.

Derivative Work. A work based on a preexisting copyrightable work that requires the permission of the original copyright holder before it can be reproduced.

Discretionary Function. An act or deed that involves the exercise of personal judgment, conscience, or discretion of the decision maker.

Disparate Impact. A neutral policy or employment practice that has a discriminatory effect or overtone.

Disparate Treatment. A practice or policy that is discriminatory.

Due Process. The formulation and implementation of certain rules and procedures to govern hearings and other administrative actions that are designed to protect the rights of others.

E

Employment-at-will. Employment that can be terminated by either employer or employee at any time for any or no reason.

Estoppel. A defense that is asserted when one has reasonably and in good faith relied on the fraudulently or misrepresented facts of another. Prevents one from arguing a previously established truth.

F

Fair Use. The use of a limited amount of a copyrighted work without obtaining permission of the copyright owner. Fair use is usually measured in relation to the totality of the work and the market effect.

Fidelity. The ability to remain loyal to one's obligations and commitments.

G

Good Faith. Sincere, honest belief, no ill or illegal intent.

H

Hostile Work Environment. A form of sexual harassment in which the employee is subjected to unwelcome sexual innuendos, comments, or physical behaviors.

I

Immunity. A legal exemption from lawsuits that is granted to certain individuals.

Injunction. A court order to prevent or enforce an action.

Injunctive Relief. A court order commanding an action or prohibiting the continuation of an action.

In Loco Parentis. An early theory describing the faculty-student relationship that translates into faculty standing "in the place of parents" and thus had widespread authority of students.

J

Judicial Deference. See academic deference.

Justice. Being fair and treating everyone equally.

L

Liberty Interest. A right to be free to engage in one's chosen profession and be free from arbitrary restraint.

Limited Immunity. See qualified immunity.

M

Monograph. A scholarly book or pamphlet on a specific and limited topic.

Moral Turpitude. Conduct that involves dishonesty, fraud, or unethical behavior.

N

Negligence Theory. A theory describing the faculty-student relationship as based on a defined duty, that if breached would subject the education institution to liability for damages that were caused by the breach.

Nontenured. Lack of job security. Faculty members can be dismissed without the safeguard of due process of law.

O

Offer. The act of presenting a promise to refrain from doing something that one has a right to do or to do something that one is not obligated to do.

P

Patent. An agreement between the government and the inventor that grants exclusive use to the inventor for a certain period of time and excludes others from making, selling, or using it without permission of the patent holder.

Plaintiff. The person who brings or initiates a lawsuit against another person or entity.

Preliminary injunction. An injunction granted prior to a full hearing on the facts or merits of the case to prevent irreparable or irreversible harm.

Prima Facie Case. The production of enough evidence by a person to rule in that person's favor, unless the opposing party can produce rebuttal evidence.

Procedural Due Process. The guarantee of notice and a right to a hearing before the deprivation of a liberty or property interest.

Promisee. The recipient of the promise.

Promisor. The person making a promise.

Property Interest. A legal recognizable right one has in a certain position, course of action, or acquired benefit.

Prospective Relief. Refers to future actions or conduct; an action that becomes effective or operative in the future.

Protected Activity. An activity protected by law; activities that are permissible and encouraged.

Punitive Damages. Damages that are designed to punish an individual for gross and egregious behavior or conduct.

Q

Qualified Immunity (Limited Immunity). Immunity from civil liability for state employees or public officials in the performance of their discretionary duties that are done in good faith and do not violate established rights.

Quash. To make void, subdue, or terminate.

Quid Pro Quo. A form of sexual harassment in which one's employment and/or employment benefits is dependent on compliance with a sexual demand, usually from a boss or someone in a superior position.

R

Redact. The removal of certain, usually confidential information from reports or documents.

Reduction in Force (RIF). A decrease in the number of faculty or staff due to financial or economic reasons.

Refereed Journal. Review of manuscripts by scholars and experts in the area on a particular topic, which incorporates a blind-review process.

Retaliatory Discharge. The illegal termination or firing of an employee in response to his or her lawful actions or conduct.

Retroactive Relief. A request to provide relief for something that happened in the past.

S

Sovereign Immunity. The government's immunity from being sued and the state's immunity from being sued in federal court by the state's own citizens.

Subject-Matter Jurisdiction. The Court's authority to hear a case based on the nature and subject of the case. For example, a criminal court will not have the authority to hear workers' compensation cases.

Subpoena. A written court order directing the person to appear in court or to produce certain documents or records (subpoena duces tecum).

Substantive Due Process. The use of a fair, orderly, and unbiased process in making decisions or taking certain actions; avoidance of capricious and arbitrary procedures and decision making.

Summary Judgment. A dismissal of a case without a trial because there are no disputed facts.

Syllabus. A document that describes an academic course and outlines required components of the course, such as textbooks, grading policies, and evaluation methods.

T

Tangible Means of Expression. Expression that is visible, concrete, and capable of being understood and comprehended.

Tenure. A right to continual employment granted to faculty members who have met predetermined criteria that protects them from dismissal without due process of law.

Termination for Cause. A discharge or firing of an employee for valid reasons.

Top-Tier Journals. Journals with high academic standards and reputation based on the required rigorous evaluation process and focus on valid and scholarly research methodologies.

Tort Liability. Liability or legal responsibility for the injury of another person. Torts relate to civil as opposed to criminal or contract actions.

Treatise. A scholarly written argument including a systematic presentation of the facts, principles, and logical reasoning involved to reach the conclusions.

U

Utilitarianism. The ethical theory based on the belief that one's actions should be determined by the act that creates the greatest good for the greatest number of people.

V

Veracity. One's adherence to telling the truth.

Vicarious Liability. The legal doctrine that allows the supervisor or employing entity to respond to or answer for the negligence of subordinates or employees.

W

Work Made for Hire. A copyrightable work that is done by a specially commissioned independent contractor or by an employee acting within the scope of his or her employment and is owned by the employer.

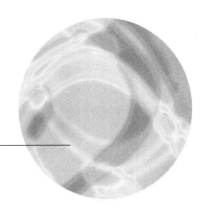

Appendix A
How to Read a Legal Case

Comments	Actual Case
Style or Caption of the case identifies the person(s) bringing the lawsuit (plaintiff-Betty Bender) and the person(s) defending the lawsuit (defendant-Alderson-Broaddus College). The term "appellant" indicates that Bender lost the lawsuit at the trial level or is unhappy with the ruling and has appealed to a higher court to hear the case. The college won at the trial level and must now defend against the appeal (Appellee).	BETTY BENDER, Plaintiff Below, Appellant v ALDERSON-BROADDUS COLLEGE, Defendant Below, Appellee
No. 30458 is the Court's docket number. Supreme Court of Appeals of West Virginia is the court hearing the appeal.	No. 30458 SUPREME COURT OF APPEALS OF WEST VIRGINIA
The case can be found in volume 212 of the state reporter, W. Va., on page 502; or volume 575 of the regional reporter, S.E.2d on page 112; or online in Lexis Nexis using the citation, 2002 W. Va. LEXIS 174. The case was argued to the appeals court on September 18, 2002, and decided/filed on October 31, 2002.	212 W. Va. 502; 575 S.E.2d 112; 2002 W. Va. LEXIS 174 September 18, 2002, Submitted **October** 31, 2002, Filed

Prior history provides the history of the case.

PRIOR HISTORY: [***1] Appeal from the Circuit Court of Barbour County. Civil Action No. 00-C-52. The Honorable Alan D. Moats, Judge.

Disposition states the court's ruling, which affirms or upholds the trial court's ruling.

DISPOSITION: AFFIRMED.

Syllabus: Identifies major principles of law. In some cases, the major principles of law may be presented under headnotes. A headnote contains a major topic and a number that correlates with the number in the narrative of the case. An example of a headnote is as follows: [1] Civil Procedure
"A circuit court's entry of summary judgment is reviewed *de novo*." Syl. Pt. 1, *Painter v Peavy*, 192 W.Va. 189, 451 S.E.2d 755 (1994).
Number 3 as:
[3] Colleges and Universities "The initial responsibility for determining the competence and suitability of persons to engage in professional careers lies with the professional schools themselves and if the conduct of educators is not high-handed, arbitrary or capricious, the courts of this state should give substantial deference to the discretion of officials of colleges and universities with respect to academic dismissals and such decisions are not ordinarily reviewable by the courts." Syl. Pt. 3, *North v W.Va. Bd. of Regents*, 175 W.Va. 179, 332 S.E.2d 141 (1985).

SYLLABUS:

1. "A circuit court's entry of summary judgment is reviewed *de novo*." Syl. Pt. 1, *Painter v Peavy*, 192 W.Va. 189, 451 S.E.2d 755 (1994).

2. "A motion for summary judgment should be granted only when it is clear that there is no genuine issue of fact to be tried and inquiry concerning the facts is not desirable to clarify the application of the law." Syl. Pt. 3, *Aetna Casualty & Surety Co. v Federal Ins. Co. of N.Y.*, 148 W.Va. 160, 133 S.E.2d 770 (1963).

3. "The initial responsibility for determining the competence and suitability of persons to engage in professional careers lies with the professional schools themselves and if the conduct of educators is not high-handed, arbitrary or capricious, the courts of this state should give substantial deference to the discretion of officials of colleges and universities with respect to academic dismissals and such decisions are not ordinarily reviewable by the courts." Syl. Pt. 3, *North v W.Va. Bd. of Regents*, 175 W.Va. 179, 332 S.E.2d 141 (1985). [***2]

4. Legal challenges to academic decisions of private institutions of higher education are subject to judicial review under an arbitrary and capricious standard.

Identifies the names of the lawyers who argued the appeal.

COUNSEL: Basil R. Legg, Jr., Clarksburg, West Virginia, Attorney for the Appellant.

Amy M. Smith, Nancy W. Brown, Steptoe & Johnson, Clarksburg, West Virginia, Attorneys for the Appellee.

Identifies a nonparty individual or organization who files a brief (written legal argument) on behalf of one of the appellees or the appellant. Amicus Curiae means "friends of the court."

Michael John Aloi, Manchin & Aloi, PLLC, Fairmont, West Virginia, Attorney for Amicus Curiae, West Virginia Independent Colleges & Universities, Inc.

Justice Albright wrote the Court's opinion.

Justice McGraw disagrees with the ruling of the other justices and will write separately to indicate his/her opinion.

JUDGES: JUSTICE ALBRIGHT delivered the Opinion of the Court. JUSTICE McGRAW dissents and reserves the right to file a dissenting opinion.

OPINION BY: Albright

OPINION:

The ** identifies corresponding pages in the regional reporter (504) and state reporter (114).

Justice Albright begins the opinion with a brief procedural history and identifies the Court's ruling.

[**114] [*504] Albright, Justice:

Betty Bender (hereinafter "Appellant") appeals from the June 19, 2001, order of the Circuit Court of Barbour County by which the lower court granted summary judgment in favor of Alderson-Broaddus College (hereinafter "Appellee" or "Appellee College") on the ground that a private college may increase the academic requirements for completion of a sequential multiyear degree program after a student has enrolled and completed a portion of the program as long [***3] as the change is not arbitrary and capricious. Upon due consideration of the petition, briefs, record and arguments, we affirm the decision of the circuit court for the reasons set forth below.

A detailed version of the facts and procedural history, including the major issues addressed in the trial court, is presented.

n1 refers to the first footnote (see n1 below). Footnotes are used to further explain a point, present principles of law, or identify discrepancies in facts. In law reporters, footnotes are listed at the bottom of the page.

I. Factual and Procedural Background

Appellant became a student at Appellee College in the fall of 1996 and was accepted into Appellee's nursing program at the beginning of her sophomore year. **n1** According to Appellant, before she enrolled at the school, she and her husband met with the chair of Appellee's nursing department, Dr. Sharon Boni, to discuss the academic standards of the nursing program. Appellant asserts that Dr. Boni explained that students were required to complete the nursing program within 5 years n2 of being admitted to the Appellee College and that the minimum qualifications for graduation from the nursing program were a grade of "C" (defined also as a grade of at least seventy percent) in all required nursing courses and a cumulative grade point average (hereinafter "G.P.A.") of 2.0 on a scale of 4.0 in all course work. Appellant

	further maintains that she and her husband pointedly asked Dr. Boni during this meeting whether the Appellee College could increase [***4] these minimum academic requirements after Appellant was admitted into the nursing program. Appellant contends that Dr. Boni assured her that these academic requirements could not, by law, be changed so as to affect students already accepted into the multiyear nursing program. n3
The identification of "Footnotes" alerts the reader to the beginning of the content related to the footnotes.	- - - - - - - - - - - - - Footnotes - - - - - - - - - - - - -
	n1 Candidates for a bachelor of science degree in nursing at Appellee College are considered prenursing students; acceptance into the nursing program does not occur until after a prenursing student has successfully completed the first year of general studies.
	n2 The school requires that the three-year nursing program be completed by a student within four years after being admitted into the program, or a total of five years from admission into the school.
	n3 Dr. Boni testified that she did not remember making such statements to Appellant and her husband.
The identification of "End Footnotes" alerts the reader to the end of the footnotes and the continuation of the Court's opinion.	- - - - - - - - - - - - End Footnotes - - - - - - - - - -
Note the Court's reliance on the College's written catalog.	Statements regarding amendment of any college policies were included in various college publications available to students during the time Appellant was deciding which school [***5] to attend as well as during her term of attendance at Appellee College. The inside covers of Appellee College's 1995–1997 Catalog and 1999–2001 Catalog stated:
	The provisions of this bulletin are not to be regarded as an irrevocable contract between the student and the College. The College reserves the right to make and designate the effective date of changes in curricula, course offerings, fees, requirements for graduation, and other regulations

	at any time such changes are considered to be desirable or necessary.
Note the Court's reliance on the School of Nursing's written policies and procedures	The catalogs also contained information regarding grade point averages, but there was no reference to the grading scale. The Policy and Procedure Manual of the Department of Nursing at Appellee College, which all nursing students were required to purchase and maintain, contained the following provision regarding amendment to nursing program policies:
	Policies affecting nursing students and/or nursing faculty are developed and/or revised through the action of various nursing department committees and finalized by the Nursing Faculty Organization. Copies of revised policies will be distributed to students and faculty with discussions as appropriate.
	The Policy [***6] and Procedure Manual contained information regarding G.P.A. requirements and the current grading scale. n4 Additionally, the Student Handbook for the school years [**115] [*505] 1995–1997, 1998–2000, 1999–2001 contained the following reservation regarding college policies:
	The provisions of this handbook are not to be regarded as an irrevocable contract between the student and the College. The College reserves the right to make and designate the effective date of changes in college policies and other regulations at any time such changes are considered to be desirable or necessary.
	- - - - - - - - - - - - - Footnotes - - - - - - - - - - - - -
	n4 The nursing department's policy and procedure manual was a loose-leaf document that students updated when the faculty supplied them with revisions.
	- - - - - - - - - - End Footnotes- - - - - - - - - - -
	After deciding to attend Appellee College, Appellant completed her first year (1996–1997) of general studies and her first year in the nursing program (1997–1998) without apparent difficulty. However, in the fall of 1998, Appellant received a final grade

of "D" in two nursing courses. As a result, Appellant [***7] could not take nursing courses in the 1999 spring semester because the classes she needed to repeat due to her unsatisfactory performance were only offered during the fall semester and were prerequisites to the nursing courses offered during the spring term. Consequently, Appellant enrolled in general studies classes in the spring of 1999 and then registered in the fall of 1999 to repeat the nursing classes in which she received "D" grades.

During the fall 1998 semester, Appellee's Nursing Department Curriculum Committee embarked upon a study of the grading scale policy. According to the minutes of its September 9, 1998, meeting, this committee decided to examine data from previous years to determine if students receiving the grade of "C" with scores in the low seventy percent range were more likely to fail the National Council Licensure Examination. After reviewing all of the compiled data, the Curriculum Committee voted in October 1998 to recommend a new grading scale whereby a minimum score of 75% would be required in order to earn a "C" grade. The new grading scale was ultimately approved in December 1998, with its implementation delayed until the fall 1999 semester [***8] so the nursing students would receive advance notice of the change. n5 The revised grade scale was applied to all nursing students, including those students who had enrolled under the more lenient 70% standard. n6

- - - - - - - - - - - - - Footnotes - - - - - - - - - - - - -

n5 Appellant testified that she received multiple advance notices of the grading change and did not question whether the change would be applied to her.

n6 The minimum cumulative G.P.A. required of nursing students was also increased at this time. Although the same implementation date was established for the revised G.P.A., it was applied only to incoming freshmen.

- - - - - - - - - - - End Footnotes- - - - - - - - - - - -

	Appellant was able to meet the new grading standard in her classes during the fall 1999 semester. However, in the spring 2000 semester she failed to achieve the minimum score of 75% in one nursing class and received a grade of "D"; the score she attained in that class was above 70%, for which she would have received a grade of "C" under the policy in effect at the time of her admission to the [***9] nursing program. Because Appellant could not repeat this required class until the following spring semester, it became impossible for her to complete the nursing program within five years from her admission to the school. Therefore, Appellee academically expelled Appellant from the nursing program in May 2000.
The Court discusses the procedural history outlining what happened in the lower court. The student filed an action asking the Court to stop the nursing school from expelling her until the case could be heard. The Court refused the injunction but allowed the case to continue based on theories of breach of contract and estoppel (good faith reliance on the words and representation of nursing officials).	On August 10, 2000, Appellant filed a civil action against Appellee seeking injunctive relief as well as damages. After conducting an evidentiary hearing, the lower court issued an order on October 15, 2000, by which it denied the requested injunction but allowed the action to proceed upon the issue of damages. According to the October 15 order, the two theories on which Appellant would proceed with regard to damages were breach of contract and promissory estoppel. n7 - - - - - - - - - - - - - - Footnotes - - - - - - - - - - - - n7 Additional bases for award of damages were enumerated in Appellant's complaint; for reasons not entirely clear from the record, only the breach of contract and promissory estoppel theories were developed. - - - - - - - - - - End Footnotes - - - - - - - - - -
The Court identifies the basis of the student's breach of contract claim against the nursing program.	The sum of Appellant's argument [***10] to the lower court was that she and the college had a contractual relationship based on the representations made in or reasonably inferred from the publications of Appellee College as well as the verbal assurances made by Dr. Boni. Appellant maintained that by the terms [**116] [*506] of her contract with Appellee the nursing program grading requirements would not change during the course of her enrollment.

Therefore, when Appellee began judging Appellant's course work against a different grading standard than that in effect at the time she enrolled, Appellee breached its contract with her. Appellant alternatively argued that the facts supported an award of damages against the college under the doctrine of promissory estoppel.

After the attorneys for both sides had completed gathering their evidence (discovery), they evaluated it and asked the court to grant summary judgment in their favor, based on the theory that there are no factual disputes for a jury to determine and thus no need for a trial. Further, the applicable law supports their case.

Following discovery, the parties filed cross-motions for summary judgment which were the subject of a hearing on June 8, 2000. Subsequently, the circuit court granted summary judgment in Appellee's favor on June 19, 2001. The summary judgment order contained the following rulings by the lower court:

11. The nature of the relationship between the Plaintiff and A-B College is clearly contractual in nature; however, implicit in that contract is a right to change the college's [***11] academic degree requirements if such changes are not arbitrary and capricious.

The Court ruled for the College based on the outlined legal facts and principles.

12. In regard to the Plaintiff's claim that Dr. Boni's oral statements are binding on the college, the Court finds that whether or not Dr. Boni made the statements attributed to her by the Plaintiff is immaterial. . . . A-B College clearly had the right to unilaterally change the grading scale of the nursing program as long as such change was not arbitrary and capricious.

13. The record is devoid of any facts to establish the action of A-B College in modifying its grading scale as arbitrary and capricious. . . .

It is from the June 19, 2001, order that Appellant filed the instant appeal.

II. Standard of Review

The appeals court identifies the legal standard upon which it can hear and will decide appeals.

As we held in syllabus point one of *Painter v Peavy*, 192 W.Va. 189, 451 S.E.2d 755 (1994), "[a] circuit court's entry of summary judgment is reviewed *de novo*." We have also recognized that: "A motion for summary judgment should be granted only

De novo means "a new trial." The Court will hear the evidence as if it was a new trial. The Court identifies the law related to summary judgment.	when it is clear that there is no genuine [***12] issue of fact to be tried and inquiry concerning the facts is not desirable to clarify the application of the law." Syl. Pt. 3, *Aetna Casualty & Surety Co. v Federal Ins. Co. of N.Y.*, 148 W.Va. 160, 133 S.E.2d 770 (1963). **III. Discussion**
Discussion of the law and incorporated facts, starting with the errors that the student-appellant asserts were made in the trial court's ruling.	At issue in this case is not whether a contract existed between the parties. Rather, Appellant assigns error to the lower court's finding that the actions of Appellee were not arbitrary and capricious under the terms of the contract. More specifically, Appellant argues that Appellee College acted arbitrarily and capriciously when it changed and applied a different grading scale to her work than that which was in place when she enrolled in the nursing program and such behavior amounted to a breach of contract or, in the alternative, the basis for a successful promissory estoppel claim.
The Justice notes the Court's previous ruling and identifies the supporting citation.	Initially we note that this Court previously has adopted the mainstream position that judicial review of purely academic decisions of a post-secondary school is decidedly limited. *North v W.Va. Bd. of Regents*, 175 W.Va. 179, 184-85, 332 S.E.2d 141, 146-47 (1985). [***13] The New York Court of Appeals aptly summarized the public policy basis for showing judicial deference in this regard by saying:
Court incorporates well-known general principles of law from different courts and identifies the citations.	When an educational institution issues a diploma to one of its students, it is, in effect, certifying to society that the student possesses all of the knowledge and skills that are required by his chosen discipline. In order for society to be able to have complete confidence in the credentials dispensed by academic institutions, however, it is essential that the decisions surrounding the issuance of these credentials be left to the sound judgment of the professional educators who monitor the progress of their students on a regular basis. *Olsson v. Board of Higher Ed.*, 49 N.Y.2d 408, 402 N.E.2d 1150, 1153, 426 N.Y.S.2d 248 (N.Y. 1980). Some federal courts have observed that the judiciary is particularly

ill-equipped to evaluate a school's academic decisions with respect to the health care field. *See, e.g., Doherty v Southern Coll. of Optometry*, 862 F.2d 570 (6th Cir. 1988); *Jansen v Emory Univ.*, 440 F. Supp. 1060 (N.D. Ga. 1977), *aff'd*, [**117] [*507] 579 F.2d 45 (5th Cir. 1978); [***14] *Connelly v Univ. of Vermont and State Agric. Coll.*, 244 F. Supp. 156 (D. Vt. 1965).

The foregoing notwithstanding, this Court has not condoned absolute judicial deference with regard to academic decisions made by institutions of higher education. We announced in *North v West Virginia Board of Regents*, 175 W.Va. 179, 332 S.E.2d 141 (1985), when judicial review of such decisions is appropriate by saying in syllabus point three that: the initial responsibility for determining the competence and suitability of persons to engage in professional careers lies with the professional schools themselves and if the conduct of educators is not high-handed, arbitrary or capricious, the courts of this state should give substantial deference to the discretion of officials of colleges and universities with respect to academic dismissals and such decisions are not ordinarily reviewable by the courts.

175 W.Va. at 181, 332 S.E.2d at 143. In other words, when faced with a claim that the actions of a university or college with regard to academic decisions [***15] are arbitrary and capricious, then the historical deference granted by courts to the judgment of higher education institutions is set aside. n8 Although the controversy in *North* concerned the dismissal of a medical student from a public institution, we see no reason why the same arbitrary and capricious standard should not apply to the comparable decisions of a private institution. A number of jurisdictions have adopted this position. *See, e.g., Ishibashi v Gonzaga Univ.*, 2000 Wash. App. LEXIS 1494, WL 1156899 (Wash. App. August 11, 2000); *Goodwin v Keuka Coll.*, 929 F. Supp. 90, (W.D.N.Y. 1995); *Frederick v Northwestern Univ. Dental School*, 247 Ill. App. 3d 464, 617 N.E.2d 382, 187 Ill. Dec. 174 (Ill. App. Ct. 1993); *Love v Duke Univ.*, 776 F. Supp. 1070 (M.D.N.C. 1991); *Babcock v New Orleans Baptist Theological Seminary*, 554

The Court notes that although case law regarding academic/judicial deference is strong, it is not absolute and identifies their previous ruling on the issue.

The Court notes that the *North* case, decided by them involved a public institution; they will apply the same principles of law on the issue to a private institution. It then identifies other Courts (cases with citations) that have adopted the same position.

Court states its basis for upholding the decision made in the trial court.	So. 2d 90 (La.Ct.App. 1989); *Abbariao v Hamline Univ. School of Law*, 258 N.W.2d 108 (Minn. 1977); *DeMarco v Univ. of Health Sciences/Chicago Medical School*, 40 Ill. App. 3d 474, 352 N.E.2d 356 (Ill. App. Ct. 1976); [***16] *Frank v Marquette Univ.*, 209 Wis. 372, 245 N.W. 125 (Wis. 1932). Consequently we hold that legal challenges to academic decisions of private institutions of higher education are subject to judicial review under an arbitrary and capricious standard. Therefore, we find as a matter of law that the lower court in the instant case applied the correct standard of review.
	- - - - - - - - - - - - - - Footnotes - - - - - - - - - - - -
	n8 We recognize that courts have adopted different standards of review when educators' decisions are based upon disciplinary rather than academic matters. Only the latter arises in the case before us.
	- - - - - - - - - - - End Footnotes - - - - - - - - - -
The Court addressed the student-appellant claim that the College had acted in an arbitrary and capricious manner. The Court identifies the legal principle that guides its decision.	We now turn to an examination of whether the actions of the Appellee College in the case before us were arbitrary and capricious. In applying this standard we are guided by this Court's holding in syllabus point three of *In re Queen*, 196 W.Va. 442, 473 S.E.2d 483 (1996), wherein we said that the arbitrary and capricious standard of review presumes the actions taken "are valid as long as the decision is supported by [***17] substantial evidence or by a rational basis." *Id.* at 444, 473 S.E.2d at 485. We are also mindful that we have previously recognized that an "action is arbitrary and capricious when it is unreasonable, without consideration, and in disregard of facts and circumstances of the case." *State ex rel. Eads v Duncil*, 196 W.Va. 604, 614, 474 S.E.2d 534, 544 (1996) (citation omitted).
The Court renders a decision based on its review of the facts and the guiding law.	Based upon our review of the record as explained below, we do not believe Appellee College acted arbitrarily or capriciously in instituting its modified grade scale. Given Appellee's clear and express reservation for making policy changes, as stated in the college's catalogs, handbooks and procedure manuals during the relevant period, it was reasonable for Appellee to

expect students to anticipate and comply with changes made to its grading scale. An update of degree requirements is often necessary in a profession such as nursing and, as disclosed in the record, the college undertook the study of the grading scale out of concern with the performance of its graduates on the nursing board examination. A letter in the record from the Board of Examiners for Registered Professional [***18] Nurses to Appellee's nursing department supports this concern since it related that the pass rate on the nursing board [**118] [*508] examination by the school's graduates was below the established standard. Likewise, the manner in which the modification was studied, adopted, and implemented by the school reflects a balance of concern for the welfare not only of the institution but also of the student population. The record shows that a variety of data was examined and an extensive review process was conducted by the school before the modification to the grade scale was made. We note further that although the grade modification was approved in December 1998, the change was not implemented until the fall 1999 semester, which the record reflects was done in order to enable the Department of Nursing to provide ample advance notification to its students. The school's concern with adequate advance notice of the change is borne out through Appellant's testimony, which revealed that she received information regarding the implementation of a grade scale modification in the following ways: memorandum from Dr. Boni, dated July 23, 1999; verbal instruction during the mandatory health sciences orientation on August 24, 1999; [***19] and verbal explanation by all of her nursing instructors as well as through written materials the instructors distributed to their classes. Furthermore, and perhaps most important, the record shows that the college made bona fide efforts to assist the students in meeting the revised grading standard. There is documentation in the record of Appellant being routinely apprised by her instructors regarding her academic progress in a class and that the instructors extended offers of various types of assistance with studying when Appellant began experiencing difficulty in her class

	performance. Even after Appellant was dismissed from the nursing program, Appellee encouraged Appellant to complete her degree at the college in a field of study more suited to her abilities. Based upon this and other undisputed and substantial evidence in the record, the actions of the college in modifying and implementing the modification of its grade scale were not unreasonable, arbitrary or capricious. Consequently, we affirm the decision of the circuit court. n9
	- - - - - - - - - - - - - Footnotes - - - - - - - - - - -
Once the Court ruled in favor of the school of nursing on the first legal issue, the second issue is no longer valid or suitable for the Court to address.	n9 Our affirmance of the lower court's finding that Appellee had the right to change the grading scale of the nursing program so long as the amendment was not made arbitrarily or capriciously renders Appellant's promissory estoppel argument moot. This too is in keeping with the ruling of the lower court in its summary judgment order.
	- - - - - - - - - - - End Footnotes - - - - - - - - - - -
	[***20]
The Court notes that it will not uniformly sanction modification of grading scales.	To be clear, our decision today does not constitute the wholesale approval of grading scale modifications by institutions of higher education. Certainly, we may have reached a different conclusion had the evidence not shown that the grading scale change undertaken by the college reflected a measure of concern for the enhancement of the student's educational experience as well as advancement of the institution's reputation and goals.
The Court's final ruling, which upheld or affirmed the lower court's decision.	Accordingly, we affirm the June 19, 2001, order of the Circuit Court of Barbour County granting summary judgment in favor of Appellee College. Affirmed.
Justice McGraw disagrees with the ruling of the majority of Justices and authors an opinion outlining the basis of his disagreement. Dissenting opinions often provide a review of the case from a different perspective. He starts with a review of the facts and states why a different opinion should be reached.	**DISSENT BY:** McGraw **DISSENT:** McGraw, Justice, dissenting: Ms. Bender started a challenging nursing program under certain conditions, and I believe she should have been able to complete the program under the same conditions that applied when she started. Ms. Bender signed up, if you will, for a

10-mile race, but during the running of it, the school decided to add an extra mile. While a Marine Corps drill instructor might make such a change for psychological reasons, I don't think the school should have been able to do that to Ms. Bender.

Several details of the [***21] program suggest that the school's choice of scheduling classes make it difficult to complete, even under the best of circumstances. One must finish in five years, but many required courses are only offered once a year. As the majority points out, Ms. Bender lost a semester when poor grades required her to repeat a class. We do not know why it is Ms. Bender performed poorly that semester, but certainly she is not the first student to do so. A student might face the birth of a child, the death of a parent, or a serious illness during his or her course of study, any of which might result in a poor outcome for grades. But under the program as described, that [**119] [*509] student faces a difficult challenge in completing the program, caught between a limited schedule and a five year limit.

But in spite of the scheduling obstacles created by the school, Ms. Bender still completed the program, and would have successfully graduated if the school had applied the same rules her last semester that it had established at the beginning. Instead, Ms. Bender finds herself with her degree not quite complete, and with no opportunity to complete it. After spending several years of her life working toward the goal [***22] of a degree, she has been told by the school to try something else.

Obviously it is important for all of Ms. Bender's potential future patients that she be well educated and well trained. But I don't believe that the difference between a 70 and a 75 necessarily makes her a bad nurse. I imagine that there were other nursing students who finished the program one year before Ms. Bender did who scored between 70% and 75% in a class and still passed that class and graduated from the program. No reasonable person would suggest that such individuals, now nurses, should be sent back to school.

My comments in no way imply that a school should not have the ability to change the requirements of one of its programs. Education is a constantly changing endeavor, and schools must be free to incorporate new advances into their existing curriculum. However, if a school does make such a change, I feel it should allow students who began their study before that change to finish under the old rules, or it should at least make some allowance when that change prevents a student from graduating.

In short, I think that the school made a deal with Ms. Bender when it enrolled her and took her tuition money, [***23] and she should have had the benefit of that deal throughout her studies. The majority indicates that Ms. Bender held up her end, and I believe the school should have been required to hold up its end as well.

Therefore, I respectfully dissent.

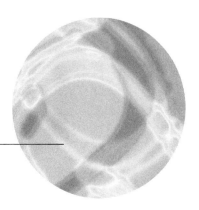

Appendix B
How to Research Legal Topics

GOVERNMENTAL STRUCTURE

Researching the law requires knowledge of the governmental structure and sources of the law. The three branches of government at the federal level, depicted in the diagram below, consist of the executive, legislative, and judiciary branches.

The U.S. Constitution is the highest law of the land. It applies to public institutions and organizations and more directly applies to higher education through the First, Fifth, and Fourteenth Amendments. The legislative branch makes laws that must be consistent with the Constitution; the executive branch enforces the law and the judiciary interprets the law.

At the state level, a similar structure exists, with the state's Constitution comprising the highest law of the land for that state. The following diagram depicts the branches of government at the state level.

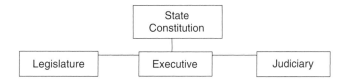

Each of the different branches of government provides a different source of law. The Legislature branch, through Congress, at the federal level or the state's legislative body creates statutory law. Agencies create administrative law, usually to enforce statutory law. Judicial law, often referred to as common law, is created based on legal principles enunciated by courts. For example, the state's legislative body creates the Nurse Practice Act (NPA)(Statutory Law). The NPA provides for the creation of a state agency, the state board of nursing to develop rules and regulations to enforce the act (administrative law). Court decisions related to issues involving the NPA will create a body of case law and guiding legal principles (common law).

LEVELS OF COURT

Trial Courts hear the initial case and render a decision. The case is heard by a jury or a judge (bench trial). Jury and judges for bench trials hear the evidence to determine issues of fact (fact-finding process). The judge also determines issues of law, such as the type of evidence that will be admitted in the case. At the state level, these courts may be referred to as Circuit Courts or District Courts. Usually court decisions and opinions are not written for publication at this level. At the federal level, trial courts are called the U.S. District Court. These decisions are published in the Federal Supplement reporter.

Midlevel or Intermediate Appeals Courts hear cases appealed from the trial level. These courts usually do not engage in a fact-finding process but address allegations of errors in law. For example, the appeals court will not rehear the facts on whether a faculty member was dismissed for cause, but will hear allegations that the trial court improperly disallowed significant data or evidence (errors in law). Lawyers file written legal arguments (briefs) and usually argue their cases in front of judges. One judge will write the court's decision that contains the legal issue(s), case facts, legal principles, court's decision and rationale. At the federal level, the appeals court is called the U.S. Court of Appeals. The decision of the appeals court at the state level is binding on all the lower courts within that jurisdiction. The decision is published in the state reporter and the appropriate regional reporter. At the federal level, the decision is binding on all district courts within that jurisdiction or outlined boundaries. These decisions are published in the Federal reporter.

The Supreme Court Justices hear cases appealed from intermediate-level appeals courts, involving issues of law. They will also hear cases when discrepancies in opinions exist among the various appeals courts to clarify the law. If the Court refuses to hear an appealed case, it will simply write certiorari denied (cert. denied). The decision of the appeals court stands. At the state level, a decision rendered by the Supreme Court is binding on all state courts. These decisions are published in the state and appropriate regional reporter. At the federal level, a decision by the U.S. Supreme Court is binding on all federal and state courts. These decisions are published in the United States Reports or Supreme Court Reporter.

SOURCES OF LAW

Federal Level

Statutory Law: *United States Code* (USC)
                          Commercial Editions:
                          United States Code Service (USCS) or *United States Code Annotated* (USCA)

Statutory Law. When researching the law, it is important to know the statutory citation. Within the Code are Numbered Titles that respond to various topics. For example Title 29 of the USC refers to Labor and Title 42 refers to The Public Health and Welfare. The Title is further divided into Chapters and chapters are then divided into specific topics. For example, 42 USCS § 1983 is the topic that discusses "Civil action for deprivation of human rights." Section (§) 1983 is frequently relied on to bring lawsuits against public officials.

Administrative Law: *Federal Register* contains all agency-issued federal administrative rules, including executive and independent agencies.
Code of Federal Regulations (CFR) contains administrative rules grouped according to topic. 34 C.R.F § 104.3 (k)(1)

Judicial Law: Specific Reporters that correspond to the level of the Court rendering the decision. Cases are found in specific reporters.

United States Supreme Court:—
US Reports (524 US 742) refers to volume 524 of the United States Report and the case starts on page 742)
Supreme Court Reporters (S Ct) (42 S Ct 1211)
United States Court of Appeal
Federal Reporter, Third Series (F3d), F2d for the Second Series, or F for the First Series (the higher the series number, the more recent the case. For example, 52 F3d 9 (2nd Cir 1994) refers to a case found in volume 52 of the Federal Reporter, Third Series, starting on page 9. The Second Circuit heard the case in 1994. The Courts of Appeal are divided into 13 Circuits and each circuit contains several states (Box B.1).
United States District Courts
Federal Supplement (F Supp.) 770 FSupp 895 (SDNY 1991) refers to a case found in volume 770 of the Federal Supplement, starting on page 895. The case was heard by the U.S. District Court for the Southern District of New York in 1991.

State Level

Statutory Law: Law passed by state legislative bodies is found in the State's Statutory Code.
The Code of Virginia, or the Code of Virginia Annotated is referenced as Va Code Ann. A complete citation is written

Court of Appeals and Corresponding States

Box B.1

1st Circuit	Maine, Massachusetts, New Hampshire, Puerto Rico, Rhode Island
2nd Circuit	Connecticut, New York, Vermont
3rd Circuit	Delaware, New Jersey, Pennsylvania, Virgin Islands
4th Circuit	Maryland, South Carolina, North Carolina, Virginia, West Virginia
5th Circuit	Louisiana, Mississippi, Texas
6th Circuit	Kentucky, Michigan, Ohio, Tennessee
7th Circuit	Illinois, Indiana, Wisconsin
8th Circuit	Arkansas, Iowa, Minnesota, Missouri, Nebraska, North Dakota, South Dakota
9th Circuit	California, Oregon, Arizona, Washington, Montana, Idaho, Nevada, Alaska, Hawaii, Guam, Northern Mariana Islands
10th Circuit	Colorado, Kansas, New Mexico, Oklahoma, Utah, Wyoming
11th Circuit	Alabama, Florida, Georgia
District of Columbia Circuit	Washington, D.C.

as Va Code Ann § 2.2-2639 (2004). The name of the state's code book will vary among the states. For example in Georgia, the Code book is called the Official Code of Georgia Annotated (OCGA) and in Nevada, Nevada Revised Statutes Annotated (NRS).

Administrative Law: Laws passed by agencies are usually found in the State Administrative Code or Administrative Register. For example, in Virginia, administrative law is found in the *Virginia Administrative Code.*

Judiciary Law: Specific Reporters that correspond to the level of the state court rendering the decision. Cases are found in state or the corresponding regional reporters. Parallel case citations provide state and regional information. For example, 80 P3d 676; 7 Cal Rptr 3d 576. The exact versions of the case are found in volume 80 of the Pacific Reporter, Third Series on page 676 and in volume 7 of the California Reporter, Third Series on page 576. There are 7 Reporters, each containing several states (see Box B.2). The Reporters usually contain cases heard by the midlevel appeals court and the state's supreme court.

Regional Reporters and Corresponding States

Atlantic Reporter (A, A2d or A3d)	Connecticut, Delaware, D.C., Vermont, Rhode Island, Maine, New Hampshire, Maryland, New Jersey, Pennsylvania
North Eastern Reporter (NE, NE 2d or NE 3d)	Illinois, Indiana, Massachusetts, New York, Ohio
North Western Reporter (NW, NW 2d, or NW 3d)	Iowa, Michigan, Minnesota, Nebraska, North Dakota, South Dakota, Wisconsin
Pacific (P, P 2d, or P 3d)	Alaska, Arizona, California, Colorado, Hawaii, Idaho, Kansas, Montana, Nevada, New Mexico, Oklahoma, Oregon, Utah, Washington, Wyoming
South Eastern (SE, SE 2d, or SE 3d)	Georgia, North Carolina, South Carolina, Virginia, West Virginia
South Western (SW, SW 2d, or SW 3d)	Arkansas, Kentucky, Missouri, Tennessee, Texas
Southern (So, So 2d, So 3d)	Alabama, Florida, Louisiana, Mississippi

RESEARCHING THE LAW

An ideal starting point is to identify the search terms, descriptors, or fact words, such as "faculty tenure" or "wrongful termination," in the index of the resource book. If the specific terms are not found, the researcher should formulate or conceptualize broader topics or the index may refer the researcher to a broader heading. For example, faculty tenure may be found under the heading Colleges and Universities and wrongful termination under the heading of Employment. Whenever possible, the researcher should review primary sources before relying on secondary sources, which are interpretations of primary sources.

Primary Sources

Primary Sources or the actual law can be found in:

- State or federal constitution
- State or federal statutes
- Administrative rules and regulations
- Judicial cases (case law)

Secondary Sources

Secondary sources consist of:

Encyclopedias: Provide a written overview of a particular topic. They are excellent as a starting point to gain more information on the topic.

Treatises: A written scholarly and comprehensive analysis of a particular topic.

Law Review Articles: May be associated with law schools, such as the Harvard Law Review, or by associations or organizations, such as The College and University Law Journal. Law review articles provide excellent coverage of a topic and are broad in scope and scholarly, and incorporate numerous references.

Newspapers: Are issued on a predetermined schedule and contain news and commentaries on certain topics, cases and related events. Newspapers may be at the state level, such as the Virginia Law Weekly or at the national level, such as the National Law Journal.

The Internet

The Internet provides access to a large variety of computer networks to conduct legal research. It has become a major research tool for finding legal topics, although it is not logically arranged or organized.

The researcher can connect to the World Wide Web (WWW) by using a web browser, such as Netscape. On Netscape's home page, the researcher can type in a search term, such as faculty tenure, and is connected to numerous publications containing these terms. The researcher can also type in a specific address to be connected to a legal web site. For example, the address www.law.harvard.edu will connect the researcher to the web page for Harvard Law School. Various search options are then available, such as viewing the law review publication *Harvard Law Review*.

Online research databases such as Westlaw and Lexis contain an organized search for legal materials. They contain primary and secondary sources on the desired topics. These databases often require a subscription.

Other Internet resources for legal research include:

http://www.findlaw.com is a good legal research site. It is organized and user friendly.

http://www.abanet.org is the Internet site for the American Bar Association.

http://law.cornell.edu is the web site for Cornell Law School and is an excellent resource for a wide range of legal topics.

http://romingerlegal.com provides links to case law, statutes, and regulations.

http://www.catalaw.com contains numerous legal catalogs and organizes indexes of law and government.

Index

Pages followed by *b* indicate box; those followed by *t* indicate table.

Index